Codes and Consequences

Codes and Consequences

Choosing Linguistic Varieties

Edited by
Carol Myers-Scotton

New York   Oxford
OXFORD UNIVERSITY PRESS
1998

Oxford   New York

Athens   Auckland   Bangkok   Bogota   Bombay
Buenos Aires   Calcutta   Cape Town   Dar es Salaam
Delhi   Florence   Hong Kong   Istanbul   Karachi
Kuala Lumpur   Madras   Madrid   Melbourne
Mexico City   Nairobi   Paris   Singapore
Taipei   Tokyo   Toronto   Warsaw

and associated companies in
Berlin   Ibadan

Copyright © 1998 by Carol Myers-Scotton

Published by Oxford University Press, Inc.
198 Madison Avenue, New York, New York 10016

Oxford is a registered trademark of Oxford University Press

Library of Congress Cataloging-in-Publication Data
Codes and consequences : choosing
linguistic varieties / edited by Carol Myers-Scotton
p.   cm.
Includes bibliographical references and index.
ISBN 0-19-511522-8; 0-19-511523-6 (pbk.)
1. English language—Discourse analysis.
2. English language—Social aspects.
3. English language—Variation.
I. Myers-Scotton, Carol.
PE1422.C63   1998
401'.41—dc21   98-7061

1 3 5 7 9 8 6 4 2

Printed in the United States of America
on acid-free paper

ACKNOWLEDGMENTS

The editor, authors, and publisher gratefully acknowledge permission to reproduce extracts from the following:

All the Pretty Horses by Cormac McCarthy, © 1992, Alfred A. Knopf. Reprint, 1993 Vintage International. By permission of Alfred A. Knopf.

"Stylistic variation and cognitive constraint in Cormac McCarthy's *All the Pretty Horses*," © 1995 in Wade Hall and Rick Wallach (eds.) *Sacred Violence: A Reader's Companion to Cormac McCarthy*. El Paso: Texas Western Press. By permission of Texas Western Press.

The Great Gatsby by F. Scott Fitzgerald. © 1925, Charles Scribner's Sons. Copyright renewed 1953 by Frances Scott Fitzgerald Lanahan. © 1991, 1992 by Eleanor Lanahan, Matthew J. Bruccoli, and Samuel J. Lanahan as Trustees under agreement dated 7/3/75 created by Frances Scott Fizgerald Smith. Excerpts from *The Great Gatsby* ("authorized text") by F. Scott Fitzgerald. Edited by Matthew J. Bruccoli. By permission of Scribner, a division of Simon & Schuster.

As I Lay Dying by William Faulkner, from © 1930, renewed 1957. From 1985, *Faulkner, Novels 1930–1935*. New York: Library of America (Literary Classics of the United States, Inc. By permission of Random House, Inc.

The Sirens of Titan by Kurt Vonnegut, Jr. © 1959 Dell. By permisson of Kurt Vonnegut, Jr., and Dell Publishing Co.

"The Snow Man" from *Collected Poems* by Wallace Stevens. © 1923, renewed 1951 by Wallace Stevens. By permission of Alfred A. Knopf, Inc.

"The Tyger," "A Poison Tree" and an excerpt from "London" by William Blake from *Songs of Innocence and of Experience*. © 1977. New York: Oxford University Press. By permission of Oxford University Press.

I am very grateful to Travis Gordon for his fine work in formatting this volume. I wish to thank Janice L. Jake and Agnes Bolonyai for comments on my own contributions to the volume. I also appreciate the help of Cathy Bridgeman, Noreen Doughty, and CeCe Mikell as editorial assistants.

CONTENTS

CONTRIBUTORS

Amittai F. Aviram is associate professor of English and comparative literature and a consulting faculty member in the linguistics program at the University of South Carolina, where he teaches literary theory and the reading of
poetry. He has published a research monograph, *Telling Rhythm: Body and
Meaning in Poetry* (1994) and a chapbook of his own poems, *Tender Phrases, Brassy Moans* (1994). His poems have also appeared in magazines and
anthologies.

Rusty Barrett is a doctoral candidate in the linguistics department at the
University of Texas–Austin. In addition to his work on language and gender/
sexuality, he has conducted a great deal of research in Mayan linguistics.
Based on fieldwork in Guatemala, his dissertation is a grammar of Sipaka-
pense Maya.

Janice Bernsten is an associate professor of linguistics at the University of
Michigan's Flint campus. She is a sociolinguist continuing her work on the
auto factory floor. In addition, she pursues research on African linguistic
issues, especially in East and Southern Africa. She is the coauthor of a grammar of Shona designed for U.S. university students.

Trevor Howard-Hill is the C. Wallace Martin Professor of English at the
University of South Carolina. He is also the editor of the *Oxford Shakespeare
Concordances* (Oxford: Clarendon Press, 1969–1973). He has written extensively on bibliography, textual criticism, and editing and is editor of *Papers
of the Bibliographical Society of America*. His most recent book is *Middle-
ton's "Vulga Pasquin": Essays on "A Game of Chess"* (1995).

Nancy Kreml is a member of the English faculty at Midlands Technical College in Columbia, South Carolina. She received her Ph.D. in linguistics from
the University of South Carolina in 1992. She is the author of several articles
on Cormac McCarthy and on stylistics in writing about science.

Margaret Mishoe is a member of the English faculty at the University of
North Carolina–Charlotte, where she teaches English and linguistics courses. She received her Ph.D. in linguistics from the University of South Carolina in 1995. Her principal areas of research are the structure of dialects
among lower socioeconomic class speakers in the South and their use of
styleswitching.

Carol Myers-Scotton is a Carolina Distinguished Professor at the University of South Carolina where she is a professor of linguistics and English and has been director of the linguistics program. She has done extensive fieldwork in Africa on bilingual situations and has published widely on codeswitching, including two books, *Social Motivations for Codeswitching: Evidence from Africa* (1993) and *Duelling Languages: Grammatical Structure in Codeswitching* (1993), both with Oxford.

Mary Sue Sroda is director of the M.A. TESOL program at Murray State University (Kentucky) and a doctoral candidate in the linguistics program at the University of South Carolina. Her research interests are second-language acquisition and pragmatics and she has coauthored an article on perceptions of reference in young children. Her dissertation is entitled "Relevance Theory and the Markedness Model: A Cognitive Approach to Second-Language Acquisition."

Timothy Wilt is a translation consultant for the United Bible Societies. He has worked with translation teams in Africa for several years, especially in Zaire, Cameroon, and Chad. He holds a Ph.D. in linguistics from Michigan State University.

—I—

Overview

Introduction

CAROL MYERS-SCOTTON

A S THE TITLE of this volume indicates, the subject is the selection of one linguistic code (or variety) rather than one or more others and its consequences. *Code* and *variety* are cover terms for linguistic systems at any level, from separate languages to dialects of a single language to styles or substyles within a single dialect. As all linguists know, they are useful—even necessary— terms because the divisions between linguistic systems are not always discrete. In the intended meaning here, consequences are easier to label, although this does not mean they are necessarily separable, either. The consequences considered here have to do with either effects on ease of cognitive processing or social/psychological effects. However, all effects are cognitive in the sense that they depend on the addressee's making mental calculations about the speaker's intentions. (*Addressee* will be used as a cover term for *addressee* and *reader,* and *speaker* as a cover term for *speaker* and *writer.*)

Intentionality refers to the messages conveyed by utterances in addition to those which the utterances literally denote (i.e., more than the meaning of words and their combinations). Grice (1975) gave the name *implicatures* to such consequences or outcomes, and one of the ways in which Sperber and Wilson (1995) extend Grice's ideas is by referring to implicatures as both *strong* and *weak.* In my own work, I generally refer to *intentionality* rather than to *implicatures.* I see the relation between the two terms as this: Intentionality becomes apparent in implicatures.

Sperber and Wilson argue that any utterance can introduce a number of implicatures. They also reject the notion that implicatures are necessarily determinate, that speakers always have in mind a specific set of implicatures that they expect addressees to recover. They say, "Some implicatures are made so strongly manifest that the hearer can scarcely avoid recovering them. Others are made less stongly manifest" (Sperber and Wilson 1995: 197). While the analyses in this volume make specific claims about the intentional messages that choices of linguistic varieties convey, they also support the point

3

of view of Sperber and Wilson that we are dealing with open-ended sets of intentions or implicatures.

Messages of intentionality can be conveyed in various ways. The examples in Sperber and Wilson 1995 rely on the way an utterance is phrased to convey implicatures but without the type of variation in phrasing involved in a change in linguistic variety. In contrast, the data sets considered in this volume were selected to show how intentionality can arise through changes in linguistic variety, from one style to another.

Messages of intentionality are additional messages but not necessarily secondary; in fact, messages of intentionality may be the primary message in a discourse. For example, in Barrett's analysis of performances by African American drag queens (chapter 8), the message of intentionality conveyed by styleswitching is, in many ways, the main message. This message is that social categories related to gender, ethnicity, class, and sexuality are not stable. Also, based on my own discussion of Faulkner's *As I Lay Dying* (chapter 4), I would argue that the psychological effects of the style Faulkner imparts to Darl give the reader a better key to understanding Darl's character than the referential import of his monologues. In other chapters, the consequences of using one style rather than another may be more than an overlay on referentially based messages but less than the primary messages.

MARKEDNESS AND CHOICES OF VARIETIES

A major theme in this volume is how the construct of *markedness* can be related to the choice of one linguistic variety over other possible varieties. The argument developed in each of the chapters is that writers or speakers choose what can be considered *marked choices* to convey certain messages of intentionality. To varying degrees, authors discuss their data in terms of the distinction between unmarked and marked choices of linguistic varieties, a distinction formalized in the Markedness Model (Myers-Scotton chapter 2, in this volume; but also 1993).

Markedness in Structural Linguistics

Markedness, of course, is a well-known concept in structural linguistics where it has been used at least since the first half of the twentieth century to explain how linguistic systems are structured (Trubetzkoy [1939] 1969; Jakobson 1971; Battistella 1990, 1996). Specifically, markedness figures in four ways in structural analyses. First, it is an organizational construct used to describe various polarities within the different systems of language. For example, within phonology, two sounds may be related in terms of their articulatory properties, but one member is referred to as *unmarked* because it requires fewer distinctive features in its description than does the marked member. Second, markedness also is used in reference to frequency. The more unmarked member of a set is that which occurs more frequently. For example, a particular word order in dependent clauses in a given language is called unmarked, with other orders called marked. Third, and related to frequency, one member of a pair may occur as a cover term for both members. For example, in Spanish *muchachos* 'boys' functions as a cover term for both *muchachas* 'girls' and *muchachos*. Fourth, markedness is used in reference to language change. A general argument (but with many dissenting views) is that a more marked structure is susceptible to change (i.e., becoming more unmarked) whether through internally or externally motivated change.

All these uses of markedness are largely descriptive although they could also be incorporated into a theoretical (i.e., an explanatory and/or predictive) framework. For example, within the theory of universal grammar (UG), markedness relates structural features to the grammar as core versus periphery. This notion is extended in research in language acquisition. However, within UG markedness is not absolute. For example, consider head position. The unmarked version of the *head parameter* is that all languages have their heads on the same side of their complements. In a specific language, the central core may be considered unmarked with respect to head direction (e.g., in English, nouns as heads precede their complements, as in *movie about dinosaurs*). However, parts of the structure may be marked; for example, in English, determiners and adjectives precede the noun head, as in *the new movie*. (See Cook and Newson 1996 for a discussion of Chomsky and *universal grammar*.)

Markedness and Social Consequences

In my various discussions of the markedness model (MM), I use the concept of markedness in ways related to those discussed previously. However, I am not interested in linguistic forms as members of a set based on structural characteristics but rather of a set based on social or psychological import. My use of the term *markedness* is meant to imply that choices within such a set also can be characterized within a system of oppositions, with markedness as a property of oppositions. The premise underlying this approach is that all linguistic codes or varieties come to have social and psychological associations in the speech communities in which they are used. Given these associations, the use of a particular code is viewed in terms of the unmarked versus marked opposition in reference to the extent its use "matches" community expectations for the interaction type or genre where it is used: What community norms would predict is unmarked; what is not predicted is marked. However, this approach does not assume that these oppositions are necessarily categorical in reference to markedness. Rather, codes fall along a continuum as more or less unmarked. Further, there is not necessarily a single unmarked or marked choice, although there is often a dominant unmarked choice (in terms of frequency and in reference to the norms of the dominant group), especially when the situation or genre is relatively conventionalized.

The MM employs the unmarked versus marked distinction as a theoretical construct to explain the social and psychological motivations for making one code choice rather than another. The MM itself is based on the premise that, as part of their innate language faculty, all language users have a *predisposition* to view linguistic choices as more or less marked, given the social and intellectual context. That is, all persons come equipped with the *competence* to assess linguistic choices. To develop the *ability* to put this competence to use, everyone must be exposed to language use in specific interaction types in their speech community. Thus, all language users develop a sense of markedness regarding varieties in the community's linguistic repertoire for given interaction types or for given genres in writing in their community.

In brief, choices are labeled unmarked when they constitute predicted behavior, given the context; that is, they negotiate the unmarked rights and obligations set for that context. In some sense, they maintain the community's status quo. Choices are marked when they can be seen as negotiations to invoke a rights and obligations set *other than* the unmarked one for the context. (See chapter 2 in this volume for more details on the MM.)

Applying the Markedness Model to New Types of Data

Until now, I mainly employed the MM to explain choices in codeswitching in conversation. Further, even though codeswitching can occur at any structural level of language, I dealt largely with switching between two or more languages (e.g., Myers-Scotton 1988a, 1993; but see Myers-Scotton 1985, 1988b, on switching between styles and Myers-Scotton and Zhu 1983 on choice of terms of address). Because I often wrote about switching between languages in conversation whenever I presented the MM, many assumed that I intended such switching as the model's primary purview. Also, most other researchers who apply the MM in their work use it to discuss switching between languages (e.g., Gibbons 1987, Swigart 1992, Adendorff 1993, Wei 1994; but see Eastman 1985 and DeBose 1992 on style or dialect switching). Because it was never my intention to limit the MM to switching between languages, a major motivation for editing this volume is to demonstrate that the MM can be used profitably in other ways.

The goal of this volume, therefore, is to show how theoretical frameworks that include the MM—or at least the concept of markedness—can be applied profitably to other levels of language. Therefore, there are no chapters on codeswitching between languages. Instead, all the chapters deal with choices among available styles or subsets of styles (e.g., directives, in Bernsten chapter 10). The choices are among styles in English in all cases but one—and even that one treats English translations of styleswitching (Wilt chapter 5).

EXPLAINING STYLISTIC CHOICES IN DIVERSE AREAS

The table of contents gives at least a clue to the diversity of subject matter. Chapter 2 offers a general theoretical overview of the MM as I conceptualize it today. The next nine chapters offer applications of how the concept of markedness contributes to the social or psychological message in different choices of linguistic form. Although some studies are clearly within the scope of sociolinguistics, because many messages of intentionality in conversation are about a speaker's view of his or her own persona or social group memberships and relationships to other participants, the way that the authors view choices among linguistic alternatives also places this volume within cognitively based pragmatic studies as well. This is clear in the two ways that the notion of speakers as *rational actors* is developed.

First, viewing language users as rational actors means supporting the premise that speakers make choices from an *opportunity set* (i.e., their linguistic repertoires) to achieve certain goals important to them as individuals. In so doing, these speakers must calculate the costs and rewards—social or otherwise (e.g., aesthetic)—of one choice over another. This is what distinguishes these studies from sociolinguistic investigations that concentrate on language use as largely identifying the user with social group memberships or social networks.

Second, viewing language users as rational actors includes the notion that their choices demonstrate that these users not only recognize, but also *exploit*, the potential for utterances to convey intentional as well as referential meaning. As noted earlier, intentional messages enlarge the referential or social meaning. This comment about *style* conveys some of the flavor of the questions which this volume addresses:

> Whenever a speaker communicates he must make a decision as to what he chooses to make explicit and what he chooses to leave implicit. It is not as if [*I promise that Tom is coming*] communicates something different from [*Tom's coming*]. Rather, they differ in the amount of help the reader is given in recovering whatever is communicated. In other words, they differ in *style*. (Blakemore 1992: 7–8)

THE INTENDED AUDIENCE

The volume is designed to interest faculty and students in the disciplines of linguistics, literature, and foreign language. Because it deals with the explication of literature as well as spontaneous speech, it is a useful text for courses in either literary stylistics or rhetoric and composition in English departments. It also addresses issues covered in discourse analysis or (socio)pragmatics in linguistics departments. Moreover, the volume ought to be accessible to the general educated reader. Technical discussions are minimal and when they occur, technical terms are fully explained, with the nonspecialist in mind. None of the chapters has been published before, except for portions of chapter 3.

ORGANIZATION OF THE VOLUME

Following this introduction, Part I includes a chapter giving a theoretical overview of the markedness model. The five chapters in Part II deal with marked choices in literary works, ranging from Shakespeare to poetry to modern novels to Hebrew biblical narratives. Part III includes three chapters that analyze spontaneous speech. Their subject matter, however, is very diverse, ranging from directives at an auto plant to ingroup conversation among smalltown southerners to drag queen performances. Part IV consists of only one chapter, which considers ways in which to use markedness in instructing second-language learners of English on how to speak and write as communicatively competent users of the language. What differentiates almost all the chapters from discussions of stylistic effects by literary stylists is that most of the analyses are supported with quantitative evidence to corroborate the claims that are made.

The chapters vary in the extent to which the MM figures in the explanations of linguistic choices. Several of the chapters specifically use the MM as their main theoretical framework; for example, Mishoe (chapter 9) employs the MM exclusively in explaining her data set. Others use several theoretical approaches. For example, Kreml (chapter 3) utilizes the MM along with relevance theory (Sperber and Wilson). Others refer only to the general notion of markedness in regard to text types or linguistic varieties (Wilt chapter 5; Aviram chapter 6).

THE MARKEDNESS MODEL AS A RATIONAL ACTOR MODEL

In chapter 2, "A Theoretical Introduction to the Markedness Model," I present an overview of the MM as it stands today. Those familiar with earlier versions of the model will certainly recognize it; however, the current version goes beyond previous explications in emphasizing how the MM is a rational actor model. Rational actor models are concerned with explaining why actors (speakers) make the choices they do; such models view rationally based choices as the means by which actors try to achieve their goals as well as possible, thereby optimizing an outcome.

With the MM explicated as a rational actor model, linguistic choices are now cast in terms from Elster's (1989) conception of how social choices are made. I also introduce the *somatic marker hypothesis* of Damasio (1996). Features of the social context, including the speaker's social identity features, are considered structural constraints that determine an opportunity set; in the case of linguistic choices, the opportunity set is a speaker's linguistic repertoire. A speaker's opportunity set (and the structural constraints that "produce" it), thus, are external constraints on the speaker's choices. At this point, I introduce a second set of constraints that are internal to the speaker. I have in mind the speaker's innately available "markedness evaluator" and also somatic markers, as characterized by Damasio. Finally, as a third filter, rationality comes into the picture. To act rationally means that the speaker selects the "best" choice, given the degree of internal consistency of his or her desires, values, and beliefs and the available evidence.

In concluding the chapter, I emphasize that the attempt to optimize on some goal limits choices in ways that features of neither the social nor structural context can do: The important term regarding choices is not possible but feasible. By *feasible* I mean choices that are not simply accessible but deemed advantageous based on the prescriptions of rationality just stated. Such choices are necessarily the result of generally unconscious cognitive calculations.

Few of the following chapters in which specific data sets are analyzed in reference to markedness mention the MM explicitly as a rational actor model and none discusses the mechanisms of choice as outlined previously. Most are much more concerned with identifying a particular style as marked or not and with explaining the social or cognitive effects of the use of a marked style when it occurs. However, in reading my theoretical chapter together with the analyses of specific data sets, I hope the reader can see that what the authors are doing is applying my new emphasis on the mechanisms of linguistic choice (i.e., the how and why of choice).

LITERARY STUDIES

Part II consists of five chapters on literary works. It opens with chapter 3, "Implications of Styleswitching and the Narrative Voice of Cormac McCarthy's *All the Pretty Horses*," in which Nancy Kreml is concerned with how two styles play against each other. Her analysis shows that almost all of the novel is written in one style (the unmarked style) that shows the action of the novel, but action for which McCarthy does not explicitly assign cause and effect. A second style (the marked style) occurs very infrequently, but it suggests how the reader is to interpret the actions. She provides a quantitative analysis of linguistic features (e.g., length of sentences, use of metaphors, and types of lexical choices) to substantiate the existence of the two different styles.

Kreml employs both relevance theory (Sperber and Wilson 1995) and the MM, and her analysis can be seen as arguing that the two styles contrast at the level of implicature as well as in terms of their surface linguistic features. Although both styles introduce many implicatures, those in the unmarked style are left very open: By describing an event, McCarthy indicates it is important, but he leaves indeterminate *how* is it important. In contrast, implicatures arising from the more marked style are highly constrained in various ways. For example, not only is the marked style's often convoluted syntax at odds with the simple syntax of the world of action, but such structures give rise to implicatures that introduce the notions that actions are complex and have consequences, that they do not just happen. Similarly, the metaphors (e.g., *stars swarmed*), many modifications (e.g., *young thieves in a glowing orchard),* and uncommon lexical choices (e.g., *serried*) of the marked style require the reader to spend more effort in interpreting the text; such stylistic devices suggest complication—even disorder—in the type of implicatures that arise. In this way, McCarthy introduces the notion of responsibility and, as Kreml says, ultimately the moral significance of actions.

Chapter 4, "Marked Grammatical Structures: Communicating Intentionality in *The Great Gatsby* and *As I Lay Dying*," is my own contribution to analyses of data sets. The chapter considers different syntactic features in each of the novels, concluding that the marked syntactic structures in each of them require a different type of cognitive processing from the unmarked structures in each novel. The particular type of processing contributes substantially to the specific cognitive effects produced by the structures in question.

In *The Great Gatsby* I demonstrate that five narrative passages which carry "crucial" messages in the novel have more "elaborating" (versus "core") Projections of Complementizer (CPs) than do five matched passages with less than crucial messages. I argue that the difference in the number of elaborating CPs means that the crucial passages require more cognitive processing. Elaborating CPs include adverbial adjuncts and sentential complements as well as relative clauses.

In *As I Lay Dying*, I consider differences in two monologues each from eight different characters. My overall argument is that certain syntactic features distinguish the monologues of Darl, the apparent hero of the novel. Statistical analysis demonstrates that Darl's monologues show significantly more detached participial phrases than monologues of the other characters, as well as certain types of prepositional phrases. I argue that because these phrases contribute little to the propositional weight of the sentence (they do not contain tensed verbs and their arguments), Darl's monologues have a dream-like quality. My claim is that such cognitive effects are a main means by which Faulkner builds Darl's characterization.

In regard to the structures studied, the sources of stylistic effect contrast with each other. In *The Great Gatsby*, the author slows down the action by adding cognitive weight to sentences in the crucial passages; he does this by adding additional propositions to the sentences by adding elaborating CPs. I explain how this is different from the effect of merely adding more words. In *As I Lay Dying*, the author builds up the reader's view of Darl through monologues that are *not* loaded with extra propositional weight. Overall, such an analysis of both the novels emphasizes the role of the more abstract level of predicate-argument structure over surface-level considerations of style.

In chapter 5, "Markedness and References to Characters in Biblical Hebrew Narrative," Timothy Wilt argues that translators of texts need to pay attention to the markedness of certain aspects of a text to arrive at translations that are faithful to the tenor of the original. Wilt, a Bible translator himself, discusses the use of terms of address in biblical Hebrew narratives and how they are translated into English. What piqued Wilt's interest in terms of address was his noticing in the book of Judges that some historical figures, especially leaders of Israel's enemies, even after their first reference, are still referred to by their full names and titles rather than by only their proper names or even a pronoun. In a quantitative analysis, Wilt demonstrates that such full references for Israel's enemies are marked compared with the references to Israel's heroes. Elsewhere in the Bible, Wilt finds other instances of marked terms of address. He develops an argument as to why the references to enemies, as well as to other persons in other biblical texts, should include a relational phrase, suggesting that the sense of their names contributes to the development of the narrative. That is, the relational phrases foreshadow what is going to happen. For example, when an enemy is referred to as X *the crow,* the implication is that such an enemy is no more of a threat than a crow. When an enemy is referred to as X *the Sacrifice Whose Protection Was Refused,* the import is that such an outcome will befall those who stand opposed to God.

Bible translators have tended either to reproduce literally the marked terms of address or eschew them for the sake of a fluent style. Instead, Wilt suggests that the lesson to be learned is that (1) certain terms of address are marked and (2) they therefore warrant special attention. He argues that translators would be more faithful to the original if they would attempt to reproduce the intentionality conveyed by these usages with equivalently marked expressions in the target language of translation, especially when irony or humor is intended in the original. He says, "The equivalence will be not only with regard to the semantic content of expressions but also with regard to the pragmatic inferences that the original speakers expected their audiences to make."

In chapter 6, "Literariness, Markedness, and Surprise in Poetry," Amittai F. Aviram offers a characterization of poetry—and any literary text—as a sort of *virtual communication* and therefore as marked in relation to ordinary verbal communication. Aviram, a poet himself who also writes about literary theory and poetry, argues that although the primary function of ordinary (or unmarked) communication is to convey various types of meaning, the function of the literary text is aesthetic. As Aviram puts it, "the proper response to an aesthetic object . . . is contemplation, interpretation, the pleasure of discovering how the parts come together to make a whole, and a sense of wonder at its wholeness, completeness, perfection, ingenuity, and forms of surprise."

In relation to this view, Aviram disagrees with analyses of poetry which emphasize sequential aspects of a text, such as certain specific structural elements. In this sense, he is something of a contrarian in this volume in which most chapters emphasize the role that stylistic choices play in conveying—and not just adding to—the overall intentionality imparted in a literary work or conversation. Aviram claims that "stylisticians assume that what makes poetry poetry is the use of various marked linguistic devices in order to *convey meaning.* . . ." He goes on to say, "Stylisticians tend to assume that the literary text is a message like any other, only more punchy or expressive, using more elaborate devices to get the message across." Instead, he argues that the way poems work as aesthetic structures is to "deliver surprise when given the right context and when read as totalities rather than sequences of elements."

To reinforce his claims as to how literariness conditions the proper approach to reading a poem, he provides explications of a number of poems, including Emily Dickinson's "I cannot live with you," William Blake's "The Tyger" and "A Poison Tree," and Wallace Stevens's "The Snow Man."

The final chapter (chapter 7) in this part is "Villainous Boys: On Some Marked Exchanges in *Romeo and Juliet*" by Trevor Howard-Hill, a well-known editor of Shakespeare and writer about Elizabethan drama in general. In his contribution, he considers the extent to which the MM can be applied beyond conversation. His specific subject is the occurrence of *boy* as a term of address in *Romeo and Juliet*; he argues that the marked usage of *boy* is the basis for the revenge plot on which the play depends. Specifically, Howard-Hill discusses three crucial dramatic moments involving the marked use of *boy* together with repetition of *villain*. Early in the play, Capulet, the head of one of the two feuding houses, censures Tybalt, a hot-headed young man in the Capulet clan, by referring to him as *boy*. Later, Tybalt applies this term to Romeo (from the other feuding house, that of Montague) in challenging him to fight. Howard-Hill argues that the distribution of *boy* and *villain* in the play is by design, not accident. Significantly, *villain* is coupled with *boy* in the last scene of the play.

In his concluding remarks, Howard-Hill brings up the interesting question whether dramatic characters can be seen as making their own linguistic choices. He raises a number of reasons as to why dramatic speakers are not rational actors in the usual sense. For example, he points out that their words are governed by "such matters as the initial choice of genre, the principle of decorum within the general theory of genre, and the specific purposes of the playwright." He also questions what type of expectations *readers* of drama can have in the absence of the effects of performance on a stage. In the end, however, he leaves the answer open to the question about dramatic characters and their "ability" to make linguistic choices. It is a subject deserving more thought; yet, surely with a "suspension of disbelief" both readers and a theater audience can view characters as rational actors and, therefore, they can form expectations about choices that a specific character will make, given the way the character has already been developed by the playwright up to the point of a questioned choice. Both types of audiences also have the acquired ability to approach the entire drama with a sense that certain types of utterances (e.g., calling a young man *boy*) will be marked.

SWITCHING IN NATURALLY OCCURRING TALK

Part III of the volume consists of three chapters that analyze data from spontaneous discourse. In chapter 8, "Markedness and Styleswitching in Performances by African American Drag Queens," Rusty Barrett considers how African American drag queens switch among three styles in their performances.

He labels the styles as *white woman style, African American style,* and *gay style*. Although Barrett details defining features for each style, he also stresses that there is no clear line dividing them. In switching among styles in their performances, drag queens exploit the social and psychological associations of each style by mocking the associations, in a sense. For example, the unmarked association of the white woman style is with white, middle- or upper-class femininity; yet, here is a drag queen who is "none of the above," claiming this style as her own. Similarly, in switching to an African American style—especially when it is a "street" style, as is the case in many of Barrett's examples—the performer is using a spoken style at odds with her clothes and jewelry, which effect a stylish image of glamor. Finally, in switching to a gay style, again the performer projects an image at variance with her dress.

Barrett argues that African American drag queens engage in switching to make a number of social statements. First, they undermine audience assumptions that gender, ethnicity, class, and sexuality are categorical social categories. Second, drag queens demonstrate—by switching styles—that although they are capable of producing language that would allow them to fit into mainstream society (white woman style), they consciously choose to maintain their identities as African American gay men. Third, switching also emphasizes the social inequalities associated with white society. Fourth, these drag queens demonstrate that they refuse to be categorized according to a single set of social attributes.

Barrett also considers another topic in this chapter, how the types of switching which the MM delineates can be used to discuss certain asymmetries between dialect, register, and genre as types of linguistic varieties. Going beyond earlier treatments that largely simply define the three types of varieties, Barrett shows how the MM might provide a principled basis for discussing the ways in which dialects, registers, and genres relate to each other in actual use.

Chapter 9, "Styleswitching in Southern English," by Margaret Mishoe is one of the two chapters in the volume that deal with naturally occurring speech in ordinary conversation. Mishoe describes and explains styleswitches by lower-socioeconomic-class white speakers living in a small community in the North Carolina foothills.

The switches are between the two main styles in their repertoires, what Mishoe calls *home style* and *local standard*. While local standard approximates Standard American English except for its southern phonological features, home style has a number of distinctive morphological and syntactic features that separate it from both the national standard dialect and local standard. Further, a defining feature of local standard that distinguishes it from home style is that local standard is spoken at a clearly slower rate.

Mishoe defines home style as the unmarked choice in the conversations she studies, based on the fact that she could claim it was used in 95% of the conversational turns. In the twelve sequences of ingroup conversation that Mishoe studies, switches generally are marked switches from home style to local standard. For example, when Christmas presents are being unwrapped, it turns out one couple has been given a new camcorder but does not know how to use it. In asserting his expertise and right to assume control of the camcorder, one participant switches to local standard. In another example the switch is from local standard to home style. In this case, the family matriarch greets her guests for a party in local standard to establish her identity as someone who understands her duties as "hostess." However, she switches to home style as her guests are seating themselves in order to re-affirm her identity as a close friend and community member. Because the speakers are Mishoe's own relatives and their friends, the type of ingroup conversations she was able to record resonate with a homespun humor and verisimilitude not often found in the codeswitching literature. Yet, the speakers' motivations for switching all fall under the "classic" motivations that the MM attributes to speakers who make marked choices. In the main, Mishoe's speakers are negotiating a change in the personae that they wish to project and therefore a change in their interpersonal relationships in the current exchange.

The final chapter in this part, chapter 10, "Marked versus Unmarked Choices on the Auto Factory Floor," by Janice Bernsten, considers "the rules of engagement" between assembly-line workers and supervisors. Bernsten, who teaches in the auto factory town of Flint, Michigan, studies talk at work in an auto factory. In her analysis, she concentrates on how both unintentional and intentional marked choices have negative effects in an environment in which not only tasks on the assembly line are very conventionalized.

Although Bernsten was unable to gain entrance to the factory floor herself, she did collect quantitative data from sixty-four workers via a questionnaire and interviews. She found that factory floor language is direct and unmitigated. In fact, she reports that workers expect direct language from supervisors to the extent that mitigated language often receives a negative evaluation. Several of her examples vividly illustrate this. Bernsten suggests that the lack of politeness markers and the pervasiveness of bald imperatives used by both management and workers may index an attempt by each group to assert and maintain equal power.

Bernsten also comments at length about the workers' underlying knowledge of marked and unmarked behavior in the factory. This is apparent, she claims, in the way in which workers responded to hypothetical situations on the questionnaire. She points out that they showed much insight into the major differences in interpretation that minor differences in syntactic and lexical choices could make. Also, many workers wrote about possible interpretations, based on possible differences in the supervisor's perceived assumptions and motivations. As Bernsten writes, "It is evident that given social identity features (e.g., age and gender) and given linguistic choices do not mechanistically determine listeners' interpretations." Instead, perceived attitudes of the speakers play a large part in the listeners' evaluations of possible meanings.

In conclusion, Bernsten states that a practical consequence of such a study is that the findings can be used for training employeees in the most effective discourse patterns, particularly new managers coming from outside the factory culture.

TEACHING WHAT'S MARKED, WHAT'S NOT

The final study in the volume (chapter 11), "'Not quite right': Second-Language Acquisition and Markedness," clearly considers consequences in making a marked rather than an unmarked choice, even if the choices are not always between styles. The author, Mary Sue Sroda, is an experienced composition instructor, who deals with the problems of the second-language learner in mastering "appropriate" language use. As Sroda puts it, "the fundamental issue of language use for teachers of second language (L2) learners is, 'why do we say what when?'" The problem for these teachers is that instead of there being one "correct" answer, there is often a range of "right" answers, some answers that are "not quite right," and other answers that would not be acceptable at all.

Sroda claims that the MM provides an explanatory framework for the range of linguistic choices that second language learners can make that are "not quite right." Sroda proposes that the examples of "odd" language can be redefined as choices that are marked for a given rights and obligations set and, therefore, interfere with or confound communication.

Sroda develops her argument by showing in a case study how both native and nonnative speakers may make marked choices, but that there are differences in the types made across the two groups. (In the case study she presented both native and non-native speakers enrolled in freshman English with a perplexing situation: "You've locked your keys in the car. You have to call someone to bring your spare keys. You have to ask a stranger for the money to call—what do you say?") On the basis of her results and the frameworks she employs (both the MM and Sperber and Wilson's relevance theory), Sroda proposes that nonnative speakers can be taught to include certain crucial *information features* for given interaction types. In the keys-in-the-car scenario, information features that must be included to satisfy the requirements of the unmarked rights and obligations set between speaker and stranger would be "ask for money," "no keys," and "use for money." Responses which omitted "no keys" are marked because hearers cannot pragmatically recover the situation that has caused the speakers to ask for the quarter. The unmarked rights and obligations set between speaker and stranger can be maintained in spite of the imposition of the request if the speaker provides a good reason, as defined by the community.

Sroda sees the MM as useful in her emphasis on teaching students about crucial information features, as opposed to teaching them set phrases. She uses two notions from the MM in this regard. First, she states that the claim of the

MM is not that native speakers always try to make unmarked code choices but that they have the ability to make both marked and unmarked choices in interactions and through these choices do "social" work. This leads to one of Sroda's main points: Second-language learners also want to be able to make both marked and unmarked choices. She writes, "Without the ability to have the option of marked choices in their linguistic repertoires, L2 learners will never acquire a native-like pragmatic ability." Second, Sroda argues that "the ability of the MM to describe normative choices while allowing for surface variation can be of use in explaining to L2 learners how their choices are marked."

In a final section, Sroda discusses the range of marked choices that both native and nonnative speakers make in their academic writing. She argues that although there are countless discussions in the literature of composition and rhetoric about the influence that cultural knowledge has on language use, the MM operationalizes the interaction between language and culture in the concept of L1-defined rights and obligation sets; that is, what nonnative speakers need to learn is not set phrases but the way that the unmarked rights and obligations set underlies the selection of unmarked information units and lexical choices.

CONCLUSION

The diversity of subject matter in the chapters in this volume demonstrates—with vigor—how the general theoretical construct of markedness can be invoked to explain the social and psychological effects of choosing one style of a language rather than another. The specific usefulness of the MM in such analyses also seems clear, even when it has not been explicitly employed by particular authors.

In conclusion, several findings of general importance emerge. First, as is especially evident in chapter 10 on auto factory floor talk , distinguishing the unmarked choice from a marked choice (or an unmarked style from a marked style) is not just a matter of "common sense." Factory discourse differs from the discourse of the other worlds the workers inhabit. This suggests that it is not a speaker's linguistic repertoire or global norms about politeness that determine choices but, rather, the interaction-specific cognitive calculations that distinguish rational choice.

Second, what is implicit in all the chapters and made explicit in Kreml's chapter on the Cormac McCarthy novel (chapter 3) is that the interaction of styles is what gives rise to the richest implications, thereby setting up the most implicatures. That is, although each style has import on its own, the fact that each style is necessarily perceived in terms of a markedness relationship offers us insights into that import that would not be available *without the opposition.* Contrast is not everything, but it is a major constraining force on interpretation.

REFERENCES

Adendorff, Ralph D. 1993. Ethnographic evidence of the social meaning of Fanakalo in South Africa. *Journal of Pidgin and Creole Languages* 8: 1–28.

Battistella, Edwin L. 1990. *Markedness: the evaluative superstructure of language.* Albany: State University of New York Press.

———. 1996. *The logic of markedness.* New York: Oxford University Press.

Blakemore, Diane. 1992. *Understanding utterances.* Oxford: Blackwell.

Cook, Vivian, and Mark Newson. 1996. 2nd ed. *Chomsky's universal grammar, an introduction.* Oxford: Blackwell.

Damasio, Antonio. 1996. The somatic marker hypothesis and the possible functions of the prefrontal cortex. *Philosophical Transactions of the Royal Society of London B* 351: 1313–1420.

DeBose, Charles. 1992. Codeswitching: black English and standard English in the African-American linguistic repertoire. *Journal of Multilingual and Multicultural Development* 13: 157–167.

Eastman, Carol M. 1985. Establishing social identity through language use. *Journal of Language and Social Psychology* 4: 1–20.

Elster, Jon. 1989. *The cement of society.* Cambridge: Cambridge University Press.

Gibbons, John. 1987. *Code-mixing and code choice: a Hong Kong case study.* Clevedon, Avon: Multilingual Matters.

Grice, H. P. 1975. Logic and conversation. In *Syntax and semantics,* vol. 3, ed. Peter Cole and Jerry L. Morgan, 198–211. New York: Academic Press.

Jakobson, Roman. 1971. *Selected writings,* Vol. 2: *Word and language.* The Hague: Mouton.

Li, Wei. 1994. *Three Generations, two languages, one family.* Clevedon, England: Multilingual Matters Ltd.

Myers-Scotton, Carol. 1985. "What the heck, sir?" Style shifting and lexical colouring as features of powerful language. In *Sequence and pattern in communicative behaviour,* ed. Richard L. Street and J. N. Cappella, 103–119. London: Arnold.

———. 1988a. Codeswitching as indexical of social negotiation. In *Codeswitching: anthropological and sociolinguistic perspectives,* ed. Monica Heller, 151–186. Berlin: Mouton de Gruyter.

———. 1988b. Self-enhancing codeswitching as interactional power. *Language and Communication* 8: 199–211.

———. 1993. *Social motivations for codeswitching: evidence from Africa.* Oxford: Oxford University Press.

Myers-Scotton, Carol [Scotton, Carol Myers], and Zhu Wanjin. 1983. *Tongzhi* in Chinese: conversational consequences of language change. *Language in Society* 12: 477–494.

Sperber, Dan and Deirdre Wilson. 1995. 2nd ed. *Relevance, communication and cognition.* Oxford: Blackwell.

Swigart, Leigh. 1992. Two codes or one? The insider's view and the description of codeswitching in Dakar. *Journal of Multilingual and Multicultural Development* 13: 83–102.

Trubetzkoy, Nikolai. 1939. *Principles of phonology.* Trans. Christiane A. M. Baltaxe. Reprint, Berkeley: University of California Press, 1969.

2

A Theoretical Introduction to the Markedness Model

CAROL MYERS-SCOTTON

IN EVERY SPEECH community, more than one way of speaking exists. That is, no community is without at least two different speech styles, and in many communities, more than one dialect or more than one language is spoken, even if some people speak only one dialect of one language. In the case of dialects and languages, these varieties typically can be associated with different social groups; that is, not everyone in the community has command of all the varieties in the community's linguistic repertoire, or not everyone uses the varieties he or she knows with the same frequencies. To a lesser extent, the same can be said for different styles or registers. Although the same styles may be more or less in everyone's repertoire, clear degrees of difference in an individual's access to different styles exists and certainly differences in when and where they are used exist. (*Varieties* is a cover term for selections at all linguistic levels so that choices between varieties include, for example, choices of one language rather than another, one dialect over another, one style or register over another, and one form of a directive or refusal over another.) Transforming these assertions about varieties and their associations with social groups and social contexts into quantitatively based facts is the bread-and-butter activity of much sociolinguistic research. One basic claim of the markedness model (MM) follows on these facts. This claim is simply that in their own language use, individuals exploit the relationships that become established in a community between a linguistic variety and who uses the variety, and where and how it is used. That is, individuals take advantage of the associations that their addressees/readers make between a variety and its typical users or uses. (From now on, I use *speaker* as a cover term for both *speaker* and *writer* and *addressee* as a cover term for both *addressee* and *reader*.) Of course, at least some other researchers who study social discourse have made the same observation. For example, Bell (1984) argues not only that individual speakers design their conversational contribution with their *audience* in mind but that the particular *design* chosen is based on the speech associated with a particular social group. Also, in claiming that speakers use certain *politeness strategies* Brown and Levinson (1987) surely imply that speakers expect that addresees will interpret these strategies as "polite" because the strategies are customarily associated with "being polite" in various ways in specific speech communities (see also Tracy 1990 for other uses of such strategies). Further, speech accommodation theory, revitalized as communication accommodation theory (CAT), relies on speakers and addressees recognizing that a speaker's choice of a particular variety is *accommodation* or *divergence* (Giles and Coupland 1991; Giles, Coupland, and Coupland 1991). And, of course, to recognize accommodation/divergence, language users have to associate varieties with particular users and "scripts" for situations.

The way in which the MM is related to the approaches cited previously is that they all accord to language users the ability to make choices regarding the varieties they employ, choices that necessarily involve cognitive calculations about their potential effect . In brief, these approaches are all cognitively based approaches. All these approaches would argue that choices are intentional in the sense that they are made to achieve certain social ends. Further, not only are speakers' intentions behind choices, but speakers make choices with the expectation that addressees will recognize a choice as carrying a particular intention. On this view, speakers' choices are not determined by their social group memberships—although their individual linguistic repertoires (what varieties are available to each individual) *are* very much so determined. Unfortunately, some researchers mistakenly equate limitations on *choices* with limitations on *repertoire* (e.g., Meeuwis and Blommaert 1994 in their criticism of the MM). I discuss the relationship between repertoire and choices further later.

The MM, as well as the other approaches cited previously, all assume that speakers are *rational* in the sense that, at some level of consciousness, they are *making choices* that do not simply reflect their social group memberships or the type of speech event in which they are participating or the structure of the event. In fact, later I argue that the MM belongs to the class of *rational actor models,* and the same could be said of these other approaches. However, although all these approaches exploit the sociopsychological associations of linguistic varieties in explaining the choices speakers make, a second claim of the MM that sets it apart in subtle but important ways is the issue of goals. To put it explicitly, the question to be answered by any of these approaches is, *To what end* are speakers exploiting the social (or psychological) relationships of linguistic varieties in a given community? In what general sense can their goals be characterized? Under the MM, the goal of speakers is to enhance rewards and minimize costs; in two words, the goal is *to optimize.* What this means is that speakers choose one variety over another because of the benefits they expect from that choice, relative to its costs. Although the other approaches just mentioned can also be considered rational actor models to an extent, they explain linguistic choices more as instances of blanket strategies than does the MM. For example, such a strategy as accommodation or politeness has a certain uniformity in the source of its explanation of choices. Under the MM, speakers may well accommodate to the addressee's style or may use politenesss strategies, but they also may not. Choices depend on the strategy that would *optimize for self*. Thus, making choices is necessarily seen under the MM as very customized. Often it will mean putting together combinations of choices; it will always mean taking account of all available evidence regarding the best strategies for the specific exchange at hand and considering the internal consistency of a set of choices. This difference is discussed further later.

While the claim of optimization as the speaker's goal has been a major ingredient in the MM since its original formulation (Myers-Scotton 1983), I made it increasingly prominent in more recent presentations (e.g., Myers-Scotton 1988a, 1988b). In the most recent publications on the MM, I began to refer specifically to the MM as a rational actor model (Myers-Scotton 1993, 1997). I develop this line here. As Elster (e.g., 1979) pointed out, such a model does not claim that people are *always* rational in their choices; however, it does claim that the premise that a choice can be explained as rationally based does *cover* the phenomenon. Next, I develop further the ways in which the MM is a rational actor model.

First I offer an up-to-date outline of the basic tenets of the MM that have appeared in the previous discussions of the model mentioned earlier. The most recent interpretations of the MM were in reference to codeswitching between languages (Myers-Scotton 1988, 1993); they may have misled some readers into thinking the model applies only to such codeswitching. This limitation is most definitely not the case; to reiterate what was said in earlier explications, the MM applies to code choices at all levels of language.

INTERPRETATION AS MORE THAN DECODING
THE LINGUISTIC SIGNAL

Like the *cooperative principle* and its related maxims (Grice 1975) and *relevance theory* (Sperber and Wilson 1995), the MM starts with the premise that comprehension of an utterance involves much more than decoding the linguistic signal. All three models include as a second premise that the gap between this decoding and what is actually meant to be communicated can be filled in by inference, a process driven by the certainty that the message carries intentionality in addition to referentiality. Further, each of these three models has its own "superpremise" that is a crucial part of the interpretation of *all* choices. In this way, they are more "global" than an approach that seeks to explain why *particular* strategies are used (e.g., politeness or accommodation strategies). For Grice (1975), the superpremise is that all participants proceed with the expectation that utterances are so framed that they are "cooperative" and that this premise will aid in recovering intended messages. For Sperber and Wilson (1995), "relevance" is the key premise. Their principle of relevance is this: "Every act of ostensive communication communicates a presumption of its own optimal relevance" (Sperber and Wilson 1995: 158). In the case of the MM, the global premise is "negotiation," encapsulated in my negotiation principle. The principle is:

> Choose the *form* of your conversational contribution such that it indexes the set of rights and obligations which you wish to be in force between speaker and addressee for the current exchange.

Clearly, the negotiation principle is modeled in its phrasing after Grice's cooperative principle. As such, it pays tribute to Grice's (1975) insight that participants interpret verbal messages with preconceived notions about forces that color how interpretation is to proceed. Like Grice's principle, the negotiation principle is intended to clue in addressees that, in addition to conveying information, the speaker has an interactional goal. However, at this point, the resemblance between the two principles ends. As noted earlier, the clue that Grice's principle gives to addressees is that they should be able to assume that speakers are being cooperative. In contrast, the negotiation principle says nothing about interactants as cooperating with each other. The only cooperation the negotiation principle necessarily implies is that both speaker and addressee approach the interaction with the same preconception about the purpose of the form of the speaker's contribution: that this form can be interpreted as indexing a negotiation. This negotiation can have one of two related concerns: Either it refers more directly to the speaker's persona itself or more to this persona *in relation to that of other participants in the interaction.* (In many ways, of course, the speaker's persona can never stand on its own but only in a contrastive/complementary relationship with that of others.)

An important aspect of all three of these models in which there is an intentional message implied is that successful communication depends on having all participants "involved"—at least to the extent that they recognize that either "cooperation" or "relevance" or "negotiation" is a crucial basis for interpretation. In this way, all instances of language use must be joint enterprises in some sense. This view of language is not novel today, of course, at least in many circles. For example, the thesis of *Using Language* is that "Language use is really a form of *joint action*" (Clark 1996: 3). Further, the view that language use involves some sort of "co-construction" is a major premise in the many studies under the rubric of *conversation analysis*. However, just because these various views share the idea of joint enterprise does not mean all their premises are complementary. Conversation analysis, for example, emphasizes the contribution of the surface structural features of a conversation to the ultimate meaning that participants derive from an interaction. Sequential organization in particular is a major feature studied. In contrast, the three models under discussion in this section (Grice's cooperative principle model, Sperber and Wilson's relevance theory, and my MM) would say that in addition to the referential messages in words and their configurations, the critical messages in discourse are in mental calculations of what is being inferred, not in how surface structures are aligned. Thus, the "joint enterprise" for these models is at the cognitive level. That is, such models are based on the idea that speakers "know" that they can employ utterances for more than referential messages and that they know that addressees know this also and therefore will be looking for organization at this level. Note that although in all three of these models an intentional message is implied, only in the MM is this "extra" message sociopsychological in nature, not referential. This is not to say that the other two models could not be so modified as to refer to sociopsychological inferences; however, as conceputalized, they do not.

OUTLINING THE MARKEDNESS MODEL

I turn now to the components of the MM. First, the MM presupposes that as part of their linguistic capacity—or their general cognitive capacity—all speakers have what I have called *a markedness metric* and which I now prefer to call *a markedness evaluator*. (*Metric* implies discrete and linear measuring; this is not how I now realize markedness should be conceived.) The existence of a markedness evaluator implies that the capacity to conceptualize markedness is part of any innate competence. Conceptualizing markedness means possessing the potential to develop two abilities: (1) the ability to recognize that linguistic choices fall along a multidimensional continuum from more unmarked to more marked and that their ordering will vary, depending on the specific discourse type, and (2) the ability to comprehend that marked choices will receive different receptions from unmarked choices. Actually, to develop either of these abilities requires exposure to the use of unmarked and marked choices in actual community discourse, in the same way that a speaker requires exposure to a language in use to acquire its grammatical structures. (Innateness requires a data base to be instantiated.) From this exposure, language users develop the general understanding of markedness in relation to alternative linguistic varieties for a given interaction type and "know" that making marked choices has different consequences from making unmarked choices.

I argue later how this exposure actually sets up "readings of markedness" in the markedness evaluator in a way very similar to how Damasio (1994, 1996) claims that somatic markers are set up in the body and in the brain's representation of the body that have to do with "survival" at a number of levels. In referring to his somatic marker hypothesis, he states, "The hypothesis rejects attempts to limit human reasoning and decision making to mechanisms relying, in an exclusive and unrelated manner, on either conditioning alone or cognition alone" (Damasio 1996: 1413). As should become clearer as this chapter proceeds, the MM's argument is in a similar vein. Speakers can make links between the use of a linguistic variety and its effect in a certain situation; this linking is a form of associative learning. These linkages are only set up through experience with language in use. While the MM definitely recognizes the crucial role of the speaker's actual experience with social factors, the model argues that speakers do not make choices of linguistic varieties on the basis of such direct linkages in a cause-and-effect fashion. Instead, the MM builds in a device that will prune multiple options and multiple future outcomes in some way. This device is a cognitive device, the markedness evaluator. It takes these individual linkages as input and appraises them with reference to the theoretical construct of markedness. Markedness, then, is best considered as *a means to compare* the effects associated with one particular linkage between the use of a linguistic variety with linkages associated with other varieties. Choices then are biased by the readings of markedness for linkages contained in the markedness evaluator.

To repeat, even though the markedness evaluator has an innately based presence (whether as a task-specific module or—more likely—as the output of specific weightings in general neural networks), it comes with no innate evaluations. Rather, it only comes programmed with the ability (and bias) to make evaluations. When the speaker is exposed to language in use, this experience provides the basis for the assessments the evaluator will make. It does this by taking the linkages that experience has shown hold between a certain choice for a given discourse and its outcome in relation to an individual's position in a given speech community. These markedness readings are always relative in three ways. First, they are interaction-specific. Second, they are dynamic, meaning they are subject to change with changing circumstances, even within a single interaction; that is, what was a marked choice—in regard to the relationship between participants at the outset of an interaction—can become an unmarked choice in the process of negotiation. Finally, they always involve multidimensional ordering, meaning choices are more or less marked, not categorically marked.

Note that choices are seen as more or less unmarked for a particular *rights and obligations set* (RO set). "Rights and obligations" is a theoretical construct for referring to what participants can expect in any given interaction type in their community. For example, a person who calls a business establishment on the phone and asks to speak to a particular employee can expect that the receptionist will either connect her to that employee or take a message if the employee is not available. The term *rights and obligations* does not generally refer to actual "rights" in any legal or moral sense; for example, a customer standing at the cash register in a drugstore with an item he wishes to buy in plain view cannot *a priori* sue the idle salesperson at the cash register who ignores him for more than a minute or so. (However, of course, the salesperson's boss can fire him for neglect of duty.) In reference to some types of behavior, *rights and obligations* is another term for *norms,* codes of behavior that are established and maintained by the social group. Norms are discussed further later.

The unmarked RO set for a given interaction type (or genre, if literary works are the subject) is derived from whatever situational features are salient for the community for that interaction type. As I noted in *Social Motivations* (1993), I do not attempt to specify what those situational features are. I avoid doing so for three reasons: First, the same situational features are not relevant in all interaction types (or genres) or across all communities. For example, in one type, socioeconomic status or occupation may be relevant, but in another it may not. When I made an initial visit to a law firm recently, I was careful to "dress as a professional"; the attorney I was to see already knew my occupation, but I thought I might get better treatment from the receptionist if she could infer my status. However, men who are emptying my garbage container in front of my house while I write this do not care whether I am a professional person or a blue-collar worker; it will not change how "well" they empty my garbage cart. Second, the content of a situational feature may change. For example, what qualifies a person to be considered a member of ethnic group *x* may change because the defining features of that ethnic group may change. Third, the hierarchical relation of one feature to another feature in an interaction type may change. This change can happen within the interaction itself when the topic changes. For example, the relative expertise of group members regarding how a particular technological device, such as a camcorder, works may be relatively unimportant until using the device becomes a goal in a group (Mishoe chapter 9, this volume). Hierarchial relations of features can change over time as well. For example, participants may revise their views of how much certain technological skills are to be valued, or gender or ethnic group may take on increased salience over other features as national political debate centers on these features. At the same time, it is true that one can predict that some factors will figure in the establishment of the unmarked RO set in many interaction types. These factors include the main social identity features of participants (e.g., age, sex, ethnic group, socioeconomic status, and occupation) as well as topic/ goal and setting.

Another reason I avoided attempting to come up with a taxonomy of the features necessary to characterize the relations of participants in an un- marked RO set is that such attempts very quickly run into problems because a binary opposition along the lines of relevant versus irrelevant is hard to apply. What should count as "relevant"? Some features seemingly must be specified, but what about others which are desirable? And what about "ir- relevant"? Is there a difference between calling a feature *overspecified* and

calling it *out of place?* In addition, even to classify two participants in relation to a "must specify" criterion is difficult. For example, consider the
relative statuses of the speaker versus addressee in Sroda's keys-in-the-car
situation (chapter 11, this volume) in which the speaker who has locked his
or her keys in the car asks a stranger for a quarter to call a friend. From one
point of view, the stranger has higher status in this interaction and deserves
deference, because the speaker is asking a favor. However, from another
point of view, to think that he or she has the "right" to ask a stranger for a
quarter, the speaker almost necessarily must consider that some "egalitarian
norm" prevails, making his or her status as far as the interaction type is
concerned (if not this particular interaction) equal to that of the stranger.

Thus, it is difficult to specify exhaustively and discretely the situational
features that go into determining the unmarked RO set for a given interaction type. Further, to assume that such a specification, such a taxonomy, has
any explanatory value on its own is a mistake. I return to this point later in
a discussion of how truly explanatory comprehensive models of language
use are valuable, even in their "infancy."

In sum, utilizing the input of their experiences in their community and the
cognitive equipment in their markedness evaluator, speakers (and addressees) are able to arrive at readings of markedness of two types. First, they can
establish the outlines of the unmarked RO set for a particular interaction type.
To do this, they take into account whatever situational features are salient,
given a specific community and interaction type. These features may well
include participants, topic, and setting. Second, they calculate the relative markedness of code choices (i.e., linguistic varieties) to index the unmarked RO set.

THE MARKEDNESS MODEL EXPLAINED

In the following sections, I present the MM as a rational actor (RA) model.
As such, the MM is integrated into a more comprehensive view of how social
behaviors arise. First, I give the maxims of the MM from the *Social Motivations* version and examples of unmarked and marked choices that show stylistic
variation. Next, I outline how RA models work in general and clarify how the
MM can be considered a type of such a model. In relation to this, I explore
research suggesting how situational and cognitive features of the MM can be
integrated into a coherent explanatory and predictive model of language use as
an instance of general participant behaviors. I also outline the steps involved in
linguistic choices according to the MM as an RA model. Finally, I offer some
reasons to attempt to formulate such a model to explain language use.

Maxims under the Markedness Model

Given specific *readings* of the markedness evaluator, speakers make code
choices with the following five maxims in mind. Although these maxims
were originally formulated to refer to naturally occurring conversations,

with a little modification, writers can apply at least the unmarked-choice and the marked-choice maxims to literary texts, and the characters in literature can apply them all.

> *The Unmarked Choice Maxim*: Make your code choice the unmarked index of the unmarked rights and obligations set in talk exchanges when you wish to establish or affirm that rights and obligations set.
>
> *The Marked Choice Maxim:* Make a marked choice which is not the unmarked index of the unmarked rights and obligations set in an interaction when you wish to establish a new rights and obligations set as unmarked for the current exchange.
>
> *The Exploratory Choice Maxim*: When an unmarked choice is not clear, use switching between speech varieties to make alternate exploratory choices as (alternate) candidates for the unmarked choice and thereby as an index of a rights and obligations set which you favor.
>
> *Deference Maxim*: Switch to a code which expresses deference to others when special respect is called for by the circumstances.
>
> *Virtuosity Maxim:* Switch to whatever code is necessary in order to carry on the conversation/accommodate the participation of all speakers present.

How Speakers Apply the Maxims

What motivates speakers to follow any one of these maxims? If speakers follow either the unmarked-choice maxim or the marked-choice maxim, it is clear that they are negotiating the RO set they see as beneficial to them in some way. To follow either the deference maxim or the virtuosity maxim has fewer direct advantages for the speaker; however, there certainly are indirect benefits. Presumably, speakers follow the deference maxim when they "want something" from the addressee; that is, speakers choose deference because they expect it will have a payoff for them, even if it is only avoided costs. Following the virtuosity maxim allows speakers to present themselves as *enablers* in that they make it possible for a conversation to take place; in this way, they put themselves in a good light. Also, by utilizing their ability to switch from one code to another they show off their linguistic repertoire and therefore show themselves as multidimensional individuals.

Note that the model assumes that different individuals have similar notions of what choices are unmarked for given situations. How can this be so, since any community includes people from different social backgrounds? The key to understanding that a particular linguistic choice is unmarked is *not* to say that it is the one that gives the most members of the community the best outcome; rather it is only the one most *expected,* and what makes it expected is that it meets the beliefs and desires of those persons in the community who have sufficient power to set norms. The fact is simply that opportunities to designate markedness are not equally distributed across a community. This inequity is also recognized in one of the propositions of an extended version of communication accommodation theory: "In formal and status-stressing situations, many speakers are likely to converge to the sociolinguistic markers and behavior of the dominant group" (Gallois, Giles, Jones, Cargile, and Ota 1995: 142). Note that the model does not operationalize markedness in its maxims. Markedness is a theoretical construct; such constructs are defined by their properties, but their existence is not subject to direct falsifiability. For example, as it is used in the MM, the major property of markedness is that different linguistic choices link different social meanings to specific RO sets in specific interaction types or genres. Theoretical constructs differ from the hypotheses derived from them because these prediction-making hypotheses must be so stated so that it is clear what type of evidence would falsify them. The relation of the hypotheses to the construct is that if the hypotheses are supported, this attests to the construct's value as a heuristic that abstracts information from data sets. Information so framed has an economy; it is an organized system, not just a description. The main argument of the MM is that the unmarked versus marked opposition is just such a heuristic.

A hypothesis identifying the unmarked choice can be derived from the construct of markedness as applied to code choice. This is the frequency hypothesis:

> One linguistic variety, structural type, or discourse pattern occurs with more frequency than other possible varieties or structures as the most unmarked index of a specific RO set in a specific interaction type.

How are the terms of this hypothesis operationalized? Languages, dialects, and styles operationalize "linguistic variety." Structural types consist of lexical, morphosyntactic and phonological patterns (e.g., what information units comprise an "ask a stranger for a quarter" scenario, as discussed in chapter 11). Note that except for linguistic variety, the unmarked choice is not a single entity, but rather a set of entities with like features (e.g., bald imperatives, some with tags, some not). And, of course, linguistic varieties themselves are not really discrete entities, either.

Speakers concur on the unmarked choice because, thanks to the markedness evaluator, they "know" (consciously, but more often unconsciously) that the unmarked choice has occurred with more frequency than other choices in like circumstances in their community. They also have tacit knowledge that other community members share this recognition.

That unmarked choices emerge when data sets are examined quantitatively is supported empirically (e.g., Scotton and Bernsten 1988; Blum-Kulka, House, and Kasper 1989). Admittedly, though, I would like to see more studies that test the hypothesis that frequency in outcome types positively correlates with the unmarked choice. Other hypotheses also can be derived from the construct of markedness, specifically ones about the types of speakers and situations (including social and intellectual climates) that favor unmarked versus marked choices. However, such a discussion goes beyond the goals of this chapter.

Earlier, I implied that the unmarked choice does not "treat" everyone "equally." Why, then, should most speakers make the unmarked choice? This point is addressed in some detail later when I discuss what it means to behave rationally. Here, suffice it to discuss why people "build" norms and behave in terms of them. One of the major proponents of RA models, Elster (1989) characterizes social norms as the "cement of society." He writes that "social norms coordinate expectations" (Elster 1989: 97). Because norms, by their very nature, depend on an often unspoken consensus, norms necessarily favor unmarked choices, which themselves depend on a consensus (i.e., the fact they occur more frequently than marked choices implies a consensus). Since speakers know that most group members (not all!) perceive social norms as legitimate, they tend to see unmarked choices in the same light. Even if they do not find norms to be legitimate, speakers generally find them to be *compelling* because of the potential costs resulting from violating them. Again, this expectation favors unmarked choices. Persons can use the "compelling" component of norms to their own advantage through their own choices. And, whether they do this by making an unmarked or a marked choice, their choice is a negotiation *to make it a norm* and thereby to bind other participants.

Thus, although each person is free to make choices on his or her own, what unites individual choices is that they are made against the same backdrop of what is unmarked or marked. This tacit knowledge not only promotes unmarked choices, as I have just argued, but also accounts for the ability of participants (who have been socialized in the community in question) to interpret marked choices; that is, at the very least, they know that a marked choice is *not* an unmarked choice.

Examples of unmarked choices should be easy to find, and they are. In a very clear example, Ervin-Tripp (1976: 123) gives what are contrasting unmarked choices for asking a physician to hand an associate a chart. From a nurse, the unmarked choice would be an embedded imperative (modal + *you* interrogative). In Ervin-Tripp's version, the nurse includes a mitigating opener and closer: *Oh, by the way, doctor, could you leave me that chart when you're through?* However, for one physician to another, the unmarked choice would be a bald imperative. In Ervin-Tripp's example, an informal attention-getter precedes the bald imperative and a tag question follows it: *Hey, Len, shoot the chart to me, willya?*

To illustrate the dynamic nature of choices and the use of a marked choice to index a new RO set, consider the following. At a university where I used to teach, a male professor whom I knew socially was named provost. One day soon after his appointment I called him on departmental business. As a conversational opener, I identified myself and said, *How are you?* Rather than respond with the unmarked choice in such an interaction between acquaintances, if not close friends (*Fine, how are you?*), he said, *What can I do for you?* This choice, marked for conversational openers between friends and even only social acquaintances, of course, was his negotiation for a new RO set in which we were not to interact as friends but as provost and faculty member.

The Markedness Model as a Rational Actor Model

In this section, I show the ways in which the MM can be considered an RA model. In doing so, I develop the argument that linguistic code choices, far from being best explained as chance behavior, or linear responses to sequencing rules in conversation, are best explained as instances of the speaker acting rationally. To act rationally simply means that a choice reflects a goal to enhance rewards and minimize costs—as I said at the outset, to optimize. Indirectly, this section is an argument to support the claims of the authors of the various chapters about the goals of the various speakers and authors who are their subjects. In a final section, I discuss the merits of explanation and prediction inherent in this approach.

RA theorists come from a variety of disciplines, including economics and sociology. My treatment of RA models relies heavily on discussions in a number of places by Jon Elster, a philosopher. I adapt many of his ideas and those of other RA researchers as a means of explaining the choice of one linguistic variety over others. The general claim of such models can be stated very simply: Choices in specific interactions are best explained as cognitively based calculations that depend on the actor's (speaker's) estimation of what actions offer him or her the greatest utility. Note that RA models are often in opposition to equity theory which Clark (1996) promotes as a major influencing factor in linguistic choices. Clark's discussion results in defining equity theory in a number of different, not necessarily complementary, ways. I can certainly agree with one view he presents and do not see it contradicting RA models: "Equity theory rests on the assumption that people try to avoid the distress they feel in inequitable situations" (Clark 1996: 292). He goes on to relate ideas about "protecting face" from Goffman (1967) and Brown and Levinson (1987) to equity theory. Again, I can see how reciprocity in protecting face does not contradict the premises of RA models that I am supporting here. However, I cannot say the same for "the equity principle" he proposes:

> In proposing a joint project, speakers are expected to pesuppose a method for maintaining equity with their addressees. (Clark 1996: 295)

The possibility that speakers make marked choices which are negotiations *against* the existing status quo is a major point in the MM. Whether this possibility is compatible with the equity principle all depends on what is meant by "maintaining equity." Clark never makes that clear. If "maintaining equity" means "achieving a mutually acceptable outcome," then the MM (and presumably other RA models) can accept "equity." Certainly, a point that needs to be stressed about the MM is that speakers' choices—and most especially marked choices—are only *negotiations*. For them to "go through," they must be accepted as an acceptable medium to all participating speakers. (Parenthetically, let me say that Clark's citation of David Lewis's insight [1969] "that language use is really people solving coordination problems" [Clark 1996: 62] *is* something I can endorse.) However, just because all participants accept a linguistic variety as an acceptable medium (and therefore accept the RO set for which it is unmarked) does not mean that they necessarily "avoid the distress they feel in inequitable situations" or that they "maintain equity with their addressees." Many times, some participants must endure inequity; it is the nature of human interactions, like it or not. Of course, Clark is correct in pointing out that there are a number of linguistic choices that can be bids to restore or maintain equity, such as deference strategies and avoidance rituals. However, the speaker in the more powerful position is not obliged to use them.

Above all, RA models are mainly concerned with explaining why actors (speakers) make the choices they do. And they explain choices as the means by which actors try to achieve their ends as well as possible. As such, RA models focus less on choices in relation to the effect of their choices on others than some other approaches that I have indicated also are cognitively based. I have in mind Bell's (1984) model of audience design, as well as Brown and Levinson's (1987) politeness model or the CAT model of Giles and his associates (1991). CAT also presents speakers as, sometimes at least, making choices based more on "social comparisons," the desirability of presenting oneself as a member of one group versus another (e.g., Giles, Coupland, and Coupland 1991: 27; Giles and Wiemann 1987). This difference in focus need not be taken as a shortcoming of any of the approaches, but it is an important difference. While speakers as rational actors include an evaluation of the effects of choices on others, the *actor* is central. Speakers seek to optimize their *own* outcomes, not those of their addressees.

A second point favors RA models over other models of language choice: RA models provide a *mechanism* that activates behavior. Rationality is such a mechanism, Elster argues. This is so because RA models provide a means of telling us how things happen on two levels. First, in its emphasis on cost-benefit analysis, an RA model necessarily explains choices as goal directed. In this way it tells us *why* choices are made. Second, rationality is also the mechanism that answers the question of *how* choices are made. According to Elster, to behave rationally includes three optimizing operations: (1) considering given desires and values and prior beliefs, to find the best action; (2) making sure that these desires, values, and beliefs are internally consistent; and (3) making sure these desires, values, and beliefs are based on available evidence. Note that to be considered rational, to simply hold intentions based on desires, values, and beliefs is not enough; the tests of internal consistency and available evidence are crucial.

SOCIAL NORMS AND RATIONAL CHOICES

Previously, I introduced the role of social norms in code choice. I implied that one reason unmarked choices develop is that they themselves are norms. However, I now argue against the view that social norms are the major mechanism in choosing among possible varieties, that choices are made merely to support norms. It is true that norms designate marked and unmarked choices, but speakers make choices.

Yet, norms certainly *do* influence speakers. Recognizing this tells us why unmarked choices are the most frequent. First, to be norms, courses of action or views have to be shared by others and they are partly sustained by the approval/disapproval of others. Even when violating norms, nonsociopathic individuals also "preserve" norms by their own feelings of embarrassment, guilt, or shame. Thus, a major reason to make the unmarked choice (i.e., within the terms of the MM, to follow a norm in one's choice of linguistic variety) is to avoid group disapproval and personal distress, as noted in the discussion of Clark (1996) earlier.

Risk aversion is a second reason for making the unmarked choice, even if making the unmarked choice (i.e., following norms) does not give the speaker what he or she might consider to be the "best" outcome. That is, a second reason for not making a marked choice which *might* optimize the outcome, which would negotiate a desired RO set, is that the speaker's subjective and objective evaluations of the probability of success tell the speaker that chances of success are low. That is, making a marked choice might not be following the stricture of rationality to base decisions on available evidence. Further, it is often simply *safer* to make the unmarked choice. Many economists (e.g., Kagel 1995) demonstrate that people are simply afraid of taking risks (i.e., risk aversion is stronger than the profit motive).

Third, another reason to opt for the unmarked choice is that making and negotiating the desired consequences of marked choices may require more effort. Selection in general has a moving target. To make marked choices that actually achieve their goals, one must recognize the "strategic" nature of the environment and assess successfully the intricacies of the interrelation of salient factors in a specific interaction and the possibility of change in their relative saliency. That is, the environment itself can change because it includes other actors who are similar to the speaker and therefore who will be trying to maximize their gains, too. (In chapter 4, I argue that processing a kind of marked choice in a novel requires more effort from the reader [addressee] than processing unmarked choices.)

Yet, at times, speakers *do* make marked choices. These are choices that do not index the unmarked RO set; therefore, in making such choices, the speaker's aim is to establish a new RO set as unmarked for the current exchange. Marked choices derive their intentional meaning from two sources. First, because a marked choice is *not* the unmarked choice for the unmarked RO set for the current exchange, its choice is a negotiation *against* that unmarked RO set. Second, it is a call for *another* RO set in its place. The choice that is marked under the *current* RO set is, in fact, unmarked in the *new* RO set which the speaker is negotiating.

THE MARKEDNESS MODEL AND THE
EVOLUTION OF SURVIVAL MECHANISMS

Note that both Elster's ideas about RA theory and mine about the MM rest on the premise that speakers are innately disposed to make decisions that they judge will result in the best outcome. In effect, such a premise assumes that actors are innately disposed toward optimizing survival. This premise receives support from empirical research which, at first glance, is very distant from a cost-benefit analysis of social behaviors and specifically of linguistic choices. This area of research is the neurobiological study of reactions to a variety of stimuli, with the organism's survival as a goal. The research of Damasio and his associates introduced earlier deals with possible functions of the prefrontal cortices. Damasio argues that "marker signs" influence the types of responses which an organism will have to stimuli. The connection with human responses to social situations, which Damasio himself suggests, is made in the following way. First, Damasio lays the groundwork by giving evidence that organisms have "preorganized mechanisms" to handle basic biological activities that contribute to survival. Organisms then develop *preferences* for assessing new events/things as "good" or "bad." He calls these preferences *somatic markers*:

> The marker signals arise in bioregulatory processes, including those which express themselves in emotions and feeling, but are not necessarily confined to those alone. This is the reason why the markers are termed somatic: they relate to body-state structure and regulation even when they do not arise in the body proper but rather in the brain's representation of the body. (Damasio 1996: 1413)

Damasio goes on to argue that somatic markers help limit "the space" necessary for decision making and also allow the organism to call on previous experience and make decisions quickly. Although such a system would have evolved to maximize basic survival,

> a very large range of other problems including those which pertain to the social realm, are indirectly linked to precisely the same framework of survival versus danger, of advantage versus disadvantage, of gain and balance versus loss and disequilibrium. It is plausible that a system geared to produce markers and signposts to guide basic survival, would have been pre-adapted to assist with "intellectual" decision making. (Damasio 1996: 1417)

In the same article, Damasio presents empirical evidence that patients with damage to the ventrodemial sector of the prefrontal cortex do not do as well as normal control subjects in a card game in which they must adopt a certain strategy to end up winning and not losing. Further, the experiment demonstrated that superior memory and IQ in control (i.e., normal) subjects did not seem to be the source of the ability to adopt the winning strategy; rather, subjects relied on their ability "to sense," overtly or not, the best strategy.

As I have indicated earlier, Damasio's somatic markers have certain similarities with the MM's markedness evaluator. Based on input from experience, the evaluator enables speakers "to sense" the degree to which alternative linguistic choices are unmarked or marked for a given interaction type. In this way, the markedness evaluator is like somatic markers in that it enables speakers to take a shortcut in the decision-making process. However, the two types of preferences the "devices" offer are somewhat different. Although somatic markers actually direct an actor toward a specific judgment for a scenario, in contrast, the markedness evaluator offers only information as to degree of markedness of a potential choice for that scenario vis-à-vis others—it does not offer the type of "good" or "bad" judgment of the somatic marker. However, it is true that in giving a reading of "more unmarked" versus "more marked" the evaluator, in effect, gives the individual the equivalent of the green light for "go" (for unmarked choices) or a yellow light for "caution" (for marked choices).

MODIFYING ELSTER'S RA MODEL FOR THE MARKEDNESS MODEL

In this sketch of the outcome process, I redraft Elster's two-filter RA model. In one of his books, Elster describes any given piece of human behavior as the end product of two successive filtering devices; I add a filter and also add other constraints to the first filter.

The first filter is the set of what Elster refers to as *structural constraints*. These are defined as "all the physical, economic, legal and psychological constraints that an individual faces" (Elster 1989: 14). In turn, these constraints produce what Elster calls an *opportunity set*. In the case of linguistic choices, I say that structural constraints are those factors generally subsumed under the term *social context*. Thus, the most important structural constraints for this analysis are the participants' social identity features (age, sex, socioeconomic status, etc.) as well as the characteristics of the discourse situation (setting, topic, etc.). In linguistic terms, an actor's opportunity set, which is a product of relevant structural constraints, is his or her linguistic repertoire.

It is true, of course, that larger societal factors affect the content and salience of an actor's individual structural constraints. For example, in some societies, if one is a woman, the chances of higher education are less great than those for men. Similarly, family connections or membership in a certain ethnic group may largely influence access to certain socioeconomic statuses. However, neither the MM specifically nor RA models in general have as their goal to explain how large-scale societal forces limit a person's access to participation in certain interaction types by limiting their linguistic repertoire. Rather, their focus is on how individuals make choices for themselves, *given* their available repertoires.

An important distinction exists between this model and "social context models" in the Labovian tradition. In those models, the social context factors (i.e., structural constraints) are correlated with linguistic choices (with the implication that they determine choices in some sense, at least). Under RA models, including the MM, what social context factors *do* is determine not *choices* but only *the speaker's opportunity set*, that is, those varieties the speaker is able to use. The distinction is very important.

In addition, I add to the first filter of structural constraints those structural features that organize discourse, particularly those having to do with sequential organization. As I noted already, many practitioners of conversation analysis see such facts as whether an utterance is a first-part or second-part member of a specific adjacency pair as limiting the possibilities—whether in content or form—as to what can fill that slot. I accept that such structural constraints are features affecting the opportunity set for a specific interaction type; however, they do not determine the actual choice from that set which the speaker makes.

All the constraints that this first filter imposes—whether the speaker's social identity features or situational variables or surface linguistic structural features of the interaction type or the specific conversational turn—are *external*. That is, speakers do not control them, at least directly.

At this point, I add, as a second filter, those features that are *internal* to the speaker but still not under conscious control. These are Damasio's somatic markers and the innately "available" markedness evaluator. Like the constraints of the first filter, speakers have no direct control over how these elements constrain the choice process. Within the terms of this filter model, what these elements do is further bias the selection of alternatives from the initial, structurally determined opportunity set, this time in terms of "successes" or "failures" based on the actor's previous factual experience, facts previously categorized in an unconscious cost-benefit analysis.

The third filter includes the mechanisms responsible for which alternative from the opportunity set is actually chosen. The main element in this filter, of course, is rationality. Earlier, I outlined how rationality operates as a mechanism: From the speaker's set of possible choices, rationality indicates the "best" choice, given the degree of internal consistency of his or her desires, values, and beliefs and the available evidence. Whereas desires, values, and beliefs are reasons for a choice, actually to act rationally means that the speaker does not just choose the most favored choice but rather the most *feasible* choice. Note that this does not mean that the actor always has self-interest in mind. Acting rationally simply means making the optimal choice, given *any* value system the actor has.

In acting rationally, the speaker does take account of social norms as a component of "the available evidence." In contrast with rationality, which is forward-looking ("I do X because I hope to achieve Y"), norms are back-ward-looking, simply having the form, "consensus has favored doing X; there-fore do X." Earlier, I outlined reasons why following norms, and therefore making the unmarked choice, is an attractive alternative for many actors.

CONCLUSION

In this final section, I characterize RA models (and, necessarily, the MM) in a theoretic sense, contrasting them in brief with other approaches to linguis-tic code choices. Elster repeatedly refers to rationality as a *normative* theory in the sense that it tells people, "if you want X, then do Y." As such, RA models are not necessarily predictive, although they are explanatory: They explain what people would do *if* they were rational and explain the choices that people actually do make, based on the assumption *that they are acting rationally*. It is in this sense that rationality is a mechanism to explain social behavior. RA models are not necessarily explanatory theories that make pre-dictions about what people *really* do, and the MM does not predict in any global sense *when* speakers will make marked versus unmarked choices (but see Myers-Scotton, chapter 4, this volume, on Fitzgerald and marked choices for "crucial passages"). However, the MM is generally predictive in the sense that it predicts how choices *will be interpreted*.

In contrast to RA models, models of linguistic choices that hold that choices depend primarily on the social context do not provide a mechanism for evaluating and making choices. Such models typically state that choices are determined by the social identities of speakers and situational factors such as topic, setting, genre, and the like. Such models ignore or, at the very least, downgrade the existence of rationally based choice. The problem is that nei-ther the situational features nor the participants' identity features of such mod-els can be considered *mechanisms of choice*. It is true that in such models pre-dictions can be correlated with observable outcomes; in fact, in this sense they can even identify the unmarked choice. A general example of such a "predic-tion" is this: "If situational features X are present, then choice Y is unmarked."

Another model of linguistic choices is contained in the various approaches to discourse under the rubric, conversation analysis (CA). Like social context models, CA does account for the data descriptively, although it takes quite a different approach to context. In fact, a main goal for CA is "to develop an empirical analysis of the nature of context" (Drew and Heritage 1992: 17). They go on to say that "'context' and identity have to be treated as inherently locally produced, incrementally developed, and, by extension, transformable at any moment" (Drew and Heritage 1992: 19).

In a sense, structural organization in CA is similar to social situational factors in the social context models because in most CA approaches, the emerging conversational structure, especially sequences, "organizes" choices. However, in the case of both social context and CA models, formulating a prediction that identifies a choice (i.e., social context models) or describes what choices are made in a specific context (i.e., CA models) is not the same as explaining why a choice obtains or, even more interestingly, why a choice is *not always* observed. That is, such "predictions" are too restrictive. Most importantly, they do not allow for—or account for—marked choices. Nor do such models provide a way for interpreting marked choices. As will become apparent, the "meat" of many of the chapters in this volume are, in fact, marked choices.

In sum, RA models, including the MM, offer a far-reaching advantage over other current models of linguistic choice. From the outset, "being rational" constrains choices in an important way: Every choice in a speaker's repertoire (opportunity set) does *not* have an equal chance of occurring. Instead, the goal to enhance rewards and minimize costs limits choices in a way that neither situational factors nor structural organization can do: The operative word regarding choices is not *possible* but *feasible*. This narrowing of choices to those that are feasible or advantageous assumes that such choices are the result of conscious or unconscious cognitive calculations.

Finally, and perhaps most important, as noted early in this chapter, although RA models such as the MM do not claim that people are always rational, they do claim that the assumption of rationality *accounts* for the data. That is, not only do RA models provide an explanation of why every potential choice does not occur with the same frequency, but they also provide a principled means for interpreting the choices that do occur.

REFERENCES

Bell, Alan. 1984. Language style as audience design. *Language in Society* 13: 145–204.
Blum-Kulka, Shoshana, Juliane House, and Gabrielle Kasper (eds.). 1989. *Cross-cultural pragmatics: requests and apologies*. Norwood, N.J.: Albex.
Brown, Penelope, and Stephen Levinson. 1987. *Politeness, some universals of language usage*. Cambridge: Cambridge University Press.
Clark, Herbert H. 1996. *Using language*. Cambridge: Cambridge University Press.
Damasio, Antonio. 1994. *Descartes's error: emotion, reason, and the human brain*. New York: Grosset/Putnam.
———. 1996. The somatic marker hypothesis and the possible functions of the prefrontal cortex. *Philosophical Transactions of the Royal Society. London B* 351. 1313–1420.
Drew, Paul, and John Heritage. 1992. Analyzing talk at work: an introduction. In

Talk at work, ed. Paul Drew and John Heritage, 3–65. Cambridge: Cambridge University Press.

Elster, Jon. 1979. *Ulysses and the sirens.* Cambridge: Cambridge University Press.

———. 1989. *The cement of society.* Cambridge: Cambridge University Press.

———. 1991. Rationality and social norms. *Archives of European Sociology* 32: 109–29.

Ervin-Tripp, Susan. 1976. Speech acts and social learning. In *Meaning in anthropology*, ed. Keith Basso and Henry Selby, 123–153. Albuquerque: University of New Mexico Press.

Gallois, Cynthia, Howard Giles, Elizabeth Jones, Aaron C. Cargile, and Hiroshi Ota. 1995. Accommodating intercultural encounters, elaborations and extensions. In *Intercultural communication theory*, ed. Richard L. Wiseman, 115–147. Thousand Oaks, Calif.: Sage Publications.

Giles, Howard, and Nikolas Coupland. 1991. *Language: contexts and consequences.* Pacific Grove, Calif.: Brooks Cole.

Giles, Howard, Nikolas Coupland, and Justine Coupland. 1991. Accommodation theory: communication, context, and consequences. In *Contexts of accommodation: developments in applied linguistics*, ed. Howard Giles, Nikolas Coupland, and Justine Coupland, 1–68. Cambridge: Cambridge University Press.

Giles, Howard, and John M. Wiemann. 1987. Language, social comparison and power. In *Handbook of communication science,* ed. Charles R. Berger and Steven H. Chaffee, 350–386. Newbury Park, Calif.: Sage.

Goffman, Erving. 1967. *The presentation of self in everyday life.* Harmondsworth: Penguin.

Grice, H. Paul. 1975. Logic and conversation. In *Syntax and semantics,* vol. 3, ed. Peter Cole and Jerry L. Morgan, 41–58. New York: Academic Press.

Kagel, John H. 1995. Auctions: a survey of experimental research. *The handbook of experimental economics*, ed. John H. Kagel and Alvin Roth, 501–559. Princeton, N.J.: Princeton University Press.

Lewis, David K. 1969. *Convention: a philosophical study.* Cambridge, Mass.: Harvard University Press.

Meeuwis, Michael, and Jan Blommaert. 1994. The "Markdness Model" and the absence of society: remarks on codeswitching. *Multilingua* 13: 387–423.

Myers-Scotton, Carol M. 1983. The negotiation of identities in conversation: a theory of markedness and code choice. *International Journal of the Sociology of Language* 44: 115–136.

———. 1988a. Codeswitching as indexical of social negotiation. In *Codeswitching: anthropological and sociolinguistic perspectives*, ed. Monica Heller, 151–186. Berlin: Mouton de Gruyter.

———. 1988b. Self-enhancing codeswitching as interactional power. *Language & Communication* 8: 199–211.

———. 1993. *Social motivations for codeswitching: evidence from Africa.* Oxford: Oxford University Press.

———. 1995. What do speakers want? Codeswitching as evidence of intentionality in linguistic choices. *SALSA II: proceedings of the second annual symposium on language and society–Austin,* ed. Pamela Silberman and Jonathan Loftin, 1–17. Austin: University of Texas Department of Linguistics.

———. 1997. Rational actor models and social discourse analysis. In *Discourse anal-*

ysis: proceedings of the first international conference on discourse analysis, ed. Emilia Ribeiro Pedro, 177–199. Lisbon: Edicoes Colibri/Associacão Portuguesa de Linguistica.

Myers-Scotton, Carol M. [Scotton, Carol Myers], and Janice Bernsten. 1988. Natural conversations as a model for textbook dialogue. *Applied Linguistics* 9: 372–384.

Sperber, Dan, and Deirdre Wilson. 1995. *Relevance, communication and cognition*. 2nd ed. Oxford: Blackwell.

Tracy, Karen. 1990. The many faces of facework. In *Handbook of language and social psychology*, ed. Howard Giles and W. Peter Robinson, 209–226. Chichester, England: John Wiley.

— II —

Stylistic Choices in Literature

3

Implicatures of Styleswitching in the Narrative Voice of Cormac McCarthy's
All the Pretty Horses

NANCY KREML

Cormac McCarthy's novels pose many problems for the reader: Issues of history, philosophy, religion, abnormal psychology, and mythology are intertwined with problems of style and structure. Adding especially to the difficulty of reading *All the Pretty Horses* (1992) is the problematic narrative voice. The narrative voice is the reader's primary access to the events of the novel and their significance, yet the experience of reading the novel is often like that of observing a play or film: We hear dialogue (often in page-long interchanges without even repeated indications of speaker identity) and see details of setting and action clearly, but without overt interpretation, without description of inner states or even of possible ambiguous tones of voice or facial expression, without clearly stated evaluations, suggestions, or judgments of characters and their actions. Nevertheless, McCarthy provides the reader access not only to the inner workings of the characters' minds but also to interpretations of the events of the novel. To understand the means by which such effects are achieved, we may turn to theories of communication of intentionality, especially relevance theory (Sperber and Wilson 1995) and the markedness model (Myers-Scotton chapter 2, this volume).

If these theories can explain the significance of the stylistic choices in *All the Pretty Horses*, they may enable a reader to choose among the widely varying interpretations of the plot and characters of the novel. To help us understand the problems of interpretation of the novel, a brief summary provides context. The protagonist, John Grady Cole, a sixteen-year-old Texan bereft of family and heritage, travels to Mexico with a friend (Rawlins) and befriends a younger man (Blevins) who rides a beautiful, but possibly stolen, horse. When Mexicans steal the horse from the boys, they regain it, but Blevins kills a man in the process and leaves the other boys. John Grady and Rawlins find a hacienda where John Grady demonstrates his remarkable ability to break and train horses. He is accepted until he falls in love with the young heiress, Alejandra, and her family apparently betrays him to the law to separate the girl from this lover, unsuitable both culturally and financially. After Blevins is killed and Rawlins wounded, John Grady defends his life in prison by killing a probably hired killer. Released from prison by some unknown external agent, John Grady makes a futile attempt to reunite with Alejandra and finally locates the beautiful horse and returns with it to Texas. At the novel's end, he is seeking its rightful owner.

Even in this precis, we see that many of the most important actions and relationships in the novel must be qualified as "apparent" or "possible," communicated only through implicature; McCarthy does not explicitly assign cause and effect for many crucial elements in the plot. John Grady's responsibility for his fate is thus a central problem in reading the novel: Is it his own self-deception and misguided idealism that lead to his losses, or is he the undeserving target of evil (especially as personified by the Mexicans and women who wrong him)? This question has been debated: Bell (1992) and Morrison (1993) see him as victimized by "the autocratic rule of families, at best, and at worst, of brute power instead of law" (Bell 1992: 926), but Luce (1995) argues that much that happens to John Grady results from his own lapses in judgment and ignorance of cultural differences.

THEORETICAL FRAMEWORKS

Because the narrative voice offers little or no overt interpretation, only recovery of the implicatures of the novel, especially those created by stylistic choices, may help the reader to resolve this question. By manipulating the interplay between a marked and an unmarked style in the narrative voice, McCarthy constrains with some precision the reader's interpretation of the implicatures of the narrative voice. An examination of these implicatures can in fact lend weight to one aspect of the argument that it is the protagonist John Grady Cole's own self-deception and misguided idealism, rather than foreign and feminine villainy, that lead to his losses. Beyond that, offering an answer to the problems posed by the ambiguities of the plot, the implicatures suggest that the world does have meaning, shaped by responsibility, cause and effect, and knowledge of consequences.

Relevance theory and other theories of the communication of intentionality enable us to see how the reader is led to recover the appropriate implicature by McCarthy's use of two sharply distinct styles in the narrative voice. In analyzing literary language, Sperber and Wilson (1995: 222) have been especially concerned with authors' use of *weak implicatures* to signal to readers the necessity to recognize or create multiple meanings of texts. In the cooperation between writer and reader, the reader must determine which contexts to use for the recovery of meaning from the text, so that multilayered and complex interpretations result when a writer leaves open the possibility of various contexts. However, multiplicity of meaning can dissolve into meaninglessness without some guidance from the writer as to which inferences can most appropriately be drawn, so writers must supply what Sperber and Wilson call "acts of ostension" (1995: 49) or noticeable signals that give hints or set limits for selection of appropriate, or most relevant, contexts.

Relevance theory's analysis of communication of intentionality helps explain McCarthy's stylistic effects: Although he makes communication rich by opening many possible implicatures, he makes it precise by using stylistic choices to constrain the reader's selection of contexts for "optimal Relevance" (Blakemore 1992: 177). This constraint is made manifest to the reader through acts of ostension.

McCarthy creates the most significant act of ostension in this novel by using two distinct styles. He sets up an unmarked style for the uninterpreted transmission of observations. He then introduces a marked style that leads the reader to question the simplicity of the unmarked; indeed, it constrains or forces us to interpret. The markedness model explains the choices of a speaker or writer as resulting from the making of rational (though not necessarily overtly conscious) choices to optimize outcome— that is, to influence the behavior of the hearer or reader (Myers-Scotton chapter 2, in this volume). In the case of the reader of literature, that behavior is primarily internal: the selection of one interpretation against another (or the maintenance of the tensions of coexistent multiple readings). The choices that produce this outcome, according to the markedness model, are the code choices that are rationally believed to satisfy the various constraints of the situation at hand (Myers-Scotton chapter 2, in this volume). In literature, these constraints are partly those in social life but partly also those created by the novelist. Each novel establishes its own linguistic community, with its own unmarked style, and "sets of rights and obligations" (Myers-Scotton chapter 2, in this volume) attendant on it, its own "cognitive environment" (Sperber and Wilson 1995: 38–46), and thus develops its own constraints.

THE NOVEL AND COGNITIVE CONSTRAINTS

As an example, a writer who intends to be read by the majority of the American public is constrained to write in English, a choice made by McCarthy in the main part of *All the Pretty Horses*; however, he may choose to represent a world that includes characters who speak Spanish and may, as McCarthy does, include untranslated Spanish dialogue. The reader must then either know Spanish, find some way of translating the Spanish passages, or remain ignorant of their content. McCarthy thus adds his own constraint (the ability to interpret Spanish) to the larger social constraint (the ability to read English). Thus, untranslated Spanish in an English text becomes for this novel the unmarked norm, though in many social contexts it would be marked.

Thus, the unmarked style of this novel assumes a world of permeable borders between languages.

This is only one example of an author's ability to create a style that is unmarked for that particular text, and thus a style that is marked for that text as well. Other obvious examples of contrast between the unmarked norm of this novel and that outside it occur in punctuation: McCarthy never uses quotation marks or indeed any punctuation to set off dialogue from narration and routinely drops apostrophes in contractions, though he maintains them for the possessive—again lessening the distinction between the narrator and the characters, between various levels of usage.

McCarthy creates a basic style for the novel that becomes the norm of discourse, a simple, straightforward, undecorated style with the same unmarked force as the linguistic and social unmarked choices of the natural world. The majority of the novel is in this style, and the simple interpretation of John Grady as wounded hero derives from it. But relevance theory explains how the styles of the narrative voice take us beyond that initial simplicity. In the natural world and in the novel, the violation of constraints is a form of communication. The writer's intention is communicated by the use of a marked choice, one that clearly violates the norms of the unmarked choices.

Such a marked choice is vividly apparent in *All the Pretty Horses*: In only a few passages McCarthy employs a style that is complex and metaphoric. The style is marked both by the salience of the features—the unusual vocabulary and occasional archaic structures—and by the quantitative differences seen in Tables 3-1, 3-2, and 3-3.[1] The use of this marked style is the act of ostension that signals to the reader the need to recover complex implicatures, to look beyond surface actions for motivations, assumptions, and misperceptions. In the use of this style we find some of the clues that lead to the more complex evaluation of John Grady's own complicity in his fate.

Finally, an even more complex message is communicated by the convergence of the two styles, signaling the possibility of the convergence of the

1. The tables are based on six passages in the marked style and six in the unmarked, equaling a total of sixty-five lines of type each (this edition has about twelve words of type per line). The frequencies are determined by counting the total number of occurrences of each feature and dividing by the number of sentences or lines. *Sentences* are considered to be groups of words ending with periods, regardless of syntactic features. McCarthy's punctuation is very deliberate (he often writes two words together to form an unhyphenated compound not found in dictionaries, he uses apostrophes for contractions rarely and quotation marks for dialogue not at all, and he does not italicize non-English words), and thus his periods must be taken as intentional division of segments of the text.

For each passage in the marked style, a passage in the unmarked is selected from as closely as possible the same segment of the book and from within ten pages when possible. The pairs of passages appear throughout the novel. Because only twenty-two passages of more than five lines in the marked style are found in the novel, and few of those occur during the second hundred pages (approximately pp. 90–230), most pairs are taken from either the earlier or the later parts of the novel. None contain dialogue. The pages and numbers of lines given for each passage refer to the printed text (McCarthy 1992). (See Appendix) simple world of action, lived out by the "heroic" protagonist and described in the unmarked, simple style, and the more complex world of meaning suggested and reflected by the marked, elaborated style. The gradual development of this fluidity between the borders of the unmarked and marked styles, like the increasing fluidity of the border between Spanish and English in the novel, also signals the emergence of a new set of relations between writer and reader: The reader of the mixed style must see the unity of action and meaning.

NARRATIVE VOICE IN TWO EXAMPLES

To show in detail the developments of these constraints, I examine the stylistic qualities of the narrative voice in two passages, using those passages to demonstrate how McCarthy teaches us to recognize the constraints he imposes. As the dominant style of the narrative voice he establishes a transparent style, with little limitation of interpretation, against which he plays a secondary, more highly constrained foregrounded style. Further, he uses the elements of the foregrounded style to signal a thematic shift, an intrusion of another level of meaning. Early in the novel, the foregrounded style occurs in fairly extended passages. As we learn to recognize its characteristics, he uses it more briefly and less often, so that a sentence or even a phrase evokes the significance of the style. This association of style and meaning becomes one of the constraints on interpretation that guide us in recovering the implications of the text.

COMPARING THE STYLES QUANTITATIVELY

McCarthy's styles are so clearly distinct that we can quantify the differences in passages easily recognizable throughout the novel. Tables 3-1, 3-2, and 3-3 detail a number of contrasts between the two styles. The tables show how different features occur in the two styles both by frequency per sentence and frequency per line of type. We must know the frequency of features per line to understand how long the sentences are in each of the two styles. If we know only the frequency per sentence, the longer sentences of the marked style will artificially inflate the number of features. Thus, the frequency per line gives a more accurate representation of the density of the reading experience. However, the frequency with which each feature occurs in a sentence is also important because co-occurrence of features in a sentence requires the reader to sustain complex syntactic relationships.

One of the more obvious differences between the two styles is in the length of sentence: The unmarked sentence has only 23.44 words per sentence, whereas the marked has 42.11. The difference is less when we contrast the words per line: 11.54 in the unmarked versus 12.32 in the marked. The difference between these frequencies results from the much higher number

Table 3-1
Syntactic Features

Features	Per Sentence		Per Line	
	Unmarked	Marked	Unmarked	Marked
words	42.11	23.44	11.54	12.31
NP+VP	1.90	3.84	.94	1.12
VP	4.06	6.52	2.00	1.91
VP+VP	.72	.42	.35	.12
copula	.21	.58	.11	.17
non-finite VP	.94	1.53	.46	.45
PP	3.13	5.63	1.54	1.65
ADJP	1.31	3.95	.65	1.15
ADVP	.38	.68	.18	.20
NPVP+NPVP	.40	1.63	.20	.48
overt COMP	.31	1.63	.15	.48
ADJP post NP	—	.55	—	.15
levels of mod.	1.53	2.89	.75	.85

of prepositional phrases in the marked style (5.63 in the marked, compared to only 3.13 in the unmarked) and other constructions requiring short connective words.

Modifiers are more common in the marked (e.g., adjectives 3.95/sentence marked to 1.31/sentence unmarked, nonfinite verbs 1.53/sentence marked to 0.94/sentence unmarked), but even more significantly, the marked has a much higher level of modification (modifiers that in turn modify other modifiers— 2.89/sentence marked to 1.53/sentence unmarked). In the marked style, too, adjectives often follow rather than precede the nouns they modify or follow intransitive verbs of motion (0 in the unmarked, 0.15 per line in the marked). The marked style also has more extremes—one-syllable words occur at the rate of 10 per line in the marked to 9.37 in the unmarked; three-syllable words at 0.49 per line, compared to 0.34 per line in the unmarked.

The syntax of the marked style is thus more complex than that of the unmarked, and the word length much more varied. The effect of these longer sentences is most obviously to foreground the language simply by the fact of the marked difference. But an additional effect is the nature of the marked style: The longer, more complex sentences and words require more effort and slow down the reader's processing of thought, thus making these passages doubly noticeable and more difficult to skim past without stopping to absorb meaning. The length and complexity of the sentences literally, almost physically, constrain the reader to find meaning.

Literary features are also much more common in the marked style: 0.20 metaphors occur per line in the marked, while 0 are in the unmarked, and such prosodic features as alliteration are also heavily used in the marked

Table 3-2
Lexicon

Features	Per Sentence		Per Line	
	Unmarked	Marked	Unmarked	Marked
words	23.43	42.11	11.54	12.30
Spanish words	.22	.37	.11	.11
English words	23.29	41.74	11.43	12.20
syllables/word:				
one	19.03	34.21	9.37	10.00
two	3.63	12.44	1.78	1.72
three	.69	1.68	.34	.49
more than three	.09	.32	.05	.09

(0.88/line) and rare in the unmarked (0.32/line). Other features are more difficult to quantify: The rhythms—the variations of stress—in the unmarked style are more nearly those of common speech, whereas those of the marked are literary or biblical (resulting in part from the higher frequency of words of more than two syllables). Again, these features not only mark the style but involve the reader more intensely in processing the language.

Perhaps the most famous of McCarthy's stylistic devices is his use of rare and arcane vocabulary, a feature that in *All the Pretty Horses* occurs almost exclusively in the marked style. Few of these words are old or rare enough to be marked as *archaic* in common dictionaries, yet the reader recognizes them as rarely occurring in common speech—*spume* (161), *isinglass* (242), *serried* (242), *espaliered* (73). This vocabulary in the marked style is itself a very

Table 3-3
Literary Features

Features	Per Sentence		Per Line	
	Unmarked	Marked	Unmarked	Marked
metaphor	—	.68	—	.20
simile	.03	42	.02	.12
appositive	.06	.32	.03	.09
parallelism	.34	.95	.17	.28
formulaic structure	—	.70	—	.23
alliteration	.66	3.00	.32	.88
assonance	.40	2.74	.23	.80
consonance	.34	1.79	.17	.52
rhyme	.13	.53	.06	.15
repetition	.32	4.22	.15	.58

specific act of ostension, requiring the reader to draw heavily on memory, inference, or dictionary. Like the use of Spanish in the novel, the use of these rarer words presupposes a reader who shares this knowledge of language or is willing to acquire it for the sake of comprehending the passage. The words themselves, like the syntax, constrain the reader to spend more time and effort on interpreting the text and thereby to feel the weight of meaning more heavily.

Though these quantified comparisons substantiate the existence of two different styles and suggest their general nature, we can understand the workings of the novel most clearly by examining several specific passages in detail. To clarify the developments of these marked and unmarked styles, I examine the stylistic qualities of the narrative voice in passages first of unmarked, then of marked, and finally of the two styles mixed to reveal how McCarthy teaches us to recognize the constraints he imposes.

THE UNMARKED STYLE

As the unmarked style of the narrative voice, McCarthy establishes a transparent style used for 97% of the passages in narrative voice (see Table 3-1), especially the narratives of action, as illustrated here in account of John Grady and Rawlins as they wait for Blevins to retrieve his stolen horse:

Passage A

The boy slid from the horse and picked his way gingerly with his bare feet across the road to the house and looked in. Then he climbed through the window.

What the hell's he doin? asked Rawlins.

You got me.

They waited. He didnt come back.

Yonder comes somebody.

Some dogs started up. John Grady mounted up and turned the horse and went back up the road and sat the horse in the dark. Rawlins followed. Dogs were beginning to bark all back through the town. A light came on.

This is by God it, aint it? said Rawlins.

John Grady looked at him. He was sitting with the carbine upright on his thigh. From beyond the buildings and the din of dogs there came a shout.

You know what these sons of bitches'll do to us? said Rawlins. You thought about that?

John leaned forward and spoke to the horse and put his hand on the horse's shoulder. The horse had begun to step nervously and it was not a nervous horse. He looked toward the houses where they'd seen the light. A horse whinnied in the dark.

That crazy son of a bitch, said Rawlins. That crazy son of a bitch. (82)

This style seems to be the simplest possible in English. Most sentences are SV(subject-verb): *the boy slid, Rawlins pulled, they rode, the leather creaked,* and so on. Verbs and their arguments stand in clear and strong relation to each other; rarely do introductory or intervening phrases interfere with the clear statement of action (only 3.13 PP (prepositional phrases) per sentence, 0.94 nonfinite verbs, including one-word modifiers—Table 3-2). The sentences are short (23.43 words per sentence—Table 3-1) and often monoclausal (1.9 clauses per sentence—Table 3-1); clauses are combined more often with *and* than with a complementizer of any kind. The directness and immediacy of the syntax embody that of the scene. We find few adjectives (1.25 per sentence—Table 3-3), either as preceders of nouns or as complements, and few adverbs (0.38 per sentence)—only 5% of all words are modifiers, whereas 14% are verbs (Table 3-2). Most of the adverbial information concerns time and place, rarely manner: *across the road, in the dark.* Both nouns and verbs are usually morphologically simple (Table 3-2 shows that only 4% of the words in the unmarked passages have more than two syllables, including *Mexican*), and of Anglo-Saxon derivation (see Table 3-2): *slid, rode, shout, high,* and so on.

This simplicity makes the correspondence between sentence form and content even more noticeable, as we can see in the beginning of the next passage (the departure of John Grady and Rawlins for Mexico):

Passage B-1
They rode out along the fenceline and across the open pastureline. The leather creaked in the morning cold. They pushed the horses into a lope. The lights fell away behind them. They rode out on the high prairie where they slowed the horses to a walk. (30)

Here, most sentences consist of subject and intransitive verb, with few direct objects in these passages—the actions happen without connections in the intransitive sentences, without an actor who acts on something else—in short, without cause and effect. The characters, especially John Grady, undertake a venture without recognizing the extent of its possible consequences, an ignorance that ultimately leads to loss, imprisonment, and death. The simplicity of the syntax also makes more prominent the semantics of the passage. Case grammar analysis of this part of the passage shows how the thematic roles—the semantic as opposed to syntactic cases of nouns and verbs according to Hurst's (1990) schema—reveal the underlying nature of the characters. Most notable is the absence of nouns acting not only as grammatical subjects but also as thematic agents, that is, as actors: The agents are *they.* When we find a noun in subject position, it is thematically the recipient of the action: *leather creaked, bell that tolled,* and, most vividly, *lights fell—* although it is actually the riders who leave the lights, these riders do not take here even the responsibility of moving through the landscape.

This is the standard style, the unmarked norm, of the novel. Remarkably, it is used for the most crucial scenes: We find it not only in scenes of getting dressed and feeding horses, buying food and closing gates but also in scenes central to the plot, such as the execution of the younger boy, Blevins (177–178), John Grady's killing of the man in prison (199–202), and the last meeting of John Grady and the Mexican heiress Alejandra (247–248), among others. In these passages the language appears limited, precise, but powerful; the style mimics the action.

However, the unmarked style is in some ways also the least constrained. By describing any action (even the buying of baloney) and therefore drawing our attention to it, McCarthy suggests that it is significant; by leaving it uninterpreted, he allows the reader to supply many contexts for its possible interpretation. As our precis of the novel shows, many essential aspects of the narrative are unknown; the lack of constraint in the telling of the story is so great that the story is not completely told.

The term *constraint* refers to the limits set on an otherwise unlimited cognitive process. According to Sperber and Wilson's (1995) formulation of relevance theory, there is no limit on the interpretations, the weak implicatures, a reader may find in a text, nor, significantly, is there any need for a reader to look beyond the most obvious strong implicatures. In Passage A, we know that Blevins goes in the window, but we do not know what happens once he is inside; we see only the horses' reactions. *There came a shout*, but we are not told who shouts nor what is said. Even the coherence of the text itself is almost completely implied; *and* is so ubiquitous, so constant, that its meaning must often be interpreted from the context (it may imply sequence, as in he *leaned . . . and spoke . . .*, contrast, as in *and it was not a nervous horse*, etc.). Similar ambiguities arise from the use of pronouns which often occur with no antecedent (the novel's initial appearance of the character Luisa, for example, on page 3), so that their reference can be recovered only from subsequent action. Throughout the novel, dialogue is not set off by quotation marks, nor are speakers designated, so that the reader must assign speech to character, possibly erroneously. Even in those scenes of crucial action, therefore, much of the interpretation is left to the reader. If the scenes of action were indeed the entire book, told only in this unmarked style, we might well read John Grady as a simple man of action. If we are not forced to look beyond his own stated motivations for supporting Blevins, for his silence at his first appearance at the ranch, for courting Alejandra, we have the right to impute to him only noble motivations, and we are not constrained to see more.

THE MARKED STYLE

Such undirected interpretation is not found in another style of the narrative voice, the marked style, which appears all the more opaque by its contrast with the transparent unmarked style. Because the unmarked style is so transparent, so unforegrounded, the appearance of the marked style suddenly draws the reader's attention to the language; in turn we are led to the significance of McCarthy's stylistic choices for understanding John Grady's character. We first recognize the style's characteristics in extended passages like the remainder of the paragraph describing the departure for Mexico:

Passage B-2

They rode out on the high prairie where they slowed the horses to a walk and the stars swarmed around them out of the blackness. They heard somewhere in that tenantless night a bell that tolled and ceased where no bell was and they rode out on the round dais of the earth which alone was dark and no light to it and which carried their figures and bore them up into the swarming stars so that they rode not under but among them and they rode at once jaunty and circumspect, like thieves newly loosed in that dark electric, like young thieves in a glowing orchard, loosely jacketed against the cold and ten thousand worlds for the choosing. (30)

The introduction of metaphor—*stars swarmed*—marks the transition of the riders from the town to the high prairie (the beginning of their journey) and stylistically marks the introduction of the marked style. Here we find subordination: *where no bell was, so that they rode, like thieves newly loosed*; and modification: *that tenantless night, the swarming stars, young thieves in a glowing orchard*. Indeed, in this passage and others like it, there are 3.84 clauses per sentence, and 1.63 complementizers, as well as 1.53 nonfinite verbs (Table 3-2).

Now we are in a world of myriad syntactic connections, though all are not what they appear to be on the surface. The simple SVO sentence pattern is contorted and obscured by intervening modifiers, inversions, ellipses. In this maze of true and false syntactic leads, the use of the marked style argues the possible falsity of the romantic heroism underlying John Grady's journey to Mexico. The complementizer *that* in *a bell that tolled* dislocates the subject from its action. Next, we find an apparent copula, *was*, actually followed by no complement *(where no bell was)* and so joins nothing. We are also misled by the elaborate repetitions, appositives, and parallel structures: *they heard* and *they rode; which . . . and which . . . ; like thieves newly loosed* and *like young thieves . . ., loosely jacketed*—all lead us to expect that the sentence has a tightly controlled syntax in which every phrase fits. But our expectations are confounded in the remainder of the sentence: *they rode . . . like young thieves . . ., loosely jacketed against the cold and ten thousand worlds for the choosing*. Parallelism of syntactic form—in this case the two sides of the coordinating conjunction *and*—suggests a corresponding parallelism of ideas, but no way does *ten thousand worlds for the choosing* parallel syntactically any phrase related to it in content, certainly not *loosely jacketed*. The false parallelism suggests a fundamentally erroneous assumption in the riders' view of their place in the world. Just as the reader erroneously assumes that the first part of the sentence will provide a pattern for the last, so the boys wrongly assume that the Mexican world they enter will match the American world they leave. Thus, the syntax of the marked style in this passage offers clear implicatures of meaning underlying the simple world of action described in the unmarked passages.

Also an index of the marked style of *All the Pretty Horses* is the lexicon. In earlier works, McCarthy used an enormous vocabulary, drawn from a surprising range of social levels, historical periods, mental disciplines, professions, and contexts. Witek (1991: 51–53) speaks of the disparity between the language of the characters and that of the narrative voice in his other novels, *Suttree* (1973) and *Blood Meridian* (1985). In *All the Pretty Horses*, however, even in the marked style most of the vocabulary is more nearly that of common speech but turned at an odd and jolting metaphoric angle by context (as with *stars swarmed*, above). Only occasionally does a word from another time or place or level of usage appear, as in the unexpectedly archaic *in that dark electric*; again, the rarity of the occurrence emphasizes its effect and its importance. The use of the word *dais* is one of the means by which the simple cowboys become the mythological figures of the final lines. In one of the later phrases, *they rode at once jaunty and circumspect*, the emphasis arises not only from the unexpected register and combination but also from the syntax, with the adjective complement (*jaunty and circumspect*) following a verb (*rode*) that is not a copula. This structure is in fact formulaic in the novel; this and other such structures (*in that N , of some AdjN*, etc.) appear only in the marked style (see Table 3-3).

Finally, the marked style foregrounds sound through repetition. Witek (1991: 56–63) and Morrison (1993: 183–186) demonstrated the function of repetition in the structure of several McCarthy novels, but we can see that repetition of sound here also marks a shift of style. Repetitions of structure and sound, especially of assonance and consonance, rhyme and alliteration, occur throughout, even in the unmarked style, but they become much stronger in the marked. In this passage, the unifying phrase is *they rode*: It recurs four times and in each case is the core of the sentence. Other repetitions also figure: *stars, swarmed, bell, dark, loose, thieves*. We hear assonance in the repeated *o* sounds—*no, bore, rode, glowing*, and *cold*—and assonance as well when the *o* gives way to *oo*—*loosed, loosely*, and *choosing*—to *or* and *ar*—*horses, swarmed, where, earth, dark, orchard*, and *worlds*—and rhyme in the series *fell* and *bell*. Alliteration, too, is strong: *stars swarmed, tenantless . . . tolled, rode . . . round, thieves . . . thousand*. The passage is thus unified by the interwoven recurrence of sound patterns. Rhythm here, too, is more varied: A complex interplay of secondary and primary stresses can give way to a sudden powerful burst of strong syllables (*ten thousand worlds*). This foregrounding of prosody marks the style more insistently as a different kind of speech.

The marked style differs cognitively from the unmarked, also. As we saw earlier, the unmarked style is less constrained; the reader is left to supply the connections between the unadorned facts presented, and thus the interpretations of them. Although the marked style often suggests more possible interpretations, it also more sharply limits those that might be most appropriate. This appears on the most obvious level in the more frequent use of modifiers and in the overt statements of precise sentence connectives (such as relative pronouns) and in the preference for overtly stated (and thus more limited) similes (*like thieves*) to more open metaphors.

The constraining function of this style is especially strengthened in Passage B-2 by the foregrounding of function words—adverbs (0.68 per sentence; Table 3-3), complementizers (1.6 per sentence; Table 3-2), and especially prepositions (3.13 per sentence; Table 3-1), the means whereby McCarthy creates the image of the riders as raised into the heavens. Dominant in reading the passage are the changing impressions of the riders first as a part of the landscape (Cheuse 1992), then as on the surface of the planet (and thereby raised in size), and finally as riding among the stars, heroic in size (an apotheosis whose falsity is underscored by the *young thieves* simile). Although the verbs account for some of the visual impression of upward movement (*rode, carried and bore*), the image grows and is sustained throughout the passage by a class of words that usually escape the attention of a reader: prepositions. At least fifteen prepositions express motion, from their riding *along* and *across* to the stars' swarming *out of* the blackness, the earth's bearing them *up into* and their being loosed *in* the starry darkness. The prepositions are further foregrounded by repetition—*out on* (ll. 3–4 and 7)—and negation—*not under but among* (l. 10). With such foregrounding, the style itself becomes further associated with constraint, in the sense of the limiting of infinite possible implicatures to the appropriate choice.

The shift to the marked style in such a sustained passage clearly functions to focus our attention on the language itself rather than on the actions the language describes. Such passages occur at several points where the reader must not so much envision characters and actions as understand those actions in their context—the context of history, the physical landscape, and the mythical, moral, even ontological universe in which those characters act. The novel opens with the most sustained of such passages—almost all of the first five pages are in this style, including John Grady's sight of his grandfather in the casket (3), a howling train (3–4), and a vision of Indian ghosts (5–6). Later, such passages color the travels of the boys before the loss and recovery of Blevins's horse (73) and the arrival at the Mexican hacienda, La Purisima (93). They tell of John Grady's love for the horses (105, 128) and for Alejandra (141) and give us his dreams of horses while in prison (161), the death of a doe (282), and the final passage where he rides away, still leading Blevins's horse (302). The use of the marked style in these passages teaches us to associate that style with such subject matter: the sudden realization of the greater dimensions of actions. In these passages, McCarthy constrains us to see that events have meaning; we are not at liberty to take them as simple actions with no significance.

MIXING MARKED AND UNMARKED STYLES

Substantial passages of five or more lines in the marked style are rare: Only 6.1 pages (about 2,600 words), or 3% of the 95,000-word novel, are in this style. The passages are not more than a paragraph each (often only part of a longer paragraph) and vary in length from 60 to 220 words. But the passages teach us their language; we learn to associate it with this kind of meaning so that we do not need a sustained passage to recognize the shift to another level of the narrative, the level of meaning. A sentence, a phrase, or even a word can be so clearly marked with this style that we recognize the sign, just as even one word of Spanish summons up Mexico.

We can see also that when the marked style is used with greater economy it may also have even more force, as in this passage narrating Don Hector's first long interview with John Rawlins:

Passage C-1

They sat at a long table of english walnut. The walls of the room were covered with blue damask and hung with portraits of men and horses. At the end of the room was a walnut sideboard with some chafing dishes and decanters set out upon it and along the windowsill outside taking the sun were four cats. Don Hector reached behind him and took a china ashtray from the side board and placed it before them and took from his shirtpocket a small tin box of english cigarettes and opened them and offered them to John Grady and John Grady took one.

Gracias, he said.

The hacendado placed the tin on the table between them and took a silver lighter from his pocket and lit the boy's cigarette and then his own.

. . .

The hacendado nodded again. He sipped his coffee. He was seated sideways to the table with his legs crossed. He flexed his foot in the chocolatecolored veal boot and turned and looked at John Grady and smiled.

Why are you here? he said.

John Grady looked at him. He looked down the table *where the shadows of the sunning cats sat in a row like cutout cats all leaning slightly aslant.* He looked at the hacendado again.

I just wanted to see the country, I reckon. Or we did. (112–113; emphasis added)

Here we can see how McCarthy's use of an image to suggest John Grady's lapse in honesty is attended by stylistic signals with which it comes to be associated in the passage. In C-1, the unmarked style dominates the narrative voice. In most passages, the characteristically direct and straightforward sentence pattern appears. Words are morphologically simple, of one or two syllables, and concrete (*english walnut, ashtray, sipped, looked*); modification is moderate and also clearly concrete (*blue damask, silver lighter, thin stream*). The language is drawn from a lexicon which is standard for the time, place, occasion, and level of society. The style suddenly shifts from unmarked to marked in two places only: the references to the shadows of the cats. Both cats and shadows appeared as images elsewhere (indeed, the book opens and closes with the image of reflection and shadow). During this apparently innocent conversation, ostensibly directed toward confirming John Grady's place in the community of horsemen, the image of the cat's shadow lurks in the background, pouncing only when John chooses falsely to deny affiliation with Blevins, a denial of reality that eventually plays a part in his dismissal from the hacienda and eventual imprisonment. The significance of the image is echoed and underscored by the abrupt change to the marked style precisely at the point in the conversation at which John Grady makes his ill-fated choice.

The first appearance of the cats actually occurs at the beginning of the conversation, when they are catalogued among the items in the room. Here in the unmarked style they are but one more item in the room, but later, when the conversation turns to the potentially threatening question of the purpose of John Grady's coming to the hacienda, the image of the cats recurs, cast in the marked style: *the shadows of the sunning cats sat in a row like cutout cats all leaning slightly aslant* (113). Stylistically this sentence differs considerably from the previous narrations of the conversation, showing the marked features we saw in B-2: the unexpected simile (*like cutout cats*), nonfinite verbs (*sunning, leaning*, and perhaps *aslant*), inverted modification (*all leaning slightly aslant* follows *cutout cats*), levels of modification (*slightly* modifies *aslant* which modifies *leaning,* which in turn modifies *cats*, etc.), and foregrounded prosody (alliteration of *s: shadows, sunning, sat, slightly*; assonance of *a: shadows, cats, aslant*; and repetition and rhyme or near-rhyme: *cats, sat, cutout, cats*). This intrusion of the marked style thus constrains our interpretation of the scene. By this time, we have learned to associate such language with the linking of actions to their larger context; it forces us to recognize John Grady's choice, the choice to lie about his reason for coming there: *I just wanted to see the country, I reckon.*

Then the conversation leaves this dangerous subject, and the cats are unmentioned during the conversation and the unmarked style narration of three pages. At the end of the interview, however, the conversation again turns to a question that should lead John Grady to discuss his connection with Blevins, and the cat image recurs:

Passage C-2
The hacendado leaned back in his chair. One of the cats rose and stretched.
  You rode here from Texas.
  Yessir.
  You and your friend.
  Yessir.
  Just the two of you?
John Grady looked at the table. *The paper cat stepped thin and slant among the shapes of cats thereon.* He looked up again. Yessir, he said. Just me and him.
The hacendado nodded and stubbed out his cigarette and pushed back his chair.
Come, he said. I will show you some horses. (116; emphasis added)

The danger lies in John Grady's choice to lie, not only because of his dishonesty to the hacendado but also because of his unwillingness or inability to recognize the evil he has already chosen. By denying his connection with

Blevins to Don Hector, he denies it to himself: *John Grady looked at the table. **The paper cat stepped thin and slant among the shapes of cats thereon.** He looked up again. Yessir, he said. Just me and him* [Rawlins] (116). The danger of this false innocence is embodied in the image of the cat, now narrowed to one of the cats, suggesting that the danger, too, is no longer general but specific: The image appears while John Grady considers yet another denial of his connection with Blevins.

The danger implicit in John Grady's refusal to accept responsibility for choice is embodied also in the startling shift of stylistic choice, which again operates to limit our interpretation of the scene—we must recognize that the conversation is connected with a greater context because we have learned to recognize the style as carrying that significance, and we know more precisely what context, because of the repetition of stylistic features from the earlier scene (C-1). The term *paper cat* is a leap into the metaphoric without warning, and the reference is extremely distant, linked to the metaphor of the cats' shadows as cutouts mentioned only once, three pages earlier, just as the word *slant* is a repetition also carried from that distant previous passage. This distant link mirrors the distant connections with Blevins deliberately ignored by John Grady. The sibilant *s* of the earlier passages recurs as well: *stepped, slant, shapes, cats*; the hissing is reinforced by the fricatives ð and θ: *the, thin, thereon* and the nasal *n*: *thin, slant, among, thereon*. There is rhyme—*paper* and *shape*—and repetition—*cat*. Again the syntax is marked, with adjective complements (*thin* and *slant*) following a verb of action rather than a copula. The word *thereon*, drawn from a more formal lexicon, is emphasized by its sentence-final position.

The marked style is thus so clearly marked, and in this extended passage so clearly associated with the intrusion of another element, that McCarthy can achieve a powerful effect with only a single sentence. We cannot miss the importance of John Grady's failure to speak; our interpretation of this is constrained by the use of the style we have come to recognize as representing a particular kind of significance. Throughout the novel, such small but powerful occurrences accumulate even more significance. Often they occur before or after some event crucial to the action, to prepare us (constrain us) to interpret that action in a certain way: a thunderstorm that will eventually lead to the loss of Blevins's horse, for example, *glowed mutely like welding seen through foundry smoke. As if repairs were under way at some flawed place in the iron dark of the world* (67); riding across the countryside, after parting from Alejandra, he thinks of universal pain as *some formless parasitic being seeking out the warmth of human souls wherein to incubate* (256). Even these brief passages occur rarely—once for every seven or eight pages of text, often clustered before and after crucial scenes—but they serve to control our understanding of much of the action narrated in the more open unmarked style. Most especially in the final sections of the book do we see the marked style as commentary on the events narrated by the unmarked. It is also in these final scenes that John Grady, by becoming more aware of the consequences of his actions, comes closer to seeing those actions as happening in that larger context (indeed, even a brief appearance of the marked style reminds us of that larger context). The mixing of the styles to some extent embodies his painfully acquired awareness of the web of cause and effect within which he acts. The reader is also constrained to recognize that the larger context of the novel includes notions of responsibility, cause and effect, and ultimately therefore a moral significance of actions.

INTERACTION OF STYLES: ACTIONS AND MEANINGS

Thus, it is the interaction of styles in this novel that allows us access to the inner workings of characters' minds and, even more, to the workings of the narrative. The unmarked style shows us the action of the novel, but action whose causes and consequences are unclear and so may mean anything or nothing. The marked style suggests the framework for recognizing the meanings of these actions and requires or constrains the reader to interpret them. Even the occasional use of the marked style offers the reader the implicatures that suggest a more precise and complex interpretation of the characters and the world of the novel. By so doing, the style limits the infinite options of interpretation and especially denies the possibility of random action, action without meaning. The convergence of styles at the end of the book thus comes to signify the necessary impingement of meaning upon action.

ACKNOWLEDGMENT: Portions of this chapter were originally printed as Kreml, Nancy (1995).

REFERENCES

Bell, Vereen. 1992. Between the wish and the thing the world lies waiting. *Southern Review* 1992: 920–927.

Blakemore, Dianne. 1992. *Understanding utterances.* Cambridge, Mass.: Blackwell.

Cheuse, Alan. 1992. A note on landscape in *All the pretty horses. Southern Quarterly* 30: 146–148.

Hurst, Mary Jane. 1990. *The voice of the child in American literature: linguistic approaches to fictional child language.* Lexington: University of Kentucky Press.

Kreml, Nancy (1995). Stylistic variation and cognitive constraint in Cormac McCarthy's *All the pretty horses.* In *Sacred violence: a reader's companion to Cormac McCarthy,* ed. Wade Hall and Rich Wallach, 137–148. El Paso: University of Texas at El Paso.

Luce, Dianne. 1995. *When you wake:* John Grady Cole's heroism in *All the pretty horses.* In *Sacred violence: a reader's companion to Cormac McCarthy,* ed. Wade Hall and Rich Wallach, 155–168. El Paso: University of Texas at El Paso.

McCarthy, Cormac. 1973. *Suttree.* New York: Random House.

————. 1985. *Blood Meridian or the evening redness in the west.* New York: Random House.

————. 1992. *All the pretty horses.* New York: Knopf.

Morrison, Gail. 1993. John Grady Cole's expulsion from paradise. In *Perspectives on Cormac McCarthy,* ed. Edwin T. Arnold and Dianne C. Luce, 173–192. Jackson: University of Mississippi Press.

Sperber, Daniel, and Deidre Wilson. 1995. *Relevance, cognition and communication.* 2nd ed. Oxford: Blackwell.

Witek, Terri. 1991. "He's hell when he's well": Cormac McCarthy's rhyming diction. *Shenandoah* 41: 51–66.

APPENDIX

Unmarked Passages (32 sentences, 750 words)

p. 6 (9 lines):

The house was built in eighteen seventy-two. Seventy-seven years later his grandfather was still the first man to die in it. What others had lain in state in that hallway had been carried there on a gate or wrapped in a wagonsheet or delivered crated up in a raw pineboard box with a teamster standing at the door with a bill of lading. The ones that came at all. For the most part they were dead by rumor. A yellowed scrap of newsprint. A letter. A telegram. The original ranch was twenty-three hundred acres out of the old Meusebach survey of the Fisher-Miller grant, the original house a oneroom hovel of sticks and wattle.

pp. 22–23 (8 lines):

 They rode together a last time on a day in early March when the weather had already warmed and the yellow mexicanhat bloomed by the roadside. They unloaded the horses at McCullough's and rode up through the middle pasture along Grape Creek and into the low hills. The creek was clear and green with trailing moss braided over the gravel bars. They rode slowly up through the open country among scrub mesquite and nopal. They crossed from Tom Green County into Coke County.

p. 74 (13 lines):

The riders got their plates and utensils out of the saddlebags and John Grady got the little enameled pot out of the blackened cookbag and handed it to Blevins together with his old woodenhandled kitchen fork. They went to the fire and filled their plates with beans and chile and took each a couple of blackened corn tortillas from a piece of sheetiron laid over the fire and walked over and sat under the willows a little apart form the workers. Blevins sat with his bare legs stretched out before him but they looked so white and exposed lying there on the ground that he seemed ashamed and he tried to tuck them up under him and to cover his knees with the tails of the borrowed shirt he wore. They ate. The workers had for the most part finished their meal and they were leaning back smoking cigarettes and belching quietly.

p. 154 (7 lines):
They sat side by side on a bench of iron slats in the little alameda. A pair of the guards stood a little ways off with their rifles and a dozen children of different ages stood in the dust of the street watching them. Two of the children were girls about twelve years of age and when the prisoners looked at them they turned shyly and twisted at their skirts. John Grady called to them to ask if they could get them cigarettes.

p. 246 (11 lines):
He offered to pay in advance but the proprietor dismissed him with a small wave of the hand. He walked out into the sun and down the street where he caught the bus back to town.

   He bought a small awol bag in a store and he bought two new shirts and a new pair of boots and he walked down to the train station and bought his ticket and went to a cafe and ate. He walked around to break in the boots and then went back to the hotel. He rolled the pistol and knife and his old clothes up in the bedroll and had the clerk put the bedroll in the storage room and he told the clerk to wake him at six in the morning and then went up to bed. It was hardly even dark.

p. 279 (17 lines):
Ascending into low hills they passed a small estancia and they dismounted and went afoot through the ruins of a cornfield and found some melons and sat in the stony washedout furrows and ate them. He hobbled down the rows and gathered melons and carried them out through the field to where the horses stood and broke them open on the ground at their feet for them to feed on and he stood leaning on the rifle and looked toward the house. Some turkeys stepped about in the yard and there was a pole corral beyond the house in which stood several horses. He went back and got the captain and they mounted up and rode on. When he looked back from the ridge above the estancia he could see that it was more extensive. There was a cluster of buildings above the house and he could see the quadrangles laid out by the fences and the adobe walls and irrigation ditches. A number of rangy and slatribbed cattle stood about in the scrub. He heard a rooster crow in the noonday heat. He heard a steady distant hammering of metal as of someone at a forge.

Marked Passages (19 sentences, 800 words)

p. 6 (9 lines):
The last of the day's light fanned slowly upon the plain behind him and withdrew again down the edges of the world in a cooling blue of shadow and dusk and chill and a few last chitterings of birds sequestered in the dark and wiry brush. He crossed the old trace again and he must turn the pony up onto the plain and homeward but the warriors would ride on in that darkness they'd become, rattling past with their stone-age tools of war in default of all substance and singing softly in blood and longing south across the plains to Mexico.

p. 30 (10 lines):
They rode out on the high prairie where they slowed the horses to a walk and the stars swarmed around them out of the blackness. They heard somewhere in that tenant-

less night a bell that tolled and ceased where no bell was and they rode out on the round dais of the earth which alone was dark and no light to it and which carried their figures and bore them up into the swarming stars so that they rode not under but among them and they rode at once jaunty and circumspect, like thieves newly loosed in that dark electric, like young thieves in a glowing orchard, loosely jacketed against the cold and ten thousand worlds for the choosing.

p. 73 (9 lines):
Bye and bye they passed a stand of roadside cholla against which small birds had been driven by the storm and there impaled. Gray nameless birds espaliered in attitudes of stillborn flight or hanging loosely in their feathers. Some of them were still alive and they twisted on their spines as the horses passed and raised their heads and cried out but the horsemen rode on. The sun rose up in the sky and the country took on new color, green fire in the acacia and paloverde and green in the roadside run-off grass and fire in the ocotillo. As if the rain were electric, had grounded circuits that the electric might be.

p. 161–162 (17 lines):
That night he dreamt of horses in a field on a high plain where the spring rains had brought up the grass and the wildflowers out of the ground and the flowers ran all blue and yellow far as the eye could see and in the dream he was among the horses running and in the dream he himself could run with the horses and they coursed the young mares and fillies over the plain where their rich bay and their rich chestnut colors shone in the sun and the young colts ran with their dams and trampled down the flowers in a haze of pollen that hung in the sun like powdered gold and they ran he and the horses out along the high mesas where the ground resounded under their running hooves and they flowed and changed and ran and their manes and tails blew off of them like spume and there was nothing else at all in that high world and they moved all of them in a resonance that was like a music among them and they were none of them afraid horse nor colt nor mare and they ran in that resonance which is the world itself and which cannot be spoken but only praised.

p. 242 (7 lines):
He crossed a dry gypsum playa where the salt crust stove under the horse's hooves like trodden isinglass and he rode up through white gypsum hills grown with stunted datil and through a pale bajada crowded with flowers of gypsum like a cave floor uncovered to the light. In the shimmering distance trees and jacales stood fugitive in the clear morning air.

p. 282 (14 lines):
The sky was dark and a cold wind ran through the bajada and in the dying light a cold blue cast had turned the doe's eyes to but one thing more of things she lay among in that darkening landscape. Grass and blood. Blood and stone. Stone and the dark medallions that the first flat drops of rain caused upon them. He remembered Alejandra and the sadness he'd first seen in the slope of her shoulders which he'd presumed to understand and of which he knew nothing and he felt a

loneliness he'd not known since he was a child and he felt wholly alien to the world although he loved it still. He thought that in the beauty of the world were hid a secret. He thought the world's heart beat at some terrible cost and that the world's pain and its beauty moved in a relationship of diverging equity and that in this headlong deficit the blood of multitudes might ultimately be exacted for the vision of a single flower.

4

Marked Grammatical Structures: Communicating Intentionality in *The Great Gatsby* and *As I Lay Dying*

CAROL MYERS-SCOTTON

Gatsby believed in the green light, the orgastic future that year by year recedes before us. It eluded us then, but that's no matter—tomorrow we will run faster, stretch out our arms farther. . . And one fine morning—So we beat on, boats against the current, borne back ceaselessly into the past.

– F. Scott Fitzgerald, [1925] 1991: 141

MANY SCHOLARS of American literature can recite these final lines of F. Scott Fitzgerald's *The Great Gatsby*. Many think the work is *the* great American novel. Fitzgerald's *style*—his evocative metaphors and similes—of course, are one reason Fitzgerald's prose is valued. For example, many readers remember such lines as *Gatsby believed in the green light* or that Daisy's voice *sounded like money*. Another twentieth-century American novelist whose style is cited as an essential part of his greatness is William Faulkner. The Faulkner work studied here is *As I Lay Dying*, the novel Faulkner himself said is the result of setting out to write a *tour de force*. In that novel, the style of each chapter represents the point of view of a particular character.

However, this chapter provides a stylistic analysis of the less obvious aspects of the style of Fitzgerald and Faulkner than either the crafting of metaphors and similes or the perfection of the point-of-view technique. Here, we consider the interplay of syntax and what I call cognitive weight. Kintsch (1974) reported that reading times increase as a function of the number of propositions in the text. Even controlling for other factors, such as the number of words in the text, does not alter the result. Different types of structures are the subject in the two different novels, but both have one feature in common: They are marked in the sense that they depart from the prevailing, or unmarked, syntax of each of the novels. Whereas the syntactic structures to be discussed are less obvious aspects of style than the stylistic features commonly associated with either Fitzgerald or Faulkner, I argue that the relation between structure and cognitive weight is perhaps an even more important aspect of their styles as the carrier of intentional messages. Specifically regarding Fitzgerald, I claim that through the syntactic structures he employed, whether consciously or unconsciously, he made sure that his "crucial passages" would stand out as "the figure in the carpet." I demonstrate that Fitzgerald adds to the import of certain passages "crucial" to the novel's central message through using structures (Longacre 1985: 86, 87) referred to as "packing the event line" or "slowing the camera down." In regard to Faulkner, I show how he amplifies especially one key character in *As I Lay Dying* by giving him a distinctive "syntactic signature" that sets his monologues off from those of other characters.

HYPOTHESES UNDER CONSIDERATION

My general hypothesis is in line with the theme of this volume: Linguistic virtuosos will exploit marked linguistic choices to convey intentional meanings in their discourse. Writers who are linguistic virtuosos either "mark" the crucial passages in their works or mark key characters to set them off from the rest of the work or the rest of the characters.

Marked choices, of course, are shifts from the expected or the norm, given the social situation or the genre involved. Although all humans have tacit knowledge that there is a multidimensional markedness continuum for every interaction type in their repertoire, what choices are more unmarked or marked is both community specific and interaction specific. Further, within a genre, such as the novel, each specific novel has its own unmarked style. Humans are innately predisposed to view linguistic choices in terms of markedness; however, specific readings of markedness depend on experience in the real world (Myers-Scotton chapter 2, this volume).

Intentional meaning refers to implicatures, to use the term of Grice (1975) and Sperber and Wilson (1995). Implicatures convey meaning in addition to that which is contained in the semantics of individual words and which is transmitted in their semantic and syntactic relationships with other words in a discourse. Although messages of intentionality may simply augment referential messages, they generally go beyond them in various ways. A major source of inference, of course, is what is generally called style—not the words themselves but, rather, the cognitive associations they call up or which are called up by one way of "saying something" out of the larger set of possible ways. In this vein, departures from expected style, for example, the fact that a marked syntactic structure is employed, are sources of implicatures or intentional meaning.

The more specific hypotheses studied here are as follows:

1. Fitzgerald marks the crucial narrative passages in *The Great Gatsby* by using syntactic structures that are demonstrably different from the

typical (or unmarked) narrative passages in the novel as a whole. That is, a sample of five key crucial passages will differ from five superficially similar passages in regard to a set of syntactic structures. "Crucial passages" mean those passages literary critics often identify as "carrying the author's message" (Matthew Bruccoli, personal communication). All the syntactic structures to be studied are discussed here, but the main investigation concerns the incidence of projections of complementizer (CP).

2. Faulkner distinguishes the "more heroic" of the characters in *As I Lay Dying*—that is, Darl and to a lesser extent Vardaman—by their extensive use of a syntactic structure, which I call *the trailing constituent*. The frequency of this structure is marked in comparison with its use by other characters. *Trailing constituent* is a cover term for both what Thompson (1983) called *detached participial phrases* and for certain types of prepositional phrases—those of condition (referring to time and location) and those of manner, process, and direction.

INDEPENDENT MOTIVATION FOR HYPOTHESES

The general hypothesis is motivated by previous theories in literary stylistics, as well as by several linguistic theories of discourse structure. First, the motivation for the general hypothesis comes from the markedness model (Myers-Scotton chapter 2, in this volume). A claim of the model is that a major component of the indexicality of any single linguistic form or variety is its markedness reading. A markedness reading refers to the extent to which the form or variety in question fits the pattern of what is unmarked or expected in a given interaction type or genre. Of course, all interpretations of linguistic choices call up schema—composed of motives, desires, ideas, and peopled events—with which a linguistic choice has become associated through experience. What is of special interest here are choices which are marked. The argument of the markedness model is that writers and speakers are motivated to employ marked choices at times just because they have the special value of evoking an "otherness." As such, they send a special message to the reader/addressee that is over and above the referential meanings they include.

Speaking of marked structures is reminiscent of the notion of *foregrounding*, that has its roots in the work of the Russian formalists. As one of the members of this school, Viktor Sklovskij, argued, the function of art is to make people aware of the world in a fresh way. A device for achieving this is *defamiliarization* or *ostranenie* (Russian) "making strange." One of Sklovskij's elaborations on this view is particularly relevant to this chapter, which claims that authors add cognitive weight to their words by making marked choices:

> [Art] exists to make one feel things, to make the stone *stony*. The purpose of art is to impart a sensation of things as they are perceived and not as they are known. The technique of art is to make objects "unfamiliar," to make forms

difficult, *to increase the difficulty and length of perception because the process of perception is an aesthetic end in itself and must be prolonged.* (quoted in Van Peer 1986: 1; emphasis added)

The formalists, as their name indicates, studied literature mainly in its formal aspects, eventually arriving at the concept of *foregrounding*. This term was introduced to the West by Garvin (1964) as a translation of the Czech *aktualisace*, employed in the work of several Prague scholars. One of the problems with the Russian formalists and the Prague school of (linguistic) structuralists, however, was a failure to indicate how one could identify what would count as defamiliarization or foregrounding. Another problem is with the way in which the Prague school looked at structure: They saw grammar— or language—as largely a surface phenomenon of items arranged in slots. That is, they operated as if linguistic forms can be separated from their conceptual structure, and they did not consider that more abstract structural hierarchies might underlie surface strings.

Recently, a model relying on the idea that nonfigurative language is unmarked whereas figurative language (including literary language) is made strange or foregrounded was criticized by Freeman (1996). Freeman seized on two notions. First, even though he does not explicitly state it, he clearly objects to interpretations that rely primarily on decomposing surface features. Second, he more explicitly opposes the notion that has always been associated with foregrounding, that literary language is "deviant" and that its effect depends on this feature. With a specific interest in characterizations of metaphor, Freeman takes this notion a step further. He attributes to the foregrounding model (he refers to it as the objectivist position) the idea that "a structure is parasitic upon ordinary language structure and that it can be explained in terms of its deviance from semantic interpretations of ordinary, non-metaphorical language interpretable by a compositional semantics . . ." (Freeman 1996: 280). According to Freeman, this model does not take account of cognitive processing but, rather, explains metaphors in terms of their deviance in reference to structural features. He writes "The 'deviance' is with respect to a language-universal set of semantic features and combinatory rules external to individual cognition." (1996: 80) As an alternative explanation to how metaphor works, Freeman offers Lakoff's (1987: xv) experientialist position. On this view, metaphor is "embodied human understanding" (Freeman 1996: 281); that is, based on their experience, humans extract schema that they use to interpret metaphors.

Contrary to Freeman, I would argue that the foregrounding model can be "rescued," especially if it is combined with the markedness model. First, there is no reason to assume that deviant means parasitic. That is, marked choices do not depend for their intentionality on unmarked choices. Rather, what markedness accomplishes in this regard is simply to highlight the fact that what is said or written is not unmarked and therefore deserves special attention. After all, the primary meaning of foregrounding is to draw attention. Second, under the markedness model, all uses of language require cognitive processing for the addressee/reader to arrive at an interpretation. Although it is possible that a compositional view of semantics and grammar may suffice for the addressee to arrive at referential meaning (but this is a controversy beyond the scope of my consideration here), it seems clear there is no way that an addressee can achieve intentional meaning without engaging in cognitive calculations. (This matter is discussed more extensively in chapter 2 in this volume; see also Sperber and Wilson 1995). Further, in the formulation of the message (the work of the writer/speaker) and in interpreting the message (the work of the reader/addressee), both parties must necessarily bring to bear their own experience, as members of the salient speech community, to achieve the desired communicative effect. That is, the process necessarily is not very different from that which defines the position for which Freeman argues: "The Experientalist position claims that we create metaphor by projecting onto an abstract *target domain* the entities and structure of a concrete *source domain*, a schematized real or vicarious bodily experience" (1996: 280–281). Thus, I see no need to equate the foregrounding model with objective, mechanistic decomposition, especially as this model is reinterpreted within the markedness model, for two reasons. First, the defining feature of a foregrounded or marked structure is not its deviancy but rather its "otherness." One must consider not only that it departs from the unmarked style but also what its markedness in the context where it occurs accomplishes, in terms of both the effects of its structure and its associations. Second, to interpret the implicatures a marked structure evokes, the reader/addressee clearly must carry out cognitive calculations, both to process the structural effects and to call up the real-world associations of the marked structure.

The idea that there should be a relation between "crucial" passages or character development and marked syntactic structures is specifically motivated by Longacre's discussion of "discourse peaks" (Longacre 1985).[1] An overall feature of discourse peaks is that the "event line" fades at a peak. The reason to orchestrate this fading is that "priority is given to marking the peak of the discourse. In effect, then, the very disappearance of the routine event-line markers is itself a marking of peak" (Longacre 1985: 85). In many different places, Longacre discusses the "conspiracy of features" found in and around peaks or climatic points in discourse. He lists ten structural features, all showing a "level of excitation peculiar to the peak as contrasted with the rest of the discourse" (Longacre 1985: 85). These include rhetorical underlining by means of repetition and paraphrase, heightened vividness by a tense shift or a person shift, or dramatic shifts toward action with many more verbs

---

1. Longacre and his students, often missionary linguists connected with the Summer Institute of Linguistics, regularly translated texts in what might be called relatively exotic languages. They championed the need for basing grammatical analysis on discourse samples long before discourse analysis as it is known today had any stature in the discipline of linguistics.

than found in other passages. I argue that Fitzgerald highlights his crucial passages by "packing the event line"; Longacre says that one way this can be accomplished is by increasing the ratio of verbs to nonverbs. However, I argue that Faulkner distinguishes his character, Darl, by doing what might be considered the opposite—by avoiding the weight that finite verbs and their arguments involve. Longacre states that the pace can be slowed by treating structures that are not usually on the event line *as if they were*; how this characterization applies to Darl's monologues is discussed later.

ANALYSIS OF STRUCTURE IN "THE GREAT GATSBY"

In the case of *The Great Gatsby*, the specific hypothesis predicts that a comparison of five narrative paragraphs containing crucial messages with five paragraphs whose contribution is more only to develop the story or event line will show different syntactic patterns in the two sets. To identify crucial passages, I consulted a leading Fitzgerald scholar, Matthew Bruccoli, for advice. Five passages he chose were paired with five nearby narrative passages. These matched the crucial passages as closely as possible in regard to both subject matter and length. The longest crucial passage has 101 words and the shortest one has 80 words, for a total of 736 words and 23 sentences versus 751 words and 25 sentences in the unmarked passages.

By examining randomly chosen narrative paragraphs throughout the novel, I confirm that the "matching" passages are representative of most narrative passages in the novel. These matching passages are defined as unmarked passages, whereas—if the hypothesis is supported—the crucial passages are defined as marked passages.

Based on Longacre's findings and claims, the specific hypothesis predicts that more structures would load the event line in the crucial passages. Four main categories were studied: (1) embedded or subordinating CPs; (2) Inflection (INFL) phrases (projections of INFL, or IPs); (3) prepositional phrases (PPs); and (4) types of verbs. I also considered other features such as (1) configurations of noun phrases (NPs); (2) conjunctions as links for IPs versus links for NPs and other XPs (X being some variable), such as verb phrases (VPs), adjective phrases (APs), and PPs. In addition, I examined participials and their functions. I used Eyeball (a computer parsing program) to count lexical categories.

To test the hypothesis, I drew detailed syntactic trees of the sentences in each set of passages. The difference in the trees of the two sets was immediately striking, supporting the hypothesis. Most obvious is that the trees for the crucial passages simply had more "foliage"; that is, the sentences included more hierarchical branching. This is so even though the average number of words per sentence (thirty-two in the crucial passages compared to thirty in the unmarked ones) was very similar.

INTERPRETATION OF RESULTS FOR "THE GREAT GATSBY"

Because it was immediately clear from the tree diagrams that the two types of passages differed so that, at least in some way, the passages containing the crucial messages were distinct from the unmarked passages, from now on the two types are referred to as the unmarked and marked passages. Figures 4-1 through 4-4 present tree diagrams that are discussed next.

Interestingly, the differences between the unmarked and marked passages have little to do with incidence of lexical categories per se. The parsing analysis program showed that there was little difference in the two types of passages in regard to the type of features often counted in discourse analysis studies (e.g., ratio of nouns to adjectives to the total number of words, or auxiliaries to the total number of verbs).

Results for Elaborating CPs

The story is quite different, however, when one considers the incidence of elaborating CPs. CPs, of course, can be either independent or dependent clauses. Only elaborating CPs were counted. This category included such CPs as the following from a marked passage: (i) adverbial adjuncts such as *when I came back from the East last autumn*; (ii) sentence complements such as *that I wanted the world to be in uniform and at a sort of moral attention forever* in the sentence [*I felt* [*that I wanted the world to be in uniform and at a sort of moral attention forever*]]; and also (iii) relative clauses such as *which is dignified under the name of creative temperament* (Fitzgerald [1925]1991: 5–6). There are many more elaborating CPs in the marked passages than the unmarked ones. The overall count is thirty-one (in the marked passages) to fifteen. This difference is statistically significant, according to a χ^2 test. (See table 4-1.)

Table 4-1
Comparisons: Modifying CPs, IPs, NP & NP (& NP)
The Great Gatsby

Category	Crucial/Marked passages (words: 736)		Unmarked Passages (words: 751)		χ^2
	N	%	N	%	
CPs	31	4.2	15	1.9	*5.564 (p <.025)
IPs	7	0.9	54	0.53	0.362[YC]
NP & NP (& NP)	4	0.54	13	1.7	*3.764[YC] (p <.10)

Note: N = number of tokens; % = proportion of category tokens expressed as a percentage of word total; 1 df; .10 and .025 = the probability level; [YC] = Yates' Correction applied; * = significant.

Incidence of IPs

The marked passages use almost twice as many IP-and-IP constructions as the unmarked ones; however, at seven versus four the frequencies are not large enough to give me confidence that this ratio would stand across a larger corpus and are not large enough to perform a test of statistical significance. (See table 4-1.) Still, when they occur, the IP-and-IP constructions are distinctive. For example, the first sentence in the marked passage from the Bruccoli edition (Fitzgerald [1925]1991: 34) shows a three-part IP-and-IP construction: *The lights grow bright (as the earth lurches away from the sun); now the orchestra is playing yellow cocktail music; and the opera of voices pitches a key higher.* These three IPs are joined by the conjunction *and.* In contrast, in the unmarked passages, this conjunction tends to link not IPs but other XPs, especially NPs, but also VPs, APs, and PPs. For example, in figure 4-4, which presents a tree diagram of a sentence from an unmarked passage, there are six NPs linked by *and.*

Incidence of Prepositional Phrases

Although the unmarked passages show more PPs, eighty-one to seventy-three, the marked passages use more PPs to show "process," "direction," or "manner" of activity or action. In the unmarked passages, PPs tend to indicate "state or condition," "time," or "place/location." For example, consider the PPs (in bold) in the sentence from one marked passage, that is illustrated as a tree diagram in figure 4-3:

> The lawn started **at the beach** and ran **toward the front door for a quarter of a mile** jumping **over sun-dials and brick walls** and burning gardens—finally it reaches the house **drifting up the side in bright vines** as though **from the momentum of its run.** (Fitzgerald [1925]1991: 9)

All but the first PP clearly show process and manner. Compare these with the PPs in a sentence from a nearby unmarked passage:

> I never saw this great-uncle, but I am supposed to look like him—**with special reference to the rather hard-boiled painting** [condition] that hangs **in my father's office** [location].

Table 4-2 presents the statistics on the incidence of PPs. If the overall incidence of PPs is considered (seventy-three in the marked passages compared to eighty-one in the unmarked passages), the difference is not statistically significant. However, when we compare the passages in regard to specific types of PPs, we see a clearly statistically significant difference. Many more PPs refer to process, manner, and direction in the marked passages ($N = 31$) than in the unmarked passages ($N = 6$). In contrast, the unmarked passages have many more PPs referring to condition, time, and location ($N = 50$) than the marked passages ($N = 20$).

Table 4-2
Comparisons: PPs, Class I PPs, Class II PPs
The Great Gatsby

Category	Crucial/Marked Passages (words: 736)		Unmarked Passages (words: 751)		χ^2
	N	%	N	%	
PPs	73	9.9	81	10.7	0.414
Class I PPs	31	4.2	6	0.79	*16.89 (p < .001)
Class II PPs	20	2.7	50	6.6	*12.856 (p < .001)

Note: N = number of tokens; % = proportion of category tokens expressed as a percentage of word total; 1 df; .001 = the probability level; * = significant.

Verbal Categories

There are more verbs in the marked passages, seventy-three to fifty-eight, although the difference is not statistically significant, as shown in Table 4-3. What is more interesting, however, is that the marked passages show more successive verbs or verbs in sequence. For example, consider the sentence from a marked passage that begins with a sequence of verbs—*The groups change more swiftly, swell with new arrivals, dissolve and form . . .*'and goes on to add more— *confident girls who weave here and there . . . become . . . the center of a group and then excited with triumph glide on . . .*' (Fitzgerald [1925]1991: 34).

Also, the marked passages show many more verbs which I call *phrasal verbs*. True, it is difficult to define a phrasal verb absolutely. Rather than try to do this, Hopper (1993), for example, simply refers to all potential candidates as *multiply articulated verbal expressions*. For an example of the problem, consider the verb in this clause: *which is dignified under the name of the*

Table 4-3
Comparisons: Vs, Phrasal Verbs
The Great Gatsby

Category	Crucial/Marked Passages (words: 736)		Unmarked Passages (words: 751)		χ^2
	N	%	N	%	
Vs	73	9.9	58	7.7	1.716
Phrasal Verbs	26	3.5	7	0.9	*10.938 (p <.001)
Ratio (PVs to Vs)		1:2.8		1:8.28	

Note: N = number of tokens; % = proportion of category tokens expressed as a percentage of word total; 1 df; .001 = the probability level; * = significant.

"creative temperament" (Fitzgerald [1925]1991: 5–6). Is the verb simply *is dignified*, or is it *is dignified under*? I define phrasal verbs in two ways. First, the category includes those verbs followed by particles which cannot easily be separated from the main verb by a parenthetical intrusion, (for example, *stretch out* in this fragment from a marked passage: *When we pulled out into the winter night and the real snow, our snow, began to stretch out beside us* . . . (Fitzgerald [1925]1991: 137). Second, the category also includes those combinations of verb + prepositions in which the preposition does not assign a thematic role on its own; that is, the thematic role of the complement is assigned only by the verb in concert with the preposition as satellite. For example, by this definition, *think of* is a phrasal verb and not a verb + a preposition heading a PP. Note that *think of* is equivalent to *consider*. This phrasal verb occurs in this sentence in a marked passage: *As I sat there, brooding on the old unknown world, I **thought of** Gatsby's wonder* . . . (Fitzgerald [1925]1991: 141). However, *dignified under* in *dignified under the name* is not a phrasal verb. Under these two criteria, of the seventy-three verbs in the marked passages, thirty-six are phrasal verbs. This means that one out of every two verbs is a phrasal verb. In contrast, in the unmarked passages, out of fifty-eight verbs, only fourteen are phrasal verbs, or one in four. This difference is statistically significant according to a χ^2 test. (See table 4-3.) Some examples of phrasal verbs from the marked passages include *turned out* in *Gatsby turned out all right at the end* (Fitzgerald [1925]1991: 6); and *tipped out* in *Laughter is easier . . . spilled with prodigality, tipped out at a cheerful word* (Fitzgerald [1925]1991: 34).

What special effects do phrasal verbs have? Hopper (1993) remarked that in contrast to simple transitive verbs, which suggest backgrounded or unwitnessed events, "multiply articulated verbal expressions" suggest an authorial perspective on the action—that is, experienced or witnessed details. I would add that because phrasal verbs may be considered as icons of an "unfolding,"[2] their presence is consistent with a view of narrative as at times constructive rather than just reportorial. If phrasal verbs carry such intentional meanings, it would be predicted that more of them should occur when the author is giving his or her perspective on events. This is just what is found in the marked (crucial) passages, of course.

STRUCTURAL TREE DIAGRAMS

The four figures included in this chapter provide structural tree diagrams of example sentences. Figures 4-1, 4-2 and 4-3 provide examples of structural

---

2. Janice L. Jake points out one potential effect of phrasal verbs is that the verb portion of verb + satellite contributes its own referential meaning and also contributes to the meaning of the entire phrasal verb. For example, in the phrasal verb *turn out*, *turn* on its own means "to change" as in *change a direction*. In combination with *out* it implies not only a change but a result in which the final outcome was not predictable from the outset.

If personality is an unbroken series of successful gestures, then there was something gorgeous about him, some heightened sensitivity to the promises of life, as if he were related to one of those intricate machines that register earthquakes ten thousand miles away.

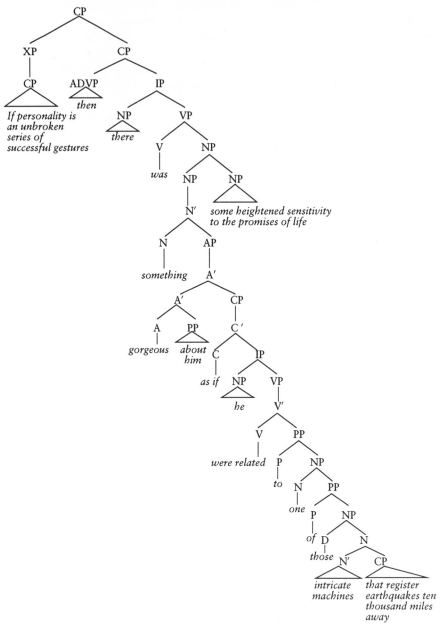

Figure 4-1
Phrase Structure Tree for a Sentence from a Crucial/Marked Passage
The Great Gatsby (1991: 6)

The lights grow brighter as the earth lurches away from the sun and now the orchestra is playing yellow cocktail music and the opera of voices pitches a key higher.

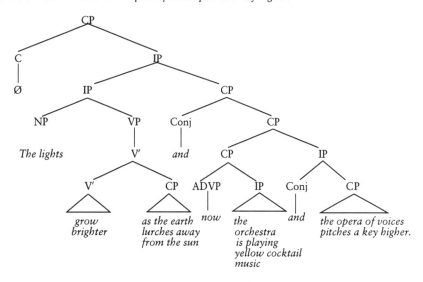

Figure 4-2
Phrase Structure Tree for a Sentence from a Crucial/Marked Passage
The Great Gatsby (1991: 34)

trees of one sentence from a marked passage. Figure 4-4 gives an example of the structural tree of a sentence from an unmarked passage. As noted earlier, the marked passages have many elaborating CPs. These can be seen in figure 4-1, for example. Note these elaborating CPs: *(i) if personality is an unbroken series of successful gestures, (ii) as if he were related to one of those intricate machines, (iii) that register earthquakes ten thousand miles away.* (The main clause or root CP is *there was something gorgeous about him.*) They also show many phrasal verbs. For example, in the sentence diagramed in figure 4-2, *lurch away* occurs: *The lights grow brighter as the earth lurches away from the sun. . . .*

DISCUSSION OF ELABORATING CPS AND CONJOINED IPS

Whereas differences in the types of PPs and the incidence of phrasal verbs across the two types of passages warrant comment, what is most striking in the comparison is the incidence of elaborating CP chaining and conjoined IP constructions in the marked passages. When there are a number of elaborating CPs and IPs within a single sentence, the sentence is more "thoughtful." But *how* is this accomplished? As background to an answer, consider that sentences in general satisfy thematic (theta) role projections—they contain

The lawn started at the beach and ran toward the front door for a quarter of a mile, jumping over sun-dials and brick walks and burning gardens—finally when it reached the house drifting up the side in bright vines as though from the momentum of its run.

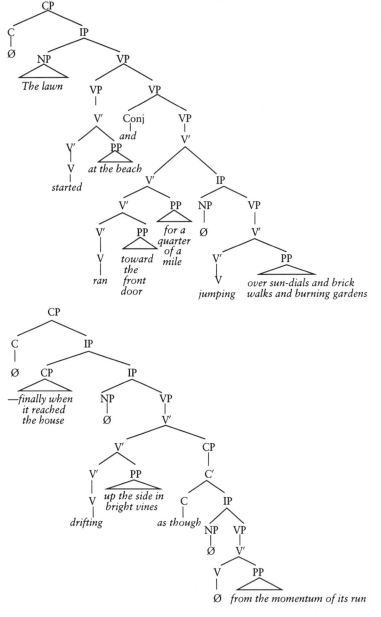

Figure 4-3
Phrase Structure Tree for a Sentence from a Crucial/Marked Passage
The Great Gatsby (1991: 9)

I remember the fur coats of the girls returning from Miss This or That's and the chatter of frozen breath and the hands waving overhead as we caught sight of old acquaintances and the matchings of invitations: "Are you going to the Ordways'? the Herseys'? the Schultzes'?" and the long green tickets clasped tight in our gloved hands.

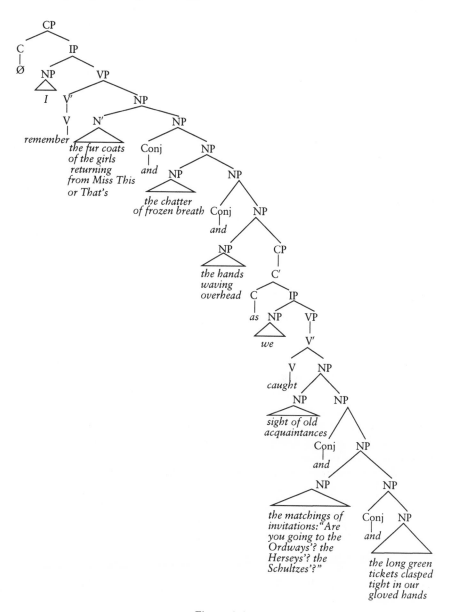

Figure 4-4
Phrase Structure Tree for a Sentence from an Unmarked Passage
The Great Gatsby (1991: 136)

thematic role assigners (verbs or prepositions) and thematic role receivers (NPs and some pronouns). Thematic roles include agent, patient, beneficiary, locative, and others. Thus, any sentence includes a verb that will specify internal thematic role requirements, and the necessary complement NPs and, in some cases, PPs to satisfy the possible subcategorized thematic roles projected by the verb and VP. Note that APs and many PPs do not satisfy thematic role requirements. Rather, as adjuncts they elaborate on already projected thematic roles. Therefore, they differ from NPs, which are prototypical complements.

The reason thematic roles concern us here is that processing the relation between thematic role assigners (e.g., a verb) and thematic role receivers (e.g., a noun) requires "cognitive energy." Thus, whenever there are numerous thematic roles presented in the same sentence, this "slows down the camera"—to rephrase Longacre's (1985) words about narrative peaks. Because CPs and IPs express thematic role requirements by containing both finite verbs and NPs, it should now be clear why the number of CPs and IPs in the marked passages is important: The more CPs and IPs there are, the more thematic role relations there are to process, even for elaborating CPs.

Having more than one CP or IP in a sentence increases cognitive weight in three ways. First, some CPs and IPs are like NPs in that they themselves can receive thematic roles. For example, as a sentential complement, a CP may function as a patient (e.g., *that the rain falls mainly on the plain* in the sentence [*I think* [*that the rain falls mainly on the plain*]]. Second, other additional adjunct CPs that are not part of the argument projection of the main verb (as the complement CP is in the sentence just discussed), "create" more thematic roles. Thus, the CP *when I came back from the East last autumn* includes thematic roles in addition to those in the main CP of the sentence. That is, the elaborating CP includes the thematic roles of actor (*I*) and direction/source (*the East*). Third, and perhaps most important, *all* additional CPs and IPs necessarily create additional propositions, all with their own cognitive weight.

Now, it is true that *any* multiplication of phrases, whether they are CPs or IPs or NPs or PPs or even APs, creates new information and therefore "slows down the camera," thus making the passage more "memorable." The difference, however, is that the information created by CPs or IPs is of *a different order* from that created by other phrases. This difference occurs because, as noted above, new propositions are created. In the case of other types of multiple phrases, the only thing added is new information. For example, multiple adjunct PPs or adjectives simply offer an elaboration on a proposition. In the case of multiple NPs, the elaboration is slightly different, but still it is only an elaboration. That is, in an NP-and-NP construction, still only one thematic role projection is satisfied, even though there are two nouns.

ANALYSIS OF "AS I LAY DYING"

I turn now to Faulkner's macabre novel, *As I Lay Dying*. This novel is the story of a poor, white rural Mississippi family and their grisly odyssey while bringing the dead body of the wife and mother of the family to town to be buried next to her kin. As it progresses, the story of the journey is told entirely through the monologues of the characters, most of whom are members of the family.

Two monologues for each of eight characters were studied, seven family members and the doctor, Peabody. The first monologue to appear in the novel for each of these persons was analyzed. The second set of monologues studied include the next one for each of the same characters that consisted largely of narration. In some cases, only part of a monologue was studied to keep all texts to approximately the same length and to treat narrative material only.[3] For the sake of brevity, I refer to all samples as monologues even if they are only portions of monologues. Again, the hypothesis is that there will be differences in syntactic structures across the passages studied (in this case, across the monologues as presentations of the characters).

To establish a baseline to serve as Faulkner's unmarked style at the time, passages from *Light in August*, written about the same time, were also analyzed. However, results show that the use of CPs, IPs, and VPs by most of the characters in *As I Lay Dying* is fairly similar to usage in narrative passages in *Light in August*. Thus, there is nothing "marked" about *As I Lay Dying* in regard to these features. Further, because there is no clear difference across characters in *As I Lay Dying* in regard to these features, any differences in characterization to be attributed to syntactic features would have to involve structures other than the relative incidence of CPs, IPs, and VPs.

Trailing Constitutents

Even in a "holistic" reading of the first monologues of the eight characters, the reader is struck by a feeling that Darl and, to a lesser extent, Vardaman, are given styles that set them apart from the other characters. Darl is the second oldest son and the hero of the novel—if there is one—whereas Vardaman is the youngest child and considered mentally "odd," even at the beginning of the novel. The difference in their style seems to have something to do with the extent to which their monologues (especially Darl's) achieved a similar length to the other monologues only by including many phrases as optional additions to the main verb and its arguments.

3. The two sets of passages studied from *As I Lay Dying* (Library of America edition 1995) are the following: Sample I: Addie (p. 114), Anse (p. 24), Cash (pp. 157–158), Darl (p. 1), Dewey Dell (p. 18), Jewel (p. 11), Vardaman (p. 36), and Peabody (p. 28). Sample II: Addie (pp. 117–118), Anse (p. 71), Cash (pp. 177–178), Darl (pp. 149–150), Dewey Dell (pp. 78–79), Vardaman (pp. 170–171), and Peabody (pp. 29–30).

Thus, my more specific hypothesis is the following:

Darl's monologues would show many more of what I call *trailing constituents* than the monologues of the other characters. Also, the monologue of Vardaman would pattern more like that of Darl than the other characters in regard to these constituents.

As noted previously, *trailing constituents* is used as a cover term for what some other writers call *detached participial phrases* (Thompson 1983) and also for certain types of prepositional phrases. Thompson defines detached participial phrases in conversation in reference to intonation patterns. She refers to them as "being set off by pauses, of exhibiting a clause-final falling intonation contour characteristic of independent clauses, or of being preceded by a clause ending with a clause-final falling intonation." She goes on to say that "these intonational signals of detachment are virtually without exception marked by commas in writing." (Thompson 1983: 43) Although Thompson's definition is useful, I used the following ways to define them. First, detached participial phrases are distinct from PPs; thus, they cannot begin with a preposition. They are also distinct from reduced relative clauses. By these two criteria, *with the water bubbling up* in *It would be quiet there then, with the water bubbling up* . . . . (Faulkner [1930]1985: 114) is not a detached participial phrase. Second, they can begin with a participial verb, which, of course, is tenseless. For example, consider this participial phrase from Darl's second monologue: *This time Jewel is riding upon it, clinging to it . . .'* (Faulkner [1930]1985: 150) Third, they may begin with a NP as subject of the participle, although these are very rare in my sample. Sometimes this subject is coreferential with a main-clause nonsubject NP, but more often it is in a part–whole relationship with the main-clause subject. This example occurs in Darl's first monologue, with the participial clause beginning with *a single broad window* (in caps): *Square, with a broken roof set at a single pitch, it leans in empty and shimmering dilapidation in the sunlight, A SINGLE BROAD WINDOW IN TWO OPPOSITE WALLS GIVING ON TO THE APPROACHES OF THE PATH* (Faulkner [1930]1985: 1).

If the trailing constituents are highlighted in the text, it is easy to see how many of these types of constituents occur in Darl's monologue . (Detached participial phrases are in caps and the prepositional phrases that show process, manner, or direction are in bold):

Jewel and I come up **from the field**, FOLLOWING THE PATH IN SINGLE FILE. Although I am fifteen feet **ahead of him**, anyone watching us **from the cottonhouse** can see Jewel's frayed and broken straw hat a full head **above my own**.

The path runs straight **as a plum-line**, WORN SMOOTH BY FEET AND BAKED BRICK-HARD BY JULY, **between the green rows of laid-by cotton, to the cottonhouse in the center of the field**, where it turns and circles the cottonhouse **at four soft right angles** and goes on **across the field** again, WORN SO BY FEET **in fading precision**.

The cottonhouse is of rough logs, from between which the chinking has long fallen. Square, with a broken roof set at a single pitch, it leans in empty and shimmering dilapidation in the sunlight, A SINGLE BROAD WINDOW IN TWO OPPOSITE WALLS GIVING ON TO THE APPROACHES OF THE PATH. Jewel, fifteen feet behind me, LOOKING STRAIGHT AHEAD, HIS PALE EYES LIKE WOOD SET INTO HIS WOODEN FACE, he crosses the floor in four strides with the rigid gravity of a cigar-store Indian dressed in patch overalls and endued with life from the hips down, and steps in a single stride through the opposite window and into the path again just as I come around the corner. In single file and five feet apart and Jewel now in front, we go on up the path toward the foot of the bluff. Tull's wagon stands beside the spring, HITCHED TO THE RAIL, THE REINS WRAPPED ABOUT THE SEAT STANCHION. In the wagon-bed are two chairs. Jewel stops at the spring and takes the gourd from the willow branch and drinks. I pass him and mount the path, BEGINNING TO HEAR CASH'S SAW. When I reach the top he has quit sawing. STANDING IN A LITTER OF CHIPS, he is fitting two of the boards together. (Faulkner [1930]1985: 1*).

Compare Darl's monologue with the first five sentences of Vardaman's monologue and similar samples from other characters, Cash and Dewey Dell:

If I jump I can go through it like the pink lady in the circus, into the warm smelling, without having to wait. My hands grab at the bushes; beneath my feet the rocks and dirt go rumbling down. Then I can breathe again, in the warm smelling. I enter the stall, TRYING TO TOUCH HIM, and then I can dry then I vomit the crying. As soon as he gets through kicking I can and then I can cry, the crying can. (Faulkner [1930]1985: 36)

Cash:

So Jewel got the team and come for me and they fixed me a pallet in the wagon and we drove across the square to the corner where Pa said, and we was waiting there in the wagon, with Dewey Dell and Vardaman eating bananas, when we see them coming up the street. Pa was coming along with that kind of daresome and hangdog look all at once like when he has been up to something he knows ma ain't going to like, CARRYING A GRIP IN HIS HAND . . . (Faulkner [1930]1985: 177)

Dewey Dell:

We picked on down the row, the woods getting closer and closer and the secret shade, PICKING ON INTO THE SECRET SHADE with my sack and Lafe's sack. Because I said will I or wont I when the sack was half-full because I said if the sack is full when we get to the woods it wont be me. I said if it don't mean for me to do it the sack will not be full and I will turn up the next row but if the sack is full, I cannot help it. (Faulkner [1930]1985: 18)

Darl's Monologues as Distinctive

A comparison across all monologues (ranging from a total of 562 to 796 words when both samples are considered) shows that Darl is very distinctive

Table 4-4
Comparisons: Detached Participial Phrases (Samples I & II)
As I Lay Dying

Character	Words	N	%
Addie	796	3	0.4
Anse	562	3	0.5
Cash	716	5	0.7
Darl	743	22	3.0
Dewey Dell	724	4	0.6
Vardaman	747	10	1.3
Peabody	730	4	0.5

$\chi^2 = {}^*34.907^{YC}$ *(p <.001)*

Note: N = number of tokens; % = proportion of category tokens expressed as a percentage of word total; 6 df; .001 = the probability level; ^{YC} = *Yates' Correction applied;* * = *significant.*

in his use of detached participial phrases. He has twenty-two, eleven in each of his monologues. Vardaman has the next largest number of these constituents, a total of ten. There are four detached participial phrases in the monologue from which the extract of Vardaman, cited previously, comes; one occurs in the extract. Cash has one detached participial phrase in the portion of the monologue quoted previously; altogether he has five of these constituents in both of his samples. In the extract from Dewey Dell's monologue, there is one detached participial phrase; in both her monologues she has a total of four. In this regard, the monologues of Cash and Dewey Dell are

Table 4-5
Comparisons: All PPs (Samples I & II)
As I Lay Dying

Character	Words	Class I PPs (process manner, direction)		Class II PPs (condition, time, location)	
		N	%	N	%
Addie	796	17	2.1	44	5.5
Anse	562	9	1.6	26	4.6
Cash	716	18	2.5	18	2.5
Darl	743	51	6.9	41	5.5
Dewey Dell	724	28	3.9	16	2.2
Vardaman	747	32	4.3	25	3.3
Peabody	730	7	1.0	34	4.7
$\chi^2 =$		*60.617 (p < .001)*		*24.32 (p < .001)*	

Note: N = number of tokens; % = proportion of category tokens expressed as a percentage of word total; 6 df; .001 = the probability level; * = significant.

typical of those of the other characters and in stark contrast with those of Darl and, to a lesser extent, those of Vardaman.

Overall statistics for all characters showing their use of detached participial phrases are found in table 4-4. With his twenty-two examples, Darl shows 3.0 detached participial phrases for every 100 words. For Vardaman, with his ten examples, the ratio is 1.3 per 100 words. Cash has five examples, but all other characters show only three or four, or fewer than 0.5 or 0.6 per 100 words. Note that these differences are significant according to a χ^2 analysis.

In addition to showing a high usage of detached participial phrases, Darl also shows a high frequency and ratio of both class I (manner, process, and direction) and class II (condition, time, and location) prepositional phrases compared to the other characters. These are in boldface in Darl's monologue included above. Darl has fifty-one PPs which encode process, manner, or direction. The high incidence of such PPs definitely sets him apart from any other character, giving him a ratio of 6.9 PPs of this type per 100 words. Vardaman follows with thirty-two PPs of this class and a ratio of 4.3 PPs of this type per 100 words. Darl is less distinctive in his use of class II-type PPs (i.e., PPs which show condition, time, or location). He has forty-one PPs in class II, but Addie has forty-four and Peabody has thirty-four. Still, overall, the distribution of findings across all eight characters is significant for both types of PPs. (See table 4-5.) Again, the results are statistically significant.

In addition to showing a high usage of both of the types of structures for which I use the cover term *trailing constituents*, an analysis of only sample I shows that Darl has many more dynamic verbs, more nouns, and more descriptive adjectives than other characters. He has fewer elaborating CPs that other characters and fewer coordinated phrases (N+N or V+V, etc.). However, reporting the details on these categories is beyond the scope of this chapter.

INTERPRETATION OF RESULTS FOR "AS I LAY DYING"

So how does this grammatical profile build Darl's character? Impression tells us that Darl is dream-like—fanciful at the same time he is pensive. In contrast, the other characters are more commonplace, as would fit our stereotypes of the rural, white, southern lower class. In her quantitative study of detached participles Thompson (1983) commented on the relative scarcity of this construction in conversation and stated that it is more typical of planned texts and therefore more often found in writing than speech. She argues that the purpose of the detached participle is to describe, not state logical or temporal relations. When the detached participle occurs, Thompson characterizes such a text as "discourse that attempts to describe by creating an image" (1983: 46). She goes on to say: "Writing that tends to spark the visual imagination, then, tends to abound in detached participles" (1983: 51). Elsewhere, she states that the detached participle "serves as a device that allows the speaker/writer to present certain material as background against which other material can be put forth as 'figure' in the Gestalt sense" (Thompson 1983: 44).

In many ways, the typical monologue in this novel is similar to conversation, and the contrast between conversation and written text is a clue to the evocative effect of Darl's syntax. Resembling conversation, the monologues of most of the other characters seem to be directed at an imaginary listener. These monologues impart facts in the relatively straightforward way of having sentences largely composed of IPs and CPs. The main task of these types of constituents, as indicated in the earlier discussion of *Gatsby*, is to introduce new propositions. They do this, of course, by virtue of the fact that the heart of such a constituent is a finite verb and NPs in the primary argument positions of subject and object. These NPs fulfill the thematic roles of agents and patients or goals and beneficiaries. However, Darl's monologue does not show this emphasis on argument structure, perhaps because his character seems less concerned with presenting information than with painting a scene. Although Darl's first monologue has more concrete nouns than that of any other character, most of these nouns are not part of the argument structure of the main clause or of elaborating CPs. They occur as thematic roles of either participials or PPs. Because these trailing constituents are not part of the main argument structure (both participials and PPs are adjuncts, not complements of the main VP in a CP), they do not modify the propositional content of the sentence but simply provide background for what is already conveyed. In this way they contrast with complements in the main VP, that is, with NPs as objects.

This lack of contribution to the main propositional weight of the sentence, this lack of attachment to finite verbs, means that some subject NPs in Darl's monologue (i.e., those in detached participial phrases) are not really anchored in any sense. They are left *floating*, if you will. Thus, the argument here is that it is this lack of relationship between the nouns and verbs (i.e., tenseless participles) in detached participial phrases and the main predicate-argument structure of the sentence that gives Darl's monologues their dreamlike and ethereal quality. To a lesser extent, the monologues of Vardaman also have this quality.

Of course other characters also have a few detached participials, but the point is that they are just that: a few. When they do occur, the effect is similar to that found in Darl's monologues. For example, the first monologue of the father, Anse, has several detached participials in the first few lines:

> Durn that road, and it fixing to rain, too. I can stand here and same as see it with second-sight, A-SHUTTING DOWN BEHIND THEM LIKE A WALL, SHUT-TING DOWN BETWIXT THEM AND MY GIVEN PROMISE. I do the best

I can, much as I can get my mind on anything, but durn them boys. (Faulkner [1930]1985: 24)

Although in many ways Anse is not a sympathetic character, these detached participials give him—just for a second—the same dream-like quality Darl has in general. For once, he evokes images rather than confining his contributions to the pedestrian. At the least, they add a reflective dimension to his portrayal.

CONCLUSION

This chapter provides evidence that in Fitzgerald's *The Great Gatsby* five passages identified as crucial in carrying the "authorial message" differ in certain syntactic ways from five matched passages which largely function only to carry the story line forward. This chapter also provides evidence that the syntax of Darl in Faulkner's *As I Lay Dying* is marked in relation to the syntax of other characters in showing many more trailing constituents. Most especially, Darl's monologues have many detached participial phrases.

Interestingly enough, the sources of stylistic effect in the two novels in reference to the structures studied are exactly opposite each other. In *Gatsby* the author slows down the action by adding "cognitive weight" to sentences in the crucial passages; he does this by adding additional propositions to the main proposition of the sentence. This is done by adding elaborating CPs containing finite verbs and their arguments (NPs). These types of structure require additional cognitive processing because the reader needs to work out the relationship between the verbs and the thematic roles contained in their arguments, roles such as agent or patient. In *As I Lay Dying* the author builds up the reader's picture of Darl by giving him monologues that are *not* packed with "extra" propositional modification of the central proposition (i.e., core CP) to process. Instead, Darl's monologues contain constituents that do not have finite verbs (detached participial phrases) or have no verbs at all (prepositional phrases). The abundance of these constituents in Darl's monologues contrasts with what is found in the monologues of the other characters. Reading such constituents provides the reader with images or impressions rather than information. The result is that the cognitive processing in terms of thematic content and the mapping of propositional content required of the reader is reduced. The net stylistic effect is that Darl himself comes across *as detached*, not so much a part of the everyday world of the cognitive processing of actor and event as the other characters but a reflective observer.

These conclusions result from a frequency count of the major components of phrase structure in paired discourse samples from the two novels, elaborating CPs in the case of *Gatsby* and detached participials in the case of *As I Lay Dying*. To reach the most interesting claim of the analysis in both novels—that stylistic effects are achieved through varying the propositional weight—one must go beyond surface-level considerations of style. This analysis emphasizes the role of the more abstract level of predicate-argument structure. Nouns and verbs and their relations, including thematic role assignment, are what affect propositional weight. Thus, this chapter argues for quantitative analysis in stylistic research, but quantification that goes beyond counting lexical categories and phrase structures only as surface configurations.

Finally, because a goal of this chapter was to show that linguistic virtuosos achieve certain effects by using marked choices, some discussion of the relevant structures as marked choices is in order. It has been argued that many linguistic choices are motivated by the wish of the speaker/author to convey messages which, in addition to conveying the referential message of words and their syntactic configurations, suggest messages that are intentional in nature. Elsewhere I commented on the fact that messages of intentionality are social or psychological in nature (e.g., Myers-Scotton 1993). With the markedness model, marked choices function as negotiations to change either the speaker's previously established persona or the interpersonal relationship with other participants. Is it a stretch of the imagination to claim that marked choices novelists make are socially or psychologically motivated? To answer this question fully is beyond the scope of this chapter. Here, suffice it to say that for novelists, marked choices, at the very least, draw attention to themselves. In so doing, they clearly signal a higher degree of authorial involvement at the point at which they occur. Can one argue that when marked choices are made, the story line becomes secondary to "something else"? I would answer "yes." I suggest that marked stylistic choices in novels are negotiations to change the writer's relationship with the reader *and* perhaps also the reader's relationship with a character. In making marked choices, writers are inviting the reader to look for "something else" beyond the referential message—in the parlance of Grice (1975) and Sperber and Wilson (1995), to look for implicatures. Marked choices invite the reader to participate in a new way, to engage in the cognitive processing necessary for "working out" additional meaning. It is in this sense that one can argue that marked choices in a novel are also socially or psychologically motivated.

ACKNOWLEDGMENT: I am extremely grateful to Longxing Wei for a good deal of help in quantifying features for this analysis.

REFERENCES

Faulkner, William. 1930. *As I lay dying*. New York: J. Cape and H. Smith. Reprint, New York: Literary Classics of the United States, 1985.
———. 1932. *Light in August*. New York: Modern Library. Reprint, New York: Literary Classics of the United States, 1985.
Fitzgerald, F. Scott. 1925. *The Great Gatsby*. New York: Charles Scribner's Sons. Reprint, Cambridge: Cambridge University Press, 1991, ed. Matthew H. Bruccoli.

Freeman, Donald C. 1996. "According to my bond": King Lear and re-cognition. In *The stylistics reader: from Roman Jakobson to the present*, ed. Jean Jacques Weber, 280–297. New York: St. Martin's Press.

Garvin, Paul. 1964. *A Prague reader on esthetics, literary structure and style*. Washington, D.C.: Georgetown University Press.

Grice, H. Paul. 1975. Logic and conversation. In *Syntax and semantics*, vol. 3, ed. Peter Cole and Jerry L. Morgan, 41–58. New York: Academic Press.

Hopper, Paul. 1993. The English verbal expression in written discourse. Paper presented at Rice University symposium on alternative linguistics in Houston, Texas.

Kintsch, Walter. 1974. *The representation of meaning in memory*. Hillsdale, N. J.: Erlbaum.

Lakoff, George. 1987. *Women, fire, and dangerous things*. Chicago: University of Chicago Press.

Longacre, Robert E. 1985. Discourse peak as zone of turbulence. In *Beyond the sentence: discourse and sentential form*, ed. Jessica Wirth, 83–98. Ann Arbor, Mich.: Karoma.

Myers-Scotton, Carol. 1993. *Social motivations for codeswitching: evidence from Africa*. Oxford: Oxford University Press.

Sperber, Dan, and Deirdre Wilson. 1995. *Relevance: cognition and communication*. 2nd ed. Oxford: Blackwell.

Thompson, Sandra A. 1983. Grammar and discourse: the English detached participial clause. In *Discourse perspectives on syntax*, ed. Flora Klein-Andreu. 43–65. New York: Academic Press.

Van Peer, Willie. 1986. *Stylistics and psychology, investigations in foregrounding*. Wolfeboro N.H.: Croom Helm.

APPENDIX

PASSAGES STUDIED FROM "THE GREAT GATSBY"

marked ([1925]1991: 5–6)

When I came back from the East last autumn I felt that I wanted the world to be in uniform and at a sort of moral attention forever; I wanted no more riotous excursions with privileged glimpses into the human heart. Only Gatsby, the man who gives his name to this book, was exempt from my reaction—Gatsby who represented everything for which I have an unaffected scorn. If personality is an unbroken series of successful gestures, then there was something gorgeous about him, some heightened sensitivity to the promises of life, as if he were related to one of those intricate machines that register earthquakes ten thousand miles away. This responsiveness had nothing to do with that flabby impressionability which is dignified under the name of the "creative temperament"—it was an extraordinary gift for hope, a romantic readiness such as I have never found in any other person and which it is not likely I shall ever find again. No—Gatsby turned out all right at the end; it is what preyed on Gatsby, what foul dust floated in the wake of his dreams that temporarily closed out my interest in the abortive sorrows and short-winded elations of men.

marked ([1925]1991: 9)

And so it happened that on a warm windy evening I drove over to East Egg to see two old friends whom I scarcely knew at all. Their house was even more elaborate than I expected, a cheerful red and white Georgian Colonial mansion overlooking the bay. The lawn started at the beach and ran toward the front door for a quarter of a mile, jumping over sun-dials and brick walks and burning gardens—finally when it reached the house drifting up the side in bright vines as though from the momentum of its run. The front was broken by a line of French windows, glowing now with reflected gold, and wide open to the warm windy afternoon, and Tom Buchanan in riding clothes was standing with his legs apart on the front porch.

marked ([1925]1991: 34)

The lights grow brighter as the earth lurches away from the sun and now the orchestra is playing yellow cocktail music and the opera of voices pitches a key higher. Laughter is easier, minute by minute, spilled with prodigality, tipped out at a cheerful word. The groups change more swiftly, swell with new arrivals, dissolve and form in the same breath—already there are wanderers, confident girls who weave here and there among the stouter and more stable, become for a sharp, joyous moment the center of a group and then excited with triumph glide on through the sea-change of faces and voices and color under the constantly changing light.

Suddenly one of these gypsies in trembling opal seizes a cocktail out of the air, dumps it down for courage and moving her hands like Frisco dances out alone on the canvas platform. A momentary hush; the orchestra leader varies his rhythm obligingly for her and there is a burst of chatter as the erroneous news goes around that she is Gilda Gray's understudy from the "Follies." The party has begun.

marked ([1925]1991: 137)

When we pulled out into the winter night and the real snow, our snow, began to stretch out beside us and twinkle against the windows, and the dim lights of small Wisconsin stations moved by, a sharp wild brace came suddenly into the air. We drew in deep breaths of it as we walked back from dinner through the cold vestibules, unutterably aware of our identity with this country for one strange hour before we melted indistinguishably into it again.

marked ([1925]1991: 141)

And as I sat there, brooding on the old unknown world, I thought of Gatsby's wonder when he first picked out the green light at the end of Daisy's dock. He had come a long way to this blue lawn and his dream must have seemed so close that he could hardly fail to grasp it. He did not know that it was already behind him, somewhere back in that vast obscurity beyond the city, where the dark fields of the republic rolled on under the night.

Gatsby believed in the green light, the orgastic future that year by year recedes before us. It eluded us then, but that's no matter—tomorrow we will run faster, stretch out our arms farther . . . . And one fine morning—

So we beat on, boats against the current, borne back ceaselessly into the past.

unmarked ([1925]1991: 6)

I never saw this great-uncle but I'm supposed to look like him—with special reference to the rather hard-boiled painting that hangs in Father's office. I graduated from New Haven in 1915, just a quarter of a century after my father, and a little later I participated in that delayed Teutonic migration known as the Great War. I enjoined the counter-raid so thoroughly that I came back restless. Instead of being the warm center of the world the middle-west now seems like the ragged edge of the universe—so I decided to go east and learn the bond business. Everybody I knew was in the bond business so I supposed it could support one more single man. All my aunts and uncles talked it over as if they were choosing a prep-school for me and finally said "Why—ye-es" with very grave, hesitant faces. Father agreed to finance me for a year and after various delays I came east, permanently, I thought, in the spring of twenty-two.

unmarked ([1925]1991: 8)

I lived at West Egg, the—well, the less fashionable of the two, though this is a most superficial tag to express the bizarre and not a little sinister contrast between them. My house was at the very tip of the egg, only fifty yards from the Sound, and squeezed between two huge places that rented for twelve or fifteen thousand a season. The one on my right was a colossal affair by any standard—it was a factual imitation of some Hôtel de Ville in Normandy, with a tower on one side, spanking new under a thin beard of raw ivy, and a marble swimming pool and more than forty acres of lawn and garden. It was Gatsby's mansion. Or rather, as I didn't know Mr. Gatsby it was a mansion inhabited by a gentleman of that name. My own house was an eye-sore, but it was a small eye-sore and it had been overlooked, so I had a view of the water, a partial view of my neighbor's lawn and the consoling proximity of millionaires—all for eighty dollars a month.

unmarked ([1925]1991: 33)

Every Friday five crates of oranges and lemons arrived from a fruiterer in New York—every Monday these same oranges and lemons left his back door in a pyramid of pulpless halves. There was a machine in the kitchen which could extract the juice of two hundred oranges in half an hour, if a little button was pressed two hundred times by a butler's thumb.

At least once a fortnight a corps of caterers came down with several hundred feet of canvas and enough colored lights to make a Christmas tree of Gatsby's enormous garden. On buffer tables, garnished with glistening hors d'œuvre, spiced baked hams crowded against salads of harlequin designs and pastry pigs and turkeys bewitched to a dark gold. In the main hall a bar with a real brass rail was set up, and stocked with gins and liquors and with cordials so long forgotten that most of his female guests were too young to know one from another.

unmarked ([1925]1991: 136)

One of my most vivid memories is of coming back west from prep school and later from college at Christmas time. Those who went farther than Chicago would gather in the old dim Union Station at six o'clock of a December evening with a few Chicago friends already caught up into their own holiday gaieties to bid them a hasty goodbye. I remember the fur coats of the girls returning from Miss This or That's and the chatter of frozen breath and the hands waving overhead as we caught sight of old acquaintances and the matchings of invitations: "Are you going to the Ordways'? the Herseys'? the Schultzes'?" and the long green tickets clasped tight in our gloved hands. And last

the murky yellow cars of the Chicago, Milwaukee & St. Paul Railroad looking cheerful as Christmas itself on the tracks beside the gate.

unmarked ([1925]1991: 140)

I spent my Saturday nights in New York because those gleaming, dazzling parties
of his were with me so vividly that I could still hear the music and the laughter faint
and incessant from his garden and the cars going up and down his drive. One night I
did hear a material car there and saw its lights stop at his front steps. But I didn't
investigate. Probably it was some final guest who had been away at the ends of the
earth and didn't know that the party was over.

5

Markedness and References to Characters in Biblical Hebrew Narratives

TIMOTHY WILT

SEVERAL YEARS AGO, a translation team and I considered how to deal with passages such as the following from the prophet Haggai, in the Hebrew Scriptures:

> I will fill this house with splendor, says the LORD of hosts. The silver is mine, and the gold is mine, says the LORD of hosts. The latter splendor of this house shall be greater than the former, says the LORD of hosts; and in this place I will give prosperity, says the LORD of hosts.[1]

In accordance with a common approach to translation,[2] I suggested that the team might want to reduce the number of *says the LORD of hosts* if such repetition would not occur in their language, as it would not, so I said, in contemporary English. Two days later, I came across the following in a Kurt Vonnegut novel:

> "As far as I'm concerned," said Constant, "the universe is a junk yard, with everything in it overpriced. I am through poking around in the junk heaps, looking for bargains. Every so-called bargain," said Constant, "has been connected by fine wires to a dynamite bouquet." He spat again.
> "I resign," said Constant.
> "I withdraw," said Constant.
> "I quit," said Constant. (Vonnegut 1950: 21)[3]

---

1. Haggai 2:7b–9. This and all other quotes from the Hebrew Scriptures are, unless otherwise indicated, cited according to the translation of the *New Revised Standard Version* (1993).

2. The approach to translation as developed by Eugene Nida and his followers (Nida and Tabor 1976: 197). Lawrence Venuti, although opposed to Nida's approach, refers to Nida as "prolific and influential" and "typical of other theorists in the Anglo-American tradition" (1995: 21).

3. A similar repetition in the speech formula occurs on page 297, where Rumfoord is the speaker.

I recalled the same pattern when later my eight-year-old daughter said, "Supper's ready, Dad. Come to the table, Dad. You sit here, Dad."[4]

As well as proving the inaccuracy of my statement concerning what "would not occur in contemporary English," the texts from Vonnegut and my daughter also point to a serious flaw in the approach to translation that I was following in my discussion with the translation team. Emphasis on the importance of using "natural" style in translation is untempered by sufficient attention to the fact that sometimes natural style involves the use of marked choices. It also overlooks the function of these marked choices and how marked choices may be represented in translation.

In this chapter, I consider some other examples of repetition in the Hebrew scriptures that represent marked choices by the narrator. Translators tend to treat them as ancient Hebrew "style," failing to recognize that in terms of comparable ancient Hebrew texts they are marked. Consequently, they have paid insufficient attention to their communicative function. In the cases to be discussed, the marked structures function to enhance humor, irony, and/or thematic development. Suggestions are made for using marked structures with equivalent communicative functions in translations.

MARKED REFERENCES TO CHARACTERS

A problem that leaps out at the reader of traditional Bible translations and troubles the translator coming at it anew is the extensive repetition of names and titles such as that found in the references to leaders of Israel's enemies in Judges 3:8. The reference to the first of these leaders, Cushan-risthathaim, is typical of this section:

> The Lord sold them into the hand of *Cushan-rishathaim King of Aram-naharaim;* and the Israelites served *Cushan-rishathaim* eight years. But . . . The Lord raised up a deliverer. . . Othniel son of Kenaz, Caleb's younger brother. The spirit of The Lord came upon him, and he judged Israel; he went out to war, and The Lord gave *Cushan-rishathaim King of Aram* into his hand; and his hand prevailed over *Cushan-rishathaim.* (Judges 3:8–10)

The enemy king is referred to four times. Each time his proper name is used, twice with his title and origin. A pronoun could have been used at least in the second occurrence and in such a short extent of text the second *King of Aram* is mnemonically unnecessary. The references to the enemy king contrast with those to Othniel where the proper name is followed by a series of unambiguous pronouns.

Similar repetition is found in Genesis 29:10:

---

4. She was smiling as she employed this highly marked repetition. I was dining with the family for the first time after a work trip, so the repetition may have been to underline my familial role. It also comes at a time when the preferred *papa* is being replaced by *dad* due to the influence of schoolmates in a new cultural setting.

Table 5-1
References to Characters in Judges 3:8

	Unmarked Pronoun	Marked Proper Name	More Highly Marked Proper Name + Relational Phrase
Israel's heroes	58 (68%)	20 (24%)	7 (8%)
Enemy leaders	15 (42%)	10 (28%)	11 (31%)

When Jacob saw Rachel, the daughter of *Laban the brother of his mother* and the flock of *Laban the brother of his mother*, Jacob went to the well, took the stone off of it, and watered the flock of *Laban the brother of his mother*.

The narrator employs marked structures to refer to Cushan-rishathaim and to Laban. Assuming referential unambiguity, the unmarked structure, in any language, employed to refer to characters after their initial introduction is that of the pronoun,[5] as used in the references to Othniel, cited earlier. In contexts in which the reference of a pronoun could be ambiguous, the unmarked structure would be the use of the proper name of a character *or* a relational phrase such as *King of Aram* or *brother of his mother*. In both instances, the use of the proper name of a character plus a relational phrase is marked: It occurs less frequently and in fewer linguistic environments and it is structurally more complex. The following sections elaborate on this observation and attempt to explain *why* the marked structures are used.

MARKED REFERENCES TO THE "ENEMY X KING OF Y"

Taking frequency as a rough indication of markedness, we compare the references to the leaders of Israel's enemies with the references to the heroes who delivered Israel, in Judges 3:8.[6] (See table 5-1.)

In reference to Israel's heroes, the unmarked, pronominal structure occurs about twice as frequently as the combined total of marked structures. But in reference to the enemy leaders, the unmarked, pronominal structure is used less often than marked structures. Particularly striking is the difference between the use of the most highly marked structure (proper name + relational phrase): It is relatively infrequent in reference to the heroes (8% or 7/85) but almost as frequent as pronouns (31% or 11/36) in reference to the enemy leaders.

If the references via proper name + relational phrase to the enemy leaders were spread throughout the accounts and used for the purpose of

5. Givon (1991: 257) and Dressler (1992: 12).

6. Pronouns are only counted once if occurring within the same clause (as proper names will occur only once per clause). In a structure such as "And X answered and [pronoun] said," the pronoun (verbal prefix) is not counted because a noun phrase rarely occurs in this context. References in direct speech are not counted.

disambiguating, these frequency counts would not be so interesting. But this is not the case: There is a clustering of their proper names which clearly stands out in contrast to the references to the heroes. Although there are more than twice as many references to the heroes than to the enemy leaders, a hero's name is repeated within a clause or in immediately adjoining clauses only once (Judges 4:9–10), but each of the enemy leaders' names is repeated at least once in this environment:

> The Lord sold them into the hand of *Cushan-rishathaim King of Aram-naharaim*; and the Israelites served *Cushan-rishathaim* eight years. . . . The Lord gave *Cushan-rishathaim King of Aram* into his hand; and his hand prevailed over *Cushan-rishathaim*. (Judges 3:8, 10)

> Then he [Ehud] presented the tribute to King *Eglon* of Moab. Now *Eglon* was a very fat man. (Judges 3:17)

> God subdued, on that day, *Jabin King of Canaan* before the Israelites. The hand of the Israelites bore harder and harder on *Jabin King of Canaan*, until they destroyed *Jabin King of Canaan*. (Judges 4:23–24)

> They [the men of Ephraim] captured the two captains of Midian, *Oreb and Zeeb*; they killed *Oreb* at the rock of *Oreb*, and *Zeeb* they killed at the wine press of *Zeeb*, as they pursued the Midianites. They brought the heads of *Oreb and Zeeb* to Gideon beyond the Jordan. (Judges 7:25)

> [Gideon] said, "Here are Zebah and Zalmunna, about whom you taunted me, saying 'Do you already have in your possession the hands of Zebah and Zalmunna'. . . ?" (Judges 8:15)[7]

Whereas this dense repetition may occur in varying parts of the battle episodes, each account, apart from the one concerning Eglon, contains the dense repetition in the closure as well. This further marks the references; it is unparalleled in all other accounts of Israel's conquest of Canaan. Of all the battle accounts, from the exodus to the appointment of Israel's own king, there are none but these, which repeatedly refer to the enemy leaders' names in the closure. Repetition of a king's name in adjoining clauses occurs only in one other narrative (Numbers 21:23). Repetition of the structure [Personal Name + king of + Territorial Name], as in *Jabin King of Canaan*, occurs in no other accounts, let alone in adjoining clauses.[8]

---

7. This quote refers to Judges 8:5–6 where the repetition of the couplet of proper names is separated from the preceding one by only the narrative-tensed formula introducing the direct speech. In 8:12 and 8:21, *Zebah and Zalmunna* are also repeated in very closely adjoined clauses; in each case, *they* could have been used unambiguously in the second occurrence.

8. References to enemy leaders in battle accounts are made in the following passages, asterisks indicating that the name of the leader is given: Exodus 14* (Pharaoh is treated like a proper name); Numbers 21:1–3, 21–31*, 33–35*; 31:1–12*; Joshua 2:2–3; 8:1–29; 10:1–27*, 28, 29–30, 33*, 36–37, 38–39; 11:1–14*, 16–20; Judges 1:5–7*; 3:7–11*, 12–25*, 4:2–24*, 7:25*, 8:5–21*; 11:12–33.

Comparison of reference strategies can also be made with accounts of encounters of enemies from within such as Korah (Numbers 16) and Achan (Joshua 7).

Having observed these highly marked references to the characters, we must now ask why they are so marked. In general terms, marking can be done primarily for structural or for thematic purposes. The observations in the preceding paragraphs indicate that structural marking (such as that used to introduce a new setting, a new character, the peak, or closure of an account) is not involved here,[9] so we look for thematic significance.

One key aspect of these prominently marked names is that they all arguably have a meaning related to the thematic development of the section in Judges that follows the report of Joshua's death. The basic perspective is given in the exposition of Judges 2:11–3:5: "abandonment of The Lord resulted in affliction by the enemies 'left to test all those in Israel' but crying out to The Lord resulted in deliverance." This perspective is then illustrated in the narratives concerning the enemy leaders. The marked use of their names suggests that the sense of their names contributes to the thematic development of the narrative[10]: *Cushan the Doubly Wicked,*[11] *Fat Calf,*[12] *He'll Understand, Captains Crow and Coyote,*[13] and *Sacrifice and Protection Refused.*[14]

A number of the marked extensions on biblical names refer to consequences which befell the name-holder. One of the salient consequences of Israel's "doing what was evil in the sight of The Lord" (Judges 2:11; 3:7,12, 12; 4:1; 6:1) was their falling victim to such disgusting rulers as these. But when Israel "cried out to The Lord" (Judges 3:9, 15; 4:3; 6:6, 7), The Lord would raise up leaders who could deliver them from *the Doubly Wicked*

9. Examples of marking for structural purposes would be the use of formulas such as "In the *n*th year of King A son of B, X son of Y began to reign" to introduce portrayal of a succeeding king's reign, "and it was after these things" to introduce a new episode, and a particle to mark story-line events (markers such as these are discussed in detail in Longacre (1989).

10. The meaning of a character's name frequently has thematic significance in biblical narratives. One example is in Hosea 1:6–9: "Gomer had a second child . . . the LORD said to Hosea, 'Name her *Unloved*, because I will no longer show love to the people of Israel. . . .' After Gomer had weaned her daughter, she became pregnant again and had another son. The LORD said to Hosea, 'Name him *Not-My-People*, because the people of Israel are not my people. . . .'" (American Bible Society 1978).

11. Or better: *King Cushan, the Scoundrel of Aram-Naharaim.*

12. The Hebrew root can mean "calf" or "round," depending on the vowel pointing. A better translation might be *Big Bull*. Its weakness is that it could suggest an image of power. But the alliteration and monosyllables would work with the context to indicate that the suggestion of power is facetious and there would be a link in English between the name, "*Bull's*" excretion (Verses 22, 24), and a common expression for pretense which would serendipitously harmonize with the Hebrew's bawdy satire.

13. Usually translated *Raven* and *Wolf*, but my translation uses terms that are more pejorative, in American English at least, while referring to closely related animals. *(Anchor Bible Dictionary* [1992] lists both *raven* and *crow* as translations for the Hebrew reference to the bird.)

14. This is probably the most frequently suggested translation of the name (e.g., Boling in Judges [1975: 155] and *HarperCollins Study Bible* [1993: 383]; Soggins (1987: 131). Others such as *wandering shade (New Jerusalem Study Bible* note) and *Salm protects* (Mendenhall in *Anchor Bible Dictionary* [1992(6): 1055]) have also been suggested and would all harmonize with the irony of this section.

kings. The Fat Calf demanding "tributes" (elsewhere, the Hebrew word can refer to temple offerings) is as easily slaughtered as calves at the altar. The enemies of the people of The Lord should be no more of a threat than a Crow or a Coyote. Such enemies are destined to become like *the Sacrifice Whose Protection Was Refused.* These accounts illustrate the nature and the outcome of those who stand opposed to God. The readers/hearers of these biblical texts are called to understand this, with the hope that they will understand more quickly than the one at the center of the accounts understood, the one who was referred to by the most highly marked structures: *King He'll Understand.*

MARKED REFERENCES TO "X THE RELATIVE OF Y"

X the relative of Y is a marked reference to a character: It is structurally more complex than the use of the character's proper name or pronoun and occurs less frequently and in fewer environments.

In introducing his discussion of the structural and thematic uses of *X ben Y,* Clines stated, "The long form . . . is not always employed when one of the [environments he identifies] arises; one can only hope to show why *X ben Y* is used when it *is* used, and one cannot usually speculate about why it is *not* used" (1972: 267). But the notion of markedness provides a simple explanation in this respect: Unmarked structures, the default choices, occur more frequently than marked structures. The degree to which the narrator wishes to mark a reference will determine how frequently he or she uses marked structures.

As Berlin pointed out, the use of relationship terms in addition to the proper name occurs thematically "to [call] attention to [to mark] specific relationships between certain characters" (1983: 18). But there is considerable variation in the degree to which the narrator marks these relationships.

TERMS OF ADDRESS IN THE STORY OF JACOB AND LABAN

In the Genesis Jacob-steals-the-blessing episode, each of the four main characters (the two parents and the two children) are referred to twice as frequently by their proper names than by the more marked structure *X the relative of Y.*[15] However, when Isaac and his parents are in the same scene (Genesis 21–25:11), just the opposite ratio occurs: The more highly marked form is used twice as frequently as the proper name.[16] When Isaac and his

15. Totals of use of proper name (e.g., *Isaac*) versus use of *X the relative of Y* (e.g., *his father Isaac*): *Isaac*—nine versus five; *Rebekah*—five versus one; *Esau*—seven versus four; *Jacob*—nine versus four).

16. When only the proper name occurs, the immediate environment would make use of the structure *X the relative of Y* awkward if not ungrammatical: "Abraham gave the name Isaac to his son" (Genesis 21:3), "on the day that Isaac was weaned" (21:8), "It is through Isaac that offspring shall be named for you" (21:12), "Isaac said to his father Abraham" (22:7); "Abraham gave all he had to Isaac" (25:5 Masoretic Text of the Hebrew); *his son* occurs in other manuscripts).

parents are not in the same scene, the structure *Isaac ben Abraham/Sara* is never used while the less marked structure *Isaac* is used about seventy times.[17]

The frequency with which the marked structure *X the relative of* Y is used hits an all-time high in the passage concerning Laban, which was quoted earlier: three times in four consecutive clauses. With little text-structural motivation for these repetitions, the prominent marking points to thematic considerations.

The intense highlighting of the familial relationship between Jacob and Laban, along with other references in the immediately following verses to the joy of family,[18] heighten the irony of the situation: Family, the crucial source of joy and support, will soon turn into a locus of bitterness and rivalry. Marking this relationship in conjunction with the flock—the wealth of Laban—foreshadows one of the key elements in the rivalry. In the verse immediately following the happy reunion scene, Laban mentions both "kinsman" and "wages." The kinsman relationship between Laban and Jacob will never again be mentioned. Their wage relationship will come to the fore.[19] The end of joy, the disruption of the extended-family unit is evident in the following references, which so sharply contrast with the exuberant discovery of *the brother of his mother:*

Jacob to Laban: . . . *my own* home and country . . . *my* wives . . . *my* children for whom I have served you . . . (Genesis 30:25–26)

The sons of Laban: Jacob has taken all that was *our father's.* . . . (31:1)

The immediately preceding verse: [Jacob] grew exceedingly rich, and had large flocks. . . .)

Narrator: Jacob saw that Laban did not regard him favorably. . . . (31:2)

Narrator: Jacob deceived Laban *the Aramean* (31:20)

Narrator: [Laban] took *his kinsman* (31:23)

Narrator: God appeared to Laban *the Aramean*

Jacob to Laban: *my* kinsfolk and *your* kinsfolk (literally, "my brothers and your brothers") (31:37)

17. The references to Lot are similar to those of Isaac. In three of the first four references to Lot (Genesis 11:27, 31; 12:4, 5), he is referred to in terms of his relationship to Abram. He is a passive character counted among Abram's other dependents and possessions. The use of the *X the relative of* Y structure accords with the references to Isaac and Jacob, mentioned earlier, used in referring to dependency relationships. It is a marked structure but, in this context, not highly marked.

In chapter 13, Lot is a wealthy adult with whom Abram must resolve territorial disputes; he is referred to simply by his unmodified proper name: *Lot* (eight times). But in chapter 14, telling of his capture by enemies, Lot's name is used only in the *X the relative of* Y structure (14:12, 16): Y equals Abram on whom Lot depends as much for rescue as he did for nurturing in his younger days.

18. The following four verses contain several references to familial relationships (*her father's kinsman; Rebekah's son; his sister's son; you are my bone and my flesh*) and to the joy of this relationship (*kissed* [twice], *wept aloud, ran, embraced*).

19. Eleven of the twenty-three occurrences in Genesis of the verb *work/labor/slave* occur in the Jacob–Laban narrative; nine out of the ten references in Genesis to *wages* occur here.

Laban devolves from Jacob's *mother's brother* to one involved in *my family* versus *your family* disputes with Jacob, to *the Aramean*: from a person familially attached to Jacob to one familially then geographically separated.

THE TRANSLATION OF MARKED REFERENCES

We now briefly consider how various translations treat marked structures by looking at how they render the Laban and the enemy king passages referred to in the preceding section.

There are three basic options for translating structures that are marked in the original text: (1) reproducing the marking patterns of the original, (2) reducing or omitting the marking patterns, or (3) replacing the marking patterns of the original with marking patterns in the target language that will have the same, or at least a similar, communicative effect.

The first option is commonly chosen by what are often referred to as *literal* translations (from Genesis 29:10):

> Now when Jacob saw Rachel, the daughter of his mother's brother Laban, and the sheep of his mother's brother Laban, Jacob went up and rolled the stone from the well's mouth, and watered the flock of his mother's brother Laban. (New Revised Standard Version 1993)

> And when Jacob saw Rachel, the daughter of his uncle Laban, and the flock of his uncle Laban, Jacob went up and rolled the stone off the mouth of the well, and watered the flock of his uncle Laban. (New Jewish Publication Society 1988)

The problem is obvious. The Hebrew underlines the thematic importance of the relationship and the flock. The English translations might possibly underline this aspect, but they also signal to the reader that the narrative was clumsily produced. The translation of the *New Revised Standard Version* sounds foreign; that of the *New Jewish Publication Society* sounds silly.

Today's English Version translates according to the second option. It translates the Genesis text as if it were completely unmarked, eliminating two of the references to the familial relationship:

> When Jacob saw Rachel with his uncle Laban's flock, he went to the well, rolled the stone back, and watered the sheep.

The English style is much better than in *New Revised Standard Version* and *New Jewish Publication Society Version* but the thematic underlining is lost.

The following suggests how the passage, in the context of the immediately preceding and following verses, could be translated by using English, rather than Hebrew, marking techniques:

> While he was speaking with them, Rachel had come near with her father's sheep, under her care. Jacob again looked at her: the daughter of his uncle, his mother's brother! He then looked at the sheep: his uncle's! He took the stone off the well so that the sheep could drink. Then, crying for joy, he kissed Rachel.

SUGGESTIONS FOR REFERENCES TO THE ENEMY LEADERS

Most, if not all, translations choose one of the first two options listed in the introduction to this section to render the references to the enemy leaders in Judges 3–8. However, they would be better translated in a way that would allow the reader to appreciate the thematic relevance of their names to the narrative's presentation. Rather than being relegated to footnotes, the meanings of these names should be represented in the text of the translation, and the humor and irony of the original kept. This could be done in various ways; thus I offer the following suggestions as examples:

> So The Lord became angry with Israel and let them be conquered by Aram-naharaim's King Cushan the Scoundrel. For eight years, they were enslaved by The Scoundrel. (Judges 3:8)

> The Lord empowered Moab's King Calf. . . . The Israelites were King Calf's slaves for eighteen years. . . . The Israelites sent a gift to Moab's Calf. . . . Then [Ehud] presented the gift to Moab's King Calf—a really fat Calf, he was. (3:12, 14, 16, 17)

> On that day, God made Canaan's King He'll Understand give way to the Israelites. Their power over him steadily increased until they destroyed He'll Understand, King of Canaan. (4:23–24)

> They killed Raven at Raven Rock and Wolf at Wolf's Winery. (7:25)

> Then Sacrifice and Protection Withheld said, "You come and kill us. . . ." So Gideon slaughtered like sacrifices those from whom protection had been withheld. . . . (Judges 8:21)

CONCLUSION

This chapter focused on the translation of marked references that are increasingly marked by repetition of the structures in narrow text space. The interpretation of this literary device is viewed as proceeding in the same way as the interpretation of the marked use of language in everyday conversation, as explained by the markedness model (Myers-Scotton chapter 2, in this volume).

Just as interlocutors choose and evaluate marked codes in terms of social values and communication goals, so, too, the producer of a literary text makes marked choices to signal communicative goals. In turn, the audience evaluates these choices in terms of literary norms shared with the speaker. The translator of literary texts may attempt to use equivalently marked expressions and structures in the target language to represent the original speech event. The equivalence will be not only with regard to the semantic content of expressions but also with regard to the pragmatic inferences that the original speakers expected their audiences to make. Similar to the switch from one language to another, when semantically unnecessary but pragmatically significant, the occurrence of an expression like *says The Lord of Hosts* three times in one verse is semantically equivalent to *says The Lord of Hosts* occurring once in the verse, or not at all if it has already been established that Yahweh is the origin of the utterance. However, the repetition is *pragmatically* significant in the text we considered, in that it rhetorically underlines the importance of the source of the message (divine, not human) and the validity of the prophet's identity as messenger (not inventor) in keeping with the religious traditions recognized by the hearers as valid.

I have indicated how translators of biblical texts tend either to reproduce fairly literally the marking patterns of the original text or to diminish or ignore them for the sake of fluent, contemporary style.

The former practice can lead the translation's audience to make inferences that were unintended by the original speaker, because the target audience tends to interpret the marked structures according to the norms of their own communicative context rather than those of the original text's communicative context. This misinterpretation is similar to that which can arise in intercultural communication when the second-language speaker uses such stylistic features as loudness, verbosity, or directness, which are not intended to be marked, or are intended to be marked but with the intention that different inferences be made than those made by the first-language speaker of the language. Miscommunication often results, especially when the hearer does not share a sympathetic bond with the struggling speaker.

On the other hand, when translators diminish or ignore the marking patterns in the original text, a more readable style may result, but the text can be significantly misrepresented as the reader will not be able, or will be less likely, to make the inferences that the original speaker desired the audience to make. In most Bible translations attempting to use contemporary language, an extreme reduction in the use of marked structures contributes to a literarily unsatisfactory leveling of style. In the case of the Judges narratives discussed previously, the stylistic leveling resulted in changing stories that were originally filled with bawdy and taunting humor to unemotional, pious narratives in the target language of translation. A more accurate representation of the original results when the translator uses marked structures in the target language that enable communicative effects similar to those intended by the original speaker's use of marked structures. There may be an overlap in the two languages' use of marked structures for similar communicative effects, but the two languages will often differ in how they mark structures to obtain similar results.

The repeated use of the proper names of Israel's enemies in the book of Judges was evaluated in terms of norms suggested by the statistical study of references to characters in other biblical narratives, especially in the subgenre of the battle accounts. It was concluded that the repetition of names was for thematic purposes, encouraging the audience to attribute significance to the meaning of the character's name as well as enabling them to identify the character. Suggestions were given for how equivalent marking could be achieved in translation.

The thematic use of repetition may be understood as a means of minimizing communicative costs. While signaling secondary themes, repetition does not foreground these themes at the expense of distracting the reader from appreciation of either the primary themes or the basic story line. In the Hebrew Scriptures, primary themes are often made explicit through speeches of key characters, including Israel's god, or through the narrator's introductory or concluding comments. The primary theme of both the Genesis and Judges narratives discussed previously is, broadly stated: The Lord takes care of his chosen people. This theme is explicitly stated by the Lord in, for example, the episode immediately preceding the Jacob-meets-Rachel episode and by the narrator in the introduction to the book of Judges.

Marked repetition is one of the narrative means used to invite the reader to consider what other themes lie behind the most transparent ones. As one literary critic says:

> If the biblical truth is explicit, then the whole truth is implicit; and the more you bring to this art of implication, the more secrets and prizes it yields. No one goes away empty-handed. But the challenge to the . . . reader is as omnipresent as the solicitude for all. (Sternberg 1987: 52)

REFERENCES

American Bible Society. 1978. *Good News Bible: the Bible in today's English version.* New York: American Bible Society.

Anchor Bible dictionary. 1992. New York: Doubleday.

Berlin, Adele. 1983. *Poetics and interpretation.* Sheffield, England: Almond.

Biblia Hebraica Stuttgartensia. 1966/77. Stuttgart: Deutsche Bibelstiftung.

Boling, Robert G. 1975. *Anchor Bible commentary on Judges.* New York: Anchor.

Clines, David J. A. 1972. *X, X ben Y* : Personal names in Hebrew narrative. *Vetus Testamentum* 22: 266–287.

Dressler, Wolfgang U. 1992. Marked and unmarked text strategies within semiotically based textlinguistics. *Language in context,* ed. Shin Ja J. Hwang and William Merrifield, 5–18. Dallas: Summer Institute of Linguistics and University of Texas–Arlington.

Givon, Talmy. 1991. Markedness in grammar: distributional, communicative and cognitive correlates of syntactic structure. *Studies in Language* 15: 335–370.

HarperCollins Study Bible: new revised standard version. 1993. New York: HarperCollins.

Longacre, Robert E. 1989. *Joseph: a story of divine providence.* Winona Lake, Ind.: Eisenbrauns.

New Jewish Publication Society. 1988. *Tanakh: the New Jewish Publications Society translation according to the traditional Hebrew text.* Philadelphia: Jewish Publication Society.

The New Jerusalem Bible. 1985. New York: Doubleday.

Nida, Eugene, and Charles Tabor. 1976. *The theory and practice of translation.* Leiden: J. Brill.

Soggins, J. Alberto. 1987. *Le livre des Juges.* Geneva: Labor et Fides.

Sternberg, Meir. 1987. *The poetics of biblical narrative: ideological literature and the drama of reading.* Bloomington: Indiana University Press.

Venuti, Lawrence. 1995. *The translator's invisibility: a history of translation.* New York: Routledge.

Vonnegut, Kurt, Jr. 1959. *The sirens of Titan.* New York: Dell.

6

Literariness, Markedness, and Surprise in Poetry

AMITTAI F. AVIRAM

POETRY VERSUS COMMUNICATION

T HAT POETRY is a marked instance of language and that poems make expressive use of marked stylistic devices in both vocabulary and syntax are known facts about poetry for decades (Jakobson 1960, 1968, 1973; Mukařovský [1948]1989). Somewhat accordingly, many scholars bring concepts from linguistics to bear upon literary texts, specifically by analyzing the *stylistic* devices that seem to make the literary text effective (Austin 1981; Epstein 1981; Fairley 1981; Freeman 1981b; Keyser 1981; Kiparsky 1981; Tarlinskaya 1987). Nevertheless, many such stylisticians commenting on poetry tend to focus on these stylistic expressive devices while often seeming to miss the point of the texts they are reading. These often inadequate, superficial readings result not from mere accident but from unexamined and incorrect assumptions about the nature of poetry and the literary text, assumptions that neglect the text's literariness in favor of what is believed to be its communicative function as a message.

Normal communication requires not only utterances but exchanges of utterances—a communicative context—to establish reference. People must be able to ask each other questions and have answers; the communicative exchange is a constant dialectic aiming toward mutual understanding. But the literary text, as Socrates points out about the "written" text in general, cannot answer any questions—it always says the same thing, no matter how things change around it (Plato 1982, 564–567 [275d–e]). By contrast, a poem, and, indeed, any literary text, is a special case of the use of language, in which the referential—and even the apparently pragmatic—sense of the utterance is permanently removed from its communicative context and therefore cannot truly be said to communicate anything at all. The literariness of the literary text is, first of all, not a matter of its inherent makeup but of how it is

101

received. Literariness is, in the first instance, a cognitive, not a physical, category. Indeed, the person who, in a lover's quarrel, responds to a partner's yelling in anger at him or her by observing, "You're so cute when you're mad," is, in a sense, transforming a communicative message into a literary text. This person is inappropriately regarding the utterance that expressed the anger as an object of contemplation and aesthetic pleasure, attending to the attractiveness of the form of expression rather than the anger it is intended to convey. A response that shows appropriate communicative engagement in this case might be fear, righteous indignation, or defensiveness rather than admiration at the display of anger as if it were intended as a work of art. But the literary text *is* intended as a work of art, even if it *represents* an utterance expressing anger.

As in the foregoing example, literariness is not so much a quality of an utterance itself but rather a quality of how an utterance is perceived, a frame of mind on the part of the hearer or reader that treats the utterance as something worthy of contemplation, discovery, and admiration rather than the conveyance of an intended message. Nevertheless, literary texts usually have formal features that prompt readers to receive them as literary rather than communicative. When the reader perceives the text as literary, the apparent communicative content of the utterance is a sort of *virtual* rather than actual communication, one that *would* only take place within an imaginary world that would provide it with a communicative context. Because that imaginary world is created only out of inferences derived from the text's signs, it has limits that distinguish it from the infinitude of the real world. Insofar as the literary text communicates an intention, it does so at a level higher than that represented directly by its own language—outside, as it were, the text's fictive frame. The fact that the literary text is bracketed off from the exchanges of normal communication also causes the text to be apprehended as a totality rather than strictly as a sequence. Whereas normal communication is a potentially endless sequence of signs and responses through time, the literary text is a completed whole unto itself, acquiring a timeless spatiality in the reader's mind (on completion of reading) at the same time that it also produces the appearance of a normal sequence.

The markedness of a literary text such as a poem then serves simultaneously to express intention and to provide the aesthetic pleasure of surprise—the two, intention and surprise, become inseparable—but only insofar as such markedness is placed within its properly literary context and the reader assumes the correct default expectations for what would be unmarked. In short, the language of a poem does not mean but *seems* to mean. The poem *means* only insofar as it uses this *seeming* within a larger context, which is not communicative in the normal sense but literary and aesthetic.

By *aesthetic*, I mean appealing to a sense of pleasure in the contemplation of the object, in its totality and as a pattern. This is the purpose, or primary function, of an aesthetic object. By contrast, the primary function of communication is to convey meaning. If one communicates effectively, the aesthetic pleasure given by the form of communication should be negligible or trivial compared to the content being communicated. Effective communication usually means clear, relatively transparent, easily understood communication, with little distraction of the listener's attention to the formal features of expression. But if an utterance is considered an aesthetic object, it does not matter so much what meaning it conveys as how the parts of the utterance work together to make a satisfactory or successful whole. Two opposite mind-sets are required for appropriate responses, respectively, to what is understood as a communicative utterance and to what is understood as an aesthetic object—a literary text. The proper response to a communicative utterance is directly relevant to the content of the utterance—a reply, an action, or an appropriate affect (e.g., fear or defensiveness in the case of angry speech). By contrast, the proper response to an aesthetic object, such as a literary text, is contemplation, interpretation, the pleasure of discovering how the parts come together to make a whole, and a sense of wonder at its wholeness, completeness, perfection, ingenuity, and forms of surprise.

Communicative messages are not subject to the same interpretive attitude as aesthetic objects because communicative messages are embedded within ongoing communicative contexts that can restrict and control their meanings. By contrast, literary texts, as aesthetic objects, are appropriate objects pondering their meanings, as they are bracketed off from any communicative contexts other than the limited, imaginary ones they imply. Much of the aesthetic pleasure of the literary text is precisely in the pondering over possible meanings and the construction of plausible patterns of meaning. By contrast, communicative messages should aim at clarity, and ambiguity is not generally a source of pleasure but of temporary frustration, remedied by further exchanges of communication intended to clarify and disambiguate.

EXAMPLE: EMILY DICKINSON'S "I CANNOT LIVE WITH YOU"

"I Cannot Live with You," a poem by Emily Dickinson, (1960: 317–318, no. 640), illustrates some of these points. It begins with the statement (or, to be more accurate in speaking about poetry, the *pseudostatement*), "I cannot live with you— / It would be Life—." We can infer that the speaker must just have been asked by someone to live with him—that someone has just proposed marriage to the speaker (and that the speaker is a woman, the person charged with either rejecting or accepting a marriage proposal). Later lines in the text clearly corroborate this inference. Thus we imagine a communicative context, in which an interlocutor, the suitor, asks a question, "Will you marry me?" and what we "hear" is the response. But we cannot infer how the interlocutor would respond to this response, nor is it a relevant consideration for the experience of the poem. The focus of the poem is, rather, on the abstruse reasons the speaker gives for declining the proposal, all of which involve, ironically, a way of living up only too well to the (Congregationalist Protestant Christian) ideal of marriage, given the inherent sex inequalities within that ideology. The poem thus allows an ideological system to play itself out against itself. The neatness with which the speaker, in all innocence, can give voice to a standard ideology in such a way as to make the fulfillment of that ideology—marriage— impossible is, itself, a source of great aesthetic pleasure: We wonder at the brilliant wit of this argument that turns so seamlessly and yet ironically against its own assumptions. At the same time, the neatness of the poem's metrical and syntactic arrangements coincides with the feeling of inevitability about its argumentative structure, again to contribute to our delight in its ironic perfection. The meter and other poetic elements do not, then, contribute to the "message" of rejecting a marriage proposal; they contribute to the surprising aesthetic effect of the text *for us*, its readers. The rejection is not aimed at us. We get to delight in the ingenuity, brilliance, and perfection of the utterance. Within the imaginary world implied by the text, the imaginary recipient of the message would not be able to enjoy these aesthetic qualities. For him, it would be a message, not a literary text. By contrast, in our real world, outside the imaginary world of the text, we, the readers, can and should take pleasure in the wit and ingenuity with which the utterance is crafted—that is, its aesthetic qualities. The reader experiences much of this aesthetic pleasure in the process of solving the riddle of the poem— figuring out that it could be imagined as the rejection of a marriage proposal and then marveling at the surprising form of logic such a rejection takes.

This chapter attempts to clarify the problems of stylistics when applied to poetry, and, in so doing, sketches a concept of the literary text—the poem— in a way that is more rationally defensible than the concept apparently held by many stylisticians. I hope that this concept of the literary text would also be more useful for teaching people how to read and appreciate poetry and other literature. I discuss the concept of literariness first, defining poetry accordingly. Then, I examine some errors that I think typify the potential pitfalls of stylistics-oriented reading. With these criticisms, I urge readings of the same texts more faithful to the concept of literariness and show how markedness functions in these readings in the realm of the literary rather than in the realm of normal communicative utterances. Finally, drawing on these examples, I review the phenomenon of markedness in relation to communication in the special case of the literary utterance, suggesting how what is "communicated" is an aesthetic experience rather than a message.

THE APPROPRIATE ATTITUDE TOWARD THE LITERARY TEXT

A literary text is *not communication* in a direct and simple sense. If the utterance takes a propositional form ("Roses are red"), it is subject to the truth test in normal conversation ("Are they really?") but not in a literary text (i.e., it matters not whether they are or not; the poem says they are, for its purposes). If the utterance takes the form of a question, it would be liable to an answer or, if a rhetorical question, a response in real life; in literature, it is only open to *literary interpretation*. The same with imperatives: In real life, one responds to "Take out the garbage!" by doing so or by refusing to do so, whereas, in reading poetry, one responds by figuring out the relevance of the seeming imperative to the rest of the seeming utterances that make up the poem as a whole, to discover the whole poem's point, its overall aesthetic effect. In poetry, even illocutionary acts have no force in the real world but only contribute elements to an aesthetic whole. If a character says "I cannot live with you," this does not mean that a real marriage proposal was declined but that the formula of rejection is presented to us in a surprising way that gives us aesthetic pleasure.

The communicative context ennabling a communicative utterance has two elements: (1) a social context of exchange, and (2) a referential context, giving the utterance meaning and relevance. The social context includes within it the possibility that the recipient of the utterance will be able to ask questions or answer the utterance in some way, either directly or indirectly (as, for instance, by writing a letter after hearing a lecture in a large lecture hall). Even the refusal to respond, the failure to respond, or the accidental impossibility of responding contributes to the social context. The referential context must be clear enough to all parties to the communication for communication to occur at all. Reference is not exclusive to propositional utterances. If I say "How are you today," it must be clear who the *you* is and which day *today* is for the utterance to qualify as normal communication. By contrast to all of this, the literary text requires (1) a reader and (2) inferrable fragments of a communicative context (with both social and referential elements) sufficient to make the utterance make imaginary sense in an imaginary world. The elements of this "world" would be insufficient to provide the infinite possible preconditions, environments, and consequences of a real utterance. The fragments of a communicative context that can be inferred from the clues in the text are just enough to make the literary text "work," that is, deliver its aesthetic effect of surprise and satisfaction. The limitation of the communicative context to these few inferrable fragments of an imaginary world gives every literary text an air of ambiguity and invites the reader to ponder its interpretive possibilities. But that same limitation, the result of the text's being bracketed from the constant give-and-take of normal communicative exchanges, is what gives the text its finitude and completeness as an aesthetic whole, so that the entirety of its pattern can be appreciated and enjoyed.

Because the communicative message and the literary text are received cognitively in completely different ways, the appropriate responses to each are different. When the speaker of Wallace Stevens's "Blanche McCarthy" exhorts, "Look in the terrible mirror of the sky," our first task is *not* to look up (and thus cease reading the poem) but to consider what the "terrible mirror of the sky" might, figuratively, mean, and thus how it will fit into that text's system of figurative signs as an aesthetic experience. When the speaker of John Keats's "Ode on Melancholy" admonishes, "No, no, go not to Lethe," we are to imagine that the utterance *would* be properly directed to an imaginary person—a virtual literary character—who is about to commit suicide. It is unlikely that we would happen to receive the message appropriately when we, ourselves, are on the verge of committing suicide and would pause long enough to read the poem through to take the rest of its admonishments. Here, as elsewhere in poetry, even the seeming message—the content of the imaginary communicative utterance in an imaginary context—is far too complex and ambiguous to serve as a practical message in a real-life situation. This richness is not a necessary feature of a literary text, but it follows naturally, on both the poet's and the reader's parts from the assumption of the appropriate frame of mind that the reader would hold in receiving a literary text rather than a communicative message.

That the appropriate response to the imperative beginning "Ode on Melancholy" is the imaginary reconstruction of a possible scene in which the utterance *would* be a communicative message introduces a crucial paradox about the literary text. This paradox is that the literary text's existence depends on the hypothetical possibility that the very same utterance, the same signs, *could* be employed in an imaginary communicative exchange within an imaginary referential context.

LITERARINESS AND THE AESTHETIC PLEASURE OF SURPRISE

Literary meaning, then, is a special case of meaning. What a literary text "communicates" to its reader is its aesthetic effect, which may be understood as some form of *surprise*. Literary texts use the material ordinarily used for communication to deliver surprise, which pleases the reader, edifies him or her, sharpens readerly skills, and performs other functions associated with aesthetic experience rather than with communication per se. Literary texts achieve surprise by means of various kinds of markedness. The very removal of the utterance from any conceivable *actual* communicative exchange and referential context already makes the utterance as a whole, by definition, *marked* as literary, and it is in part the task of the literary writer to produce sufficient linguistic evidence to make sure that the reader does *not* mistake the text for a communicative message. Verse in poetry, among its functions, sets the language of poetry off from that of normal communication, as, in verse, attention is drawn toward the mere surface of language—its pure sounds or visual appearance in writing—rather than to its meaning. This shifting of attention would be inefficient and counterproductive if the utterance were intended for communicative purposes, because the aim of a communicative utterance is, first and foremost, transparency. When a parent tells a child to wash the dishes, the parent does not want the child to dwell on the sound of the parent's consonants or the repetition of *sh* in *wash* and *dishes*. This abnormal focus on the surface of language rather than on its meaning is specific to poetry. Nonpoetic literary texts use a variety of other devices to ensure the reader's response to the text, as a whole and in the last instance, as aesthetic rather than communicative.

But the mere existence of verse in poetry is not generally sufficient to deliver surprise, except in a very vague way. Poetry produces surprise by means of marked choices against default assumptions on many different levels, all depending either on literary contexts alone or on the peculiar and paradoxical interaction between literary contexts and the nonliterary, real contexts that they imitate or to which they allude, in actual communication. For example, "Because I Could Not Stop for Death" (Dickinson, 1960: 712, no. 350; see Aviram 1994: 263–279) surprises the reader in many ways, including the following.

1. The speaker apparently has already died and is thus speaking from beyond the grave. This doesn't generally happen in real life. In literature, such speeches are usually attended by signs of the supernatural, and the speeches are often cryptic and oracular. Here, the speech is a matter-of-fact past-tense narrative of the events leading up to the speaker's present (dead) state.

2. The speaker has died, but she does not sound as if she is in heaven or hell but, rather, in a state of complete emptiness, where nothing happens. (This also makes the idea of her speaking from such a state even more unfathomable.)

3. The poem is in tetrameter quatrains (four beats per line, four lines), with the second and fourth lines truncated so that the fourth beat is observed as silence rather than being realized with a syllable of a word. This is the conventional hymn form, which would be conventionally associated, in the Christian context to which other signs in the poem allude, with praises for the happy afterlife promised to the saved Christian soul. Yet this poem contains no such praise, and thus the poem forms a sort of anti-hymn when read against the cultural context of the Christian beliefs to which it alludes or that can assumed to be known (and possibly held) by its immediate readership in nineteenth-century America.

4. The allegorial figures of the poem describe death as if it were marriage—to the figure Death. This itself is a small surprise—the bridegroom being Death. But death has long been figured in Christian literature as like a marriage—to Christ, not to death. So having Death appear in the place of Christ is another surprise.

The surprises all work together to create what appears to be the speech of a naive speaker who now knows that death leads not to heaven or hell but simply to an immense vacancy. In other words, the poem dramatizes a reversal of fundamental Christian beliefs about the afterlife. The effect of the poem does not depend on this apparent revelation being either true or false; it depends on its being imaginatively successful and giving us the pleasure of surprisingly reversing ordinary, normative expectations. All this is accomplished by an intricate network of markedness on thematic, formal, and figurative levels.

The capacity of a text to deliver pleasing surprise depends, therefore, on the specific knowledge of its readership, knowledge drawn both from life and—especially—from literature. What is delightfully surprising to one reader may be simply chaotic to another and too predictable to a third. This difference is what accounts largely for differences in literary tastes, critical receptions of various poets, and the constant changes in academic and culturewide canons of good poetry. This fact, too, creates a paradox, this time about the teaching of literature. Students appreciate a literary text insofar as they have sufficient prior knowledge to view the marked features of the new text with the delight of surprise. Yet it is that very pleasure that would motivate a student to wish to acquire sufficient knowledge—sufficient literacy—to have it in the first place. In teaching literature, we constantly find ourselves in the position of trying to get students to read things in the hope that, eventually, they will realize—always retrospectively, and often too late for us—that the texts we assigned did, in fact, give them pleasure. But this is precisely why academic canons cannot be based on prevalent popular tastes and are, in some ways, necessarily conservative. The task of teaching literacy includes that of continually reintroducing sufficient literary context from the past to make the pleasurable surprises of texts available to succeeding generations of students.

Learning to read poetry is not the same thing as learning to read messages, although the former recruits the skills of the latter to gain access to surprise and literary pleasure. Yet the approach that some linguists take, in commenting on the style of particular poems, presumes an identity between these two skills. As a result, stylisticians of high professional repute and considerable expertise in their field have, in their commentaries on poems, completely missed the surprise constituting the point of those poems and belabored issues that are somewhat more obvious. Teachers and students, in turn, read these commentaries and are likely to repeat the stylisticians' mistakes: to confuse the literary text with a communicative message, to relegate literary devices to the role of "boosters" for the message's meaning, to read parts in sequence at the expense of the whole, and to oversimplify the sense of the literary text.

MISTAKING POEMS FOR MESSAGES, STYLISTICS INVITES SUPERFICIAL READINGS

Because stylisticians assume that what makes poetry poetry is the use of various marked linguistic devices in order to *convey meaning* (i.e., to communicate) stylisticians tend to assume a given meaning for a poetic text and then elaborate all the various devices that "boost" the expression of this meaning. In many cases, the meaning they infer as their starting point is oversimplified and sometimes illogical when applied to the totality of the poem, the whole text rather than parts of it in sequential order. This superficiality, flatness, or even wrongheadedness is not simply an accident. It proceeds from the project of "revealing" the expressive devices of a text rather than, first, understanding the way literary texts such as poetry work as aesthetic structures whose function is to deliver surprise when given the right context and when read as totalities rather than sequences of elements. Stylisticians tend to assume that the literary text is a message like any other, only more punchy or expressive, using more elaborate devices to get the message across. Accordingly, the message is a sequence of signs, bearing the normal relation of beginning to end rather than a sequential elaboration of a complex structure whose parts must be remembered and held together in the reader's mind to appreciate the totality. These assumptions are incorrect and lead, ultimately, to disappointing misreadings of rich and powerful poems.

EXAMPLE: BLAKE'S "THE TYGER"

My first example of this problem is E. L. Epstein's (1981) otherwise interesting essay, "The Self-Reflexive Artefact: The Function of Mimesis in an Approach to a Theory of Value for Literature." Epstein discusses many great poems in a variety of languages, including, briefly, William Blake's "The Tyger." His general thesis is that literary value, especially in poetry, derives from the extent to which linguistic devices are used in a mimetic fashion—to *imitate* the content of the poem. Thus, Epstein's sense of the term *self-reflexivity* differs sharply from its meaning in literary theory. For Epstein, *self-reflexivity* means the "reflection" or imitation (or merely expression, representation) of the meaning of the message in its form—as if the form were a dressing or clothing for the meaning. By contrast, in modern literary theory, the term refers to the way that the literary text, bracketed off from normal communication, represents in its thematic content its own nature as a literary text. That is, the poem is "about itself." (See Aviram 1994: 17–28, 43–58, 223–246.)

In the specific case of "The Tyger," Epstein spells out quite neatly the content he finds imitated (or expressed) in the form:

> What Blake achieves in *Tyger* [sic] is a subjective mimesis, based on syntax, for a very high degree of value. It seems obvious from the poem that what Blake is conveying is his own awe at perceiving the energy that drives the universe and the poet, a force here symbolized as a tiger, a power beyond good and evil. (Epstein 1981: 187)

Obvious, indeed. He also notes, beforehand, that, after the reader does "his 'first complete reading,' as it could be called," all further readings contribute nothing new and become increasingly automatized scannings of a familiar linear pattern" (Epstein 1981: 186).

Is rereading "The Tyger" that useless? I doubt it, especially if the results of the first complete reading are as Epstein summarizes them, quoted here. Let us consider the poem as would a good *literary* reader rather than a stylistician. The good reader's goal will be, first, to read the *whole* of the poem, and to understand how the parts relate to the whole that comprises them.

It is striking that "The Tyger" is made up exclusively of questions.[1] From an interpretive point of view, these questions beg a question: Are the questions to be taken as straightforward, wherein the speaker seeks answers, or are they rhetorical questions, not intended to be answered or having self-evident answers? Rhetorical questions are marked uses of the normal question structure, which is normally assumed to seek an answer. One of the ways that rhetorical questions are marked as such is by containing within them the information that would otherwise be left for the answerer—that is, the rhetorical question contains its own answer, and thus prompts a response that accords with its implied answer.

1. What are you doing today?
2. Are you going swimming today?
3. Surely, you're not going swimming today, are you?

The third question would likely be understood, in conversation, as a rhetorical question, wherein the statement, "You are not going swimming," is contained, as it were, within the question. Whereas item 1 leaves open any possible answer suggesting a plan or activity, and item 2 leaves open either a yes or no answer, question 3 requires either assent—"Yes, you're right, it's too cloudy"—or remonstrance—"Actually, I *was* planning to swim; why not?" Question 3, in other words, is a version of the statement "You shouldn't go swimming today," or even the command, "Don't go swimming today."

In "The Tyger," the questions are not clearly rhetorical, but not clearly straightforward, either.

> Tyger tyger, burning bright
> In the forest of the night;
> What immortal hand or eye,
> Could frame thy fearful symmetry? (Blake [1789–1797]1967: plate 42)

As a rhetorical question, this sentence would be equivalent to the statement "Surely, *no* immortal hand or eye could frame thy fearful symmetry." Yet, such a statement makes no sense, semantically, within the context of social and cultural beliefs that would seem applicable to the poem. If, that is, the tiger were "created" *at all*, it would have to have been created by some sort

---

1. My reading of Blake's "The Tyger" follows, and develops, the one given by Bloom (1971: 35–39).

of immortal being—a being with powers sufficiently divine to create mortal beings, and thus, itself, immortal—whether God or a classical figure such as Prometheus or some other imaginary immortal being. In this case, then, the question is not rhetorical but straightforward, asking for the identity of the divine being who created the tiger. And yet, like a rhetorical question, this question contains within it sufficient information to make the answer necessarily one from a limited number of choices—some being that has an immortal hand or eye.

In the second quatrain, the speaker further informs our concept of the being about which the questions are posed:

> In what distant deeps or skies,
> Burnt the fire of thine eyes?
> On what wings dare he aspire?
> What the hand, dare seize the fire? (Blake [1789–1797]1967: plate 42)

The maker of the tiger must have had *wings* and must have *dared to aspire*. It would be inappropriate to speak of God as *daring* to do anything. The image in the questioner's mind seems to derive from that of Lucifer, leader of the rebel angels, in Milton's *Paradise Lost*. (The image of Daedalus aspiring to fly may be relevant but probably not as clearly so as the image of Satan.) Following this thought, the last line presumes that the tiger's maker had *seized* the fire used to make the tiger's eyes, in a way reminiscent of Prometheus's theft of fire to give to man. The transition from Lucifer to Prometheus is possible because (1) both of them are types of rebel divinity, and (2) in some sense, neither of them could really have *made* the tiger— neither the story of the Fall of the Angels nor that of Prometheus's creation of man (after which he gives man fire, against the will of the other gods) quite fits in an imaginary story of making the tiger—and, in any case, there is no actual story of the tiger's creation in canonical literature or myth. Milton's Satan specifically is incapable of creating *life*—a notion following that of Spenser's arch-demon Archimago, who can only make illusions, not real living beings. And Prometheus only creates man and steals fire to give it to man; Prometheus would not make an animal that man finds frightening. So, in both cases, the questions contain within them hypotheses that make the questions unanswerable. These are special, marked questions, because they contain enough information to act as rhetorical questions, but the answers that they would prompt if they were rhetorical questions would be patently incorrect.

One of the most problematic aspects of Epstein's reading of "The Tyger" is his assumption that the speaker of "The Tyger" is the same as the actual author of the poem, William Blake. As we have seen thus far, the speaker of the imaginary speech that the poem represents is somewhat befuddled by his own questions. He asks questions that are impossible to answer because they at once contain too much information to be open to an answer as if they were straightforward questions, and, as rhetorical questions, presume incoherent or impossible answers. The befuddlement of the speaker becomes even more dramatically obvious in the next quatrain:

> And what shoulder, & what art,
> Could twist the sinews of they heart?
> And when thy heart began to beat,
> What dread hand? & what dread feet? (Blake [1789–1797]1967: plate 42)

The first question here continues in the line of the previous ones, suggesting that whoever made the tiger must have (or have had) some great physical powers to make something of such power to terrify. But the second question seems to confuse the object of creation with the creator. The "dread feet" couldn't really be attributes of the creator. Whereas the hand would be used to make the tiger and would follow in the series of metonymies, shoulder, art, hand—as well as recalling "What immortal hand" from the opening and "What the hand dare seize the fire" in the second quatrain, *feet* are not used to create. This is not to mention that it would be hard to imagine in what way *feet* can be *dread*, except insofar as a tiger has claws on both fore and hind paws and springs to the attack on its hind legs, and thus has *dread feet*. The very confusion or misattribution of qualities from the tiger onto the creator, or perhaps vice versa, illustrates something about neither the tiger nor the creator but, rather, the speaker himself. The speaker seems to be caught up in a sort of hysteria, compatible with his inability to accept the real answer to his original question.

The mood of hysteria rises even higher in the next quatrain:

> What the hammer? what the chain,
> In what furnace was thy brain?
> What the anvil? what dread grasp,
> Dare its deadly terrors clasp? (Blake [1789–1797]1967: plate 42)

One can imagine a hammer and an anvil involved if the making of the tiger is likened to a product of the Greek god Hephaestos (Roman Vulcan), yet another potential but impossible creator, because Hephaestos also never actually makes living beings, but rather artefacts such as Achilles's shield. It is hard even to imagine how a chain would come into play here. And, although it makes some sense to think of the tiger's brain as being full of "deadly terrors," it is hard either to imagine the brain, even a tiger's brain, as the product of a hammer, an anvil, and a chain or to imagine why a "dread grasp" would be necessary to take hold of it. Most of all, the questions at this point seem to fall thick and fast, contributing to the mounting emotional pitch of the speaker.

The next quatrain both alludes again to *Paradise Lost* and makes clear to us, if it wasn't before, why the speaker is having so much trouble:

> When the stars threw down their spears
> And water'd heaven with their tears:
> Did he smile his work to see?
> Did he who made the Lamb make thee? (Blake 1789–1797]1967: plate 42)

The first three lines, again, seem to presume that it was Lucifer—or Satan, as he is known after the fall from heaven—who created the tiger, again, a doctrinal impossibility. Here, the presumption leads to a fearful imagining of Satan taking pleasure in making something terrifying to humanity. But the closing line asks the very opposite question: How could the very same God who made a soft, friendly, and woolly thing like the lamb also make the ferocious tiger? How could the God who made Good also make Evil? This last gloss of the speaker's question is further assisted by the proverbial identification of the Lamb of God with the person of Jesus, and also by the poem, "The Lamb" (Blake [1789–1794]1967: plate 8), in *Songs of Innocence*, composed a few years before *Songs of Experience*, in which "The Tyger" appears. The title, "The Tyger," may in some sense allude to this earlier poem, as both titles are generic names of animals. In "The Lamb," the speaker, who identifies himself gleefully as a child, says that the lamb was created by God, and both the lamb and the speaker (a child) typify the innocence that God has created. The contexts thus reinforce the idea that the problem the speaker has in "The Tyger," the problem pushing him into a state of hysteria, is the traditional Problem of Evil: How could God, who is good, have made evil things in this world?

The final quatrain, repeating the first but for one word, once again seems to settle—and yet not to settle—upon the alternative answer, that it was not God, but Satan, who created the tiger:

> Tyger Tyger burning bright,
> In the forests of the night:
> What immortal hand or eye,
> Dare frame thy fearful symmetry? (Blake 1789–1797]1967: plate 42)

The word *dare* recalls "One what wings dare he aspire," alluding to Lucifer's rebellion against God, as if to suggest that the creation of the tiger was, itself, a gesture of rebellion and usurpation of God's creative powers.

To review, two important points come out of our close reading of Blake's "The Tyger." First, the speaker's questions have the form of rhetorical questions insofar as they contain enough information to imply their own answers, but the answers that such rhetorical questions would prompt would be both inconsistent with each other and generally impossible according to the doctrinal and mythological contexts to which they allude. Second, the speaker's insistent questions seem to boil down to a refusal to believe the most obvious answer to the question of who made the tiger, God, because it seems impossible to the speaker that a good God could make evil things.

But the very same logic that enables us to question the assumptions that the speaker's apparently rhetorical questions assume should also enable us to question the assumptions underlying the central question, the Problem of Evil. For this problem is only relevant insofar as it is assumed, to begin with, that the tiger *is* evil, an assumption manifest with all the terms suggesting terror, fear, dread, and so on, throughout the poem. Just as the speaker has *created* for himself his own incapacity to answer his own questions by insistently posing questions that are too closed to allow the correct answer (God), so, too, he has created his own problem to begin with by assuming that the tiger is evil. In a sense quite consistent with Blake's other work, the speaker himself has "created" the tiger insofar as he has created in his own imagination the object of which he is terrified and projected that object onto the actual being, the tiger.

This idea that evil is created in the eye of the beholder is consistent with other poems in *Songs of Experience*, in particular, "A Poison Tree":

> I was angry with my friend:
> I told my wrath, my wrath did end.
> I was angry with my foe:
> I told it not, my wrath did grow.
>
> And I water'd it in tears,
> Night and morning with my fears,
> And I sunned it with smiles,
> And with soft deceitful wiles;
> And it grew both day and night,
> Till it bore an apple bright,
> And my foe beheld it shine,
> And he knew that it was mine,
>
> And into the garden stole
> When the night had veil'd the pole;
> In the morning glad I see
> My foe outstretched beneath the tree. (Blake 1789–1797]1967: plate 49)

Blake's retelling of the fall in the Garden of Eden—a story originally about the acquisition of knowledge of the difference between good and evil—draws our attention to the minimal difference between *friend* and *foe*—supported by the minimal phonological difference in the first and third lines: *I was angry with my f-*. We have no reason to know, or to think, that the friend and the foe are inherently different, until the speaker chooses to treat them differently. The speaker feels wrath equally toward his friend and his foe. What defines the foe as a foe is not that the foe incurs the speaker's wrath but that the speaker does not tell his wrath to his foe, leading eventually to disastrous consequences in which the foe lives up to his role as foe and the enmity between speaker and foe reaches the extremes of deception and death.

This idea also corresponds to the meaning of the phrase in "London," also in *Songs of Experience*, "the mind-forg'd manacles":

> I wander thro' each charter'd street
> Near where the charter'd Thames does flow

And mark in every face I meet
Marks of weakness, marks of woe.

In every cry of every man,
In every infant's cry of fear,
In every voice, in every ban,
The mind-forg'd manacles I hear. (Blake 1789–1797]1967: plate 46)

Everywhere the speaker goes, he witnesses a suffering connected to restriction and confinement—even the Thames river is "chartered" and thus not free to all. But the manacles of confinement are forged in the mind. They are, implicitly, the products of bad ideas and lack of imagination.

Finally, "The Tyger" has its own most immediate visual context to give us a strong clue to corroborate the above reading. Blake originally published his *Songs of Innocence and of Experience* himself, etching each poem by hand into a copper plate, as if to imitate medieval illuminated manuscripts, along with illustrations to the poems, some of them exquisite, which he colored in by hand painting them on the newly printed books. "The Tyger" has one such illustration: a picture of a tiger, below the words of the poem and in the bottom quarter of the page. (A tree along the right side of the page may suggest an Edenic setting and pehaps reinforce the connection with "A Poison Tree.") The tiger hardly looks frightening or terrible. If anything, with eyes wide open and shoulders low, he looks a bit frightened himself, which would make perfect sense if he is the target of the speaker's frightened— and thus frightening—projections. Even if the other literary contexts mentioned here as corroborating evidence should be considered inaccessible to the beginning reader—and they should not—still, the picture itself is evidently as much a part of the "text" of "The Tyger" as the words are.

We have come a long way from Epstein's reading of "The Tyger" as an expression of Blake's "own awe at perceiving the energy that drives the universe and the poet" (1981: 187). The shallowness of Epstein's reading comes despite his meticulous commentary on specific stylistic choices within the poem, some of which may be correct, but all of which are trivial if, to begin with, they are assumed to support an unsatisfactory reading. But the reductive, superficial reading is not an accident. Epstein's failure to recognize the various kinds of irony at play in "The Tyger" arises from the theoretical assumption that the poem is a communicative message—in this case, expressing Blake's awe—and that the task of a good reader is to notice how expressive this message is. "The Tyger" is *not* a communicative utterance. Rather, it is a dramatic exercise, involving an imaginary speech. Our task as good readers is to notice where the surprises lie in the content and form of this speech, and what sort of meaningful pattern the surprises form. This pattern gives us, simultaneously, the poem's *meaning* and its *aesthetic effect*.

The poem's surprises depend on markedness on a variety of levels, many of which require knowledge of appropriate contexts. For instance, the clash of implied answers between Satan, Prometheus, and Hephaestos depends on our recognition of literary and mythological allusions. The summary of the questions as the Problem of Evil depends somewhat on familiarity with this problem in Western thought, especially in religion. In the former case, the unmarked condition would be a single, coherent field of allusive reference, making the questions neatly rhetorical and their answers easy to produce. In the latter case, the unmarked condition would be the simple answer, yes, God made all animals, both the lamb and the tiger. Without these contexts, one cannot fully appreciate the way that the speaker seems to be answering his own questions with answers that he cannot accept and yet cannot accept the answer (God) that would seem more obviously appropriate, given his concerns, because of the Problem of Evil. And without these contexts, the reader cannot arrive at the point of noticing that the speaker is in some sense inventing his own difficulties by categorizing the tiger as "evil" from the start. The unmarked condition here would be either a celebration of the tiger as a natural creature—an attitude somewhat typical of the Age of Sensibility—or a complaint about the appearance of evil in an otherwise good world—a sentiment we might find in Renaissance literature, in which things of nature might be employed allegorically to represent moral categories such as good and evil.

Blake creates a marked utterance on this level by bringing together these two, incommensurate viewpoints—an allegorical and a sentimental view of Nature—to reveal the factitiousness of both views as products of the perceiver's projections onto the world. This last point, however, is not Blake's *message*, as such, but rather the *effect* of his drama. Poetry does not tell, it makes things happen with words.

In "The Tyger," Blake causes us to recognize the difficulties someone can get into by making moral assumptions about things in nature that have no *a priori* moral essence. In this sense, we could say that the poem "communicates" to us, but what it communicates is not a message but an experience. This experience—what happens if we have this attitude—is indistinguishable from the poem's aesthetic effect, which is the effect of surprise. Here, the surprise is, ultimately, a series of surprises: (1) the speaker is saying nothing but questions; (2) the questions can't be answered, even though they sound like rhetorical questions; (3) the questions reveal great consternation; (4) the speaker has created the cause of his own consternation; and (5) the answer to the question turns out to be "God" only in the first instance but "the speaker" or "the perceiver" in the last. It is this succession of intellectual surprises that makes the work simultaneously deep and delightful.

EXAMPLE: WALLACE STEVENS'S "THE SNOW MAN"

My second (and last) example of an unsatisfactory reading produced by a stylistician is Samuel J. Keyser's (1981) reading of "The Snow Man." Let us first recall the poem.

The Snow Man

One must have a mind of winter
To regard the frost and the boughs
Of the pine-trees crusted with snow;

And have been cold a long time
To behold the junipers shagged with ice,
The spruces rough in the distant glitter

Of the January sun; and not to think
Of any misery in the sound of the wind,
In the sound of a few leaves;

Which is the sound of the land
Full of the same wind
That is blowing in the same bare place

For the listener, who listens in the snow,
And, nothing himself, beholds
Nothing that is not there and the nothing that is. (Stevens 1954: 9)

Keyser (1981: 112–120) comes closer to a convincing reading of this poem than Epstein does with "The Tyger," but not close enough to keep him from missing the point entirely. To decide the semantic meaning of the poem, Keyser first quotes Frank Kermode and then Stevens himself, clearly according more authority to the latter than the former. Here is Kermode first:

> Out of "The Snow Man" grows the recurring metaphor of winter as a pure abstracted reality, a bare icy outline purged clean of all the accretions brought by the human mind to make it possible for us to conceive of reality and live our lives. So purged, reality has no human meaning, nor has a man; he is
>
> ... the listener, who listens in the snow,
> And, nothing himself, beholds
> Nothing that is not there and the nothing that is.
> (quoted in Keyser 1981: 119)

He continues:

> In contrast to Kermode's interpretation of *The Snow Man* we have Wallace Stevens's own explanation which he gives in a letter to Hi Simons, dated 18 April 1944: "I shall explain the Snow Man as an example of the necessity of identifying oneself with reality in order to understand it and enjoy it." (Keyser 1981: 119)

The New Critics of the early to middle twentieth century generally urged that readers view a poet's own comments about his poems, especially brief and cryptic comments in personal correspondence, with the utmost skepticism: We cannot really know how much thought or knowledge was assumed as the context for the letter, and we cannot know whether Stevens willfully, or perhaps unknowingly, reduced the complexity of his own poem for his correspondent's sake. Nevertheless, not heeding this principle, Keyser takes the beginning of the poem, the words *One must*, to indicate that the entire poem is an *admonishment* to the reader, a *behest* telling the reader that he or she *must* be or do as follows. Granted, the bulk of Keyser's comments focus—correctly—on the remarkable structure of the poem's single sentence, which is built so that the reader will complete a given portion and think that that is the whole of it, only to keep reading and find out that what he or she had thought to be a whole turns out to be only a part of a much more complex sentence.

Despite this fine insight, ironically, Keyser still allows the apparent imperative form of the opening, *One must*, to dominate his sense of the whole. He treats the complex structure of the sentence as an expressive ornament to dramatize the sense of the original imperative, in effect, "One must be like a snow man." Keyser therefore misses the point that the sentence turns out to have an altogether different, surprising meaning when read as a whole. The sentence begins as an apparent imperative but ends up actually being more like a complex conditional-resultative sentence.

It helps if we reduce the poem's sentence to something of a skeletal paraphrase. We can take advantage of the poem's many parallelisms—such as the parallel of *regard* in the first tercet and *behold* in the second, and *the frost and the boughs* and *pine trees crusted with snow* within the first tercet, as well as both of these with *the junipers shagged with ice* and *the spruces rough in the distant glitter / Of the January sun.*

> One must be a creature of winter to perceive wintry things and not perceive emotion (misery) in any of them; only a snow man, who is nothing himself (not a perceiving subject), can (as it were) perceive nothing that is not there and the nothing that is.

The sentence thus has an idiomatic structure something like that of the sentence, "You have to be heartless to know her and not love her." This latter does not urge someone to be heartless; it explains what it would have to take to avoid loving a lovable person.

Stevens's sentence is not a recommendation to become like a snow man, which would be impossible. If it were possible for the reader to become like a snow man, that would mean that the reader would bring nothing to the reality he or she perceives—would impose no conceptions such as "misery in the sound of the wind." But that would *also* have to mean that he or she would not bring any knowledge to bear on perception, even the perception of the marks on the page that are the letters and words of the poem. In short, a snow man cannot read poetry. So, if the reader were (hypothetically) successful at becoming a snow man, he or she would do so only at the expense of his or her ability to read the poem or even to know that he or she has succeeded. The snow man is *nothing himself.* Even before this, the poem gives us a strong clue in the phrase equivalent to *have a mind of winter*, that is, *have been cold a long time.* The latter phrase sounds like a reference to the dead. This does in fact make sense later on, once the reader figures out that the snow man is not a human being and that one would have to be dead—be nothing—to "see" the world the way "he" does—that is, not see at all. The poem then works, as it happens, as a nice allegory for one of the main points in this chapter: the importance of the extrinsic literary and cultural contexts brought to bear on the literary text.

The surprising shifting of the sentence in Stevens's "The Snow Man" is not a demonstration of the openness that being a snow man would entail: We cannot possibly think like a snow man, because a snow man does not, by definition—even the poem's definition—think. Rather, it is precisely the turn, from apparent injunction to actual observation about the nature of humanity, that surprises and shocks the reader out of the complacency of his post-Romantic expectations. A commonplace of Romantic thought was and continues to be the idea that humanity is alienated from Nature, in permanent exile, because of its self-consciousness. The very things that make us human—language, reason, morality, civilization—also make us somehow separated from Nature and fill us with anxiety and a sense that we do not belong where we are. With this idea comes a yearning for the blissful state of oneness with Nature. To put the thought simply (at the risk of caricature), squirrels are lucky because they never have to worry about whether they are doing the right thing and never have to wonder about the meaning of life. But whereas, in the Romantics, the object of such yearning might be a bird (such as Keats's nightingale), which may or may not in fact have some awareness of its own mortality (for all we know), Stevens's snow man is most certainly without any awareness of anything, because it is not a living being at all. Indeed, even the name for it, snow man, is the product of human projections and human creation: It is only figuratively a "man" made of snow. The unmarked condition in this case is, precisely, the expectation that one *must* have a mind of winter and be like the snow man. The surprise comes when we realize that, far from having to be a snow man, one has no possible choice of being a snow man, because being one would be neither being nor choice at all.

There is, indeed, a deeper paradox in the poem, however. The common human attributes that include the hearing of misery in the sound of the winter wind *also* include our ability to contemplate what it would be like if we were not ourselves. Imagining other subjectivities is part of the human condition because it is one of the capabilities of imaginative projection, and this includes at least trying to imagine impossible subjectivities, beings that cannot possibly be subjects at all, such as the snow man, "nothing himself." The poem does not so much *tell* us that this is an aspect of the human condition as allow us to *experience* this paradoxical fact as another result of the surprise that the poem delivers. Again, the poem's "meaning"—that is, its point—is inseparable from its aesthetic effect, its surprise, and its paradox.

Like Epstein, Keyser makes his mistake precisely because he expects the poem to *express* the author's ideas or feelings as a communicative utterance. This renders him insensible to the possibilities of surprise on the level of ideas, even though Keyser is quite sensitive to surprises in syntax. He assimilates the surprises of syntax to an incorrect reading of the content because he assumes a simplistic reading of the content to begin with and then assumes that the syntactic patterning will *enhance* or *boost* the message. This logic is very similar to that of Renaissance theorists who viewed such things as verse or poetic imagery as a kind of rhetorical "garb" to "clothe" the truth carried within the text as its message. Then as now, this confusion results in a tendency to read parts at the expense of the whole.

Perhaps most fascinating here is how the poem itself seems to prepare the way for the mistaken reading—not only by setting up the surprise but also by then addressing the very questions about reading that the mistake—and the surprising turn to correct it—would naturally pose. The poem presents to us the paradox of how, like reading, human perception always includes projection, but our ability to project can also include our imagining impossible nonsubjects as test cases, nonsubjects who, if they could exist, would *not* project when they perceived. The reader who most "truly" understands the text is the one who projects nothing at all, but this would mean that he or she actually understands nothing at all and is not in fact reading. Reading always involves distortion, even though its aim is the absence of distortion. It is this very paradox that keeps the poem from being either a simplistic recommendation to a Zen-like nonprojection or an equally simplistic celebration of human projections. Rather, it dwells on the paradox that makes (perfect) reading simultaneously possible and impossible. It takes a good enough reader to recognize, ultimately, that the poem is also saying that the perfect reading is impossible—and yet that *is* the perfect reading, because no other reading will do. This self-reflexivity—the poem allegorically representing how poems work—rather than the mimesis of imitative form that Epstein calls *self-reflexivity,* accords best with literariness. For when the utterance is removed from normal communicative and referential contexts, it can only ultimately refer to itself and illustrate the paradox of language that only *appears* to communicate—having no communicative exchange to make it do so; and yet, in a sense, that very paradox *is* what the text "communicates." Every literary text approaches this paradox of self-reflexivity in a different way, but the ultimate pleasure of surprise and fascination with the paradox of a language that has the substance but not the social circumstances of communication remains always at the end of the road of interpretation.

CONCLUSION

As we have seen, literary texts, including poems, have the function of delivering surprise, provided the reader can recognize the appropriate contexts as the unmarked conditions against which the texts' features are marked. This means that literary pleasure presupposes by its very nature literacy—or what Culler (1981) aptly calls *literary competence*. Literary competence is not a stable state, however, but an infinitely progressive accumulation. Reading is a lifelong apprenticeship in the art of literary competence, as an increasing number of texts becomes increasingly accessible to the studious reader. But what about readers who aren't there yet? How does a reader get started? Are we not faced with a closed loop, where the pleasure of reading requires prior reading, which requires the capacity for the pleasure of reading?

The pleasure of literary texts, fortunately, is available to various degrees on various levels simultaneously. At the most rudimentary, the necessary context of the appropriate "unmarked" default expectations comes from very broadly shared cultural traditions, ideas, beliefs, concepts, or images. For instance, almost everyone who has learned to read in a Western country will recognize the collocation of a *tree* with a dangerous *fruit* and a *garden* into which the *foe steals* as some sort of allusion to the Fall in the Garden of Eden, because this web of myths is so widely known in some form or other throughout Western culture, even among people who never read the Bible or Milton's *Paradise Lost*. In the case of "The Tyger," the incoherency among the specific divine figures to which the questions allude would require a fair bit of prior reading. But the fact that the speaker utters nothing but questions, and that the questions, while containing sufficient information to be rhetorical, do not seem to permit the very answers that they seem to prompt—these facts should be evident to a reader attentive to mere syntactic and rhetorical conventions and only the vaguest and broadest cultural beliefs or traditions about creation and divinity. In the case of "The Snow Man," knowledge of the Romantic tradition of yearning for an unalienated unity with Nature only provides extra elaboration beyond the more basic point, which is that the sentence winds up *not* urging the reader to be like a snow man but rather says what being a snow man would be like, if it were possible (and it turns out to be, paradoxically, quite impossible). The reader who gets this point only need read the sentence as a whole rather than stopping too soon, and need think about the logical implications of what it *would* mean to urge someone to be "nothing himself" and therefore unable to perceive anything at all, including the poem making this supposed behest. Literacy in both of these instances requires, above all, that the reader read the entire poem through, all of its sentences, trying to see a pattern in the whole and only then consider how each part contributes to that whole rather than moving sequentially and making controlling inferences at every point from limited information. The procedure of accepting parts of the whole as dominant—without sufficient attention to possible irony—characterizes normal communication rather than the reading of literary texts. A literary text is first and foremost a *whole*, an aesthetic *pattern* of effects rather than a *sequence* delivering a *message*.

The reader must attend to the literary contexts that enable a literary text to deliver surprise by means of marked effects, and the reader must view the entire poem as a completed whole, a pattern whose function is to deliver that surprise. The surprises of literary texts form aesthetically satisfying patterns, and the reader's discovery of a satisfying pattern is, itself, the major pleasurable surprise that reading and interpreting a literary text provide. These two principles, *context* and *pattern*, can guide the new reader of literature from the outset. But it is the very nature of literary texts, because they draw on literary contexts to condition markedness and form patterns of surprise, that reading leads to more reading, and more reading deepens and enriches the experience of rereading familiar literary texts, making them forever new. In a sense, reading has no beginning and no end. It has no end because the addition of more literary contexts will always enrich the experiences of markedness, pattern formation, and surprise. And it has no beginning because one must always have some sort of prior knowledge, even if only rudimentary, to find pleasure in reading a literary text. Into this beginningless and endless labyrinth of texts, the teacher leads new readers, for literacy cannot be separated from pedagogy. The first step in this journey into the world of literary texts is to understand the difference between texts and normal communication and how literariness conditions the proper approach to literature.

REFERENCES

Austin, Timothy R. 1981. Constraints on syntactic rules and the style of Shelley's "Adonais": an exercise in stylistic criticism. In *Essays in modern stylistics*, ed. Donald C. Freeman, 138–165. London: Methuen.

Aviram, Amittai F. 1994. *Telling rhythm: body and meaning in poetry*. Ann Arbor: University of Michigan Press.

Blake, William. 1789–1797. *Songs of innocence and of experience*. Facsimile reprint, New York: Oxford University Press, 1967, with introduction and notes by Geoffrey Keynes.

Bloom, Harold. 1971. *The visionary company*. Ithaca, N.Y.: Cornell University Press.

Culler, Jonathan. 1981. Literary competence. In *Essays in modern stylistics*, ed. Donald C. Freeman, 24–41. London: Metheun.

Dickinson, Emily. 1960. *The complete poems of Emily Dickinson,* ed. Thomas H. Johnson. Boston: Little, Brown.

Epstein, E. L. 1981. The self-reflexive artefact: the function of mimesis in an approach to a theory of value for literature. In *Essays in modern stylistics*, ed. Donald C. Freeman, 166–199. London: Methuen.

Fairley, Irene R. 1981. Syntactic deviation and cohesion. In *Essays in modern stylistics*, ed. Donald C. Freeman, 123–137. London: Methuen.

Freeman, Donald C. (ed.). 1981a. *Essays in modern stylistics*. London: Methuen.

———. 1981b. Keats's 'To Autumn': poetry as process and pattern. In *Essays in modern stylistics*, ed. Donald C. Freeman, 83–99. London: Methuen.

Jakobson, Roman. 1960. Concluding statement: linguistics and poetics. *Style in language*, ed. Thomas Sebeok, 350–377. Cambridge, Mass.: MIT Press.

———. 1968. Poetry of grammar and grammar of poetry. *Lingua* 21: 597–609.

———. 1973. Principes de versification. In *Questions de poétique*, ed. Tzvetan Todorov, 40–55. Paris: Seuil.

Keyser, Samuel Jay. 1981. Wallace Stevens: form and meaning in four poems. In *Essays in modern stylistics*, ed. Donald C. Freeman, 100–122. London: Methuen.

Kiparsky, Paul. 1981. The role of linguistics in a theory of poetry. In *Essays in modern stylistics*, ed. Donald C. Freeman, 9–23. London: Methuen.

Mukařovský, Jan. 1948. Standard language and poetic language. In *The critical tradition*, ed. David H. Richter, 860–868. Reprint, New York: St. Martin's Press, 1989.

Plato. 1982. *Phaedrus*. Plato in twelve volumes, Vol. I, ed. and trans. Harold North Fowler, 405–579. Cambridge, Mass.: Harvard University Press. (Numbers and letters in brackets are the canonical form of citations to standard editions of Plato.)

Stevens, Wallace. 1954. *The collected poems of Wallace Stevens*. New York: Random House-Vintage.

Tarlinskaya, Marina. 1987. Rhythm and meaning: "rhythmical figures" in English iambic pentameter, their grammar, and their links with semantics. *Style* 21(1):1–35.

7

Villainous Boys: On Some Marked Exchanges in *Romeo and Juliet*

TREVOR HOWARD-HILL

T HE FUNDAMENTAL PRINCIPLE of the markedness model, the negotiation principle, can apply to literary works of the early modern period as well as to conversations:

> Choose the *form* of your conversation contribution such that it indexes the set of rights and obligations which you wish to be in force between speaker and addressee for the current exchange. (Myers-Scotton 1993: 113)

In this formulation the "conversation contribution" is the literary work that an author wishes to contribute to the literary tradition, the "form" is the mode (fiction/nonfiction, poetry, or prose) and genre in which the work is written, the "set of rights and obligations" are the conventions of the genre that establish the reader's expectations, and the speaker and addressee are the author and reader, respectively. On the level of the literary work the significant distinction between the principle's application to literature and conversation seems to be that there is only a single speaker (collaborative works aside) and that therefore there is no exchange: A literary composition is not a conversation.[1] However powerful they may be in determining the success or failure of the author's work, or assigning meanings to it, readers have no power to alter the form of words before them or to affect the progress and outcome of the literary composition.

Nevertheless, most literary works contain conversations in which the negotiation principle and markedness may be observed in operation. Indeed, plays in particular may be considered simply a sequence of speeches and

---

1. The associated maxims on codeswitching (CS) as an unmarked choice (Myers-Scotton (1993: 114), CS as a marked choice (131), CS as an exploratory choice (142), CS as a deferential strategy (147), and the virtuosity maxim (148) are less readily applied to literature. The first two, however, seem relevant to the initial choice of genre and a change of genre (or dominant style within a work), and the exploratory maxim may relate to "experimental" literature.

conversations, providing intrinsically fertile ground for the consideration of the markedness model. Without enlarging the theoretical context further, in order not to repeat remarks made elsewhere (Howard-Hill 1996), I selected Shakespeare's *Romeo and Juliet* as a play likely to be widely familiar to illustrate the application of the model to drama.

SHAKESPEARE'S BOYS

Shakespeare's plays are full of boys, natural parts for the youths who were apprenticed to master actors and usually played the female leads.[2] Among them are great lubberly boys, wimpled, whining, purblind, wayward boys (Cupid), little scrubbed boys, peevish and prating boys, changeling boys, very dishonest paltry boys, and even sweet and lovely boys. As well, there are more than a few unembellished usages of the noun. Of the 455 occurrences of *boy* or *boys* in Shakespeare's plays, two-thirds (297) are vocatives, apparently used to refer to servants, though some of them could be marked in the particular situation. About a fifth of these have qualifying adjectives but some twenty-one of them (*my boy*, *sir boy*) can be set aside, leaving only a small number (37) that are more likely to display markedness in conversational situations.[3] These marked instances are fairly evenly divided between cases with derogatory and cases with approbatory adjectives, an observation that suggests that Shakespeare himself had no particular attitude to boydom: The dramatic situation of the moment seems more likely than the playwright's predisposition to determine how speakers characterize boys. And many of the nonvocative references to boys are objective, occurring in apparently neutral contexts.[4]

On the other hand, outside *Romeo and Juliet*, in two cases young male protagonists are designated as *boys* in conspicuously contemptuous terms. In *All's Well That Ends Well*, Bertram, the young Count Rossillion (the most unsympathetic character ever rewarded with a Shakespearian heroine), is characterized as a *proud scornful boy* by the King of France (2.3.151). Even his mother describes him as a *rash and unbridled boy* (3.2.28), and to the

2. Spevack (1969) records 352 occurrences of *boy*, 1 hyphenated compound, 9 genitives, and 93 occurrences of *boys* in the plays. *Romeo and Juliet* contributes 11 occurrences of *boy*, 2 of *boys*. For convenience, the text is quoted from the *Riverside Shakespeare* (1974) used by Spevack.

3. Even though dramatic speeches usually have on-stage auditors, substantial parts of them may offer no opportunities for negotiations, in which markedness is present, to occur. Therefore, instances of a form of address, *boy* (like *man, woman, child*), when obviously a speaker is interacting with an auditor or auditors, identify the situations in which markedness is most likely to come into play.

4. This observation, like others to this point, is made from study of the concordance rather than analysis of their broader contexts in the individual plays. Nonvocative uses of *boy* are not ignored here; indeed, often the noun with negative attributes occurs to reinforce the marked vocative usage.

parasite Parolles he is a *foolish idle boy* (4.3.215) and a *lascivious boy* (4.3.220, 300). The general feeling, both within the play and in modern criticism, is that the epithets are just.

More significant for consideration of the earlier *Romeo and Juliet* is the case of *Coriolanus*. Coriolanus is presented as a heroic but intemperate character who turns against Rome even to the extent of allying himself with his rival, Aufidius, Rome's enemy. When at last the Romans send out Coriolanus's mother, wife, and son to plead for the city to be spared, he yields. Aufidius, envious of the honor Coriolanus garnered among the Volscians, is already plotting Coriolanus's assassination when he reports that he has made a treaty for peace with Rome and accuses Coriolanus of betraying his allies:

> *Auf.* . . . He has betray'd your business, and given up,
>   For certain drops of salt, your city Rome,
>   I say "your city," to his wife and mother,
>   Breaking his oath and resolution . . .
>   . . . at his nurses's tears
>   He whin'd and roar'd away your victory . . .
> *Cor.*   Hear'st thou, Mars?
> *Auf.* Name not the god, thou boy of tears!
> *Cor.*   Ha?
> *Auf.* No more.
> *Cor.* Measureless liar, thou hast made my heart
>   Too great for what constrains it. "Boy"? O slave!
>   *[8 verses omitted]*
>   . . . "Boy," false hound!
>   If you have writ your annals true, 'tis there
>   That, like an eagle in a dove-cote, I
>   Flutter'd your Volscians in Corioles.
>   Alone I did it. "Boy"! (5.6.91–115)

Indignation spurs Coriolanus to repeat the offensive *boy* incredulously three times among a scattering of equally derogatory terms directed at his rival: *liar, slave, cur, hound*. Clearly even from these few examples, in Shakespeare's world the term *boy* was polyvalent, attracting derogatory and approbatory qualifiers according to the social situation of its use but also, even without immediate qualification, possessing either a neutral or offensive force; that is, a simple (unqualified) use of the term *boy* may be marked or unmarked.

THREE CRUCIAL DRAMATIC MOMENTS IN "ROMEO AND JULIET"

In *Romeo and Juliet* the marked usage of *boy* supplies the affective basis of the mechanism of the revenge plot on which the play depends.[5] Three crucial dramatic moments in *Romeo and Juliet* embody an interesting pattern of the marked

---

5. It is imprudent to claim any novelty of observation in Shakespearian criticism. If a reader knows of a discussion of this topic that has not come to my attention, I should very much like to learn of it.

sense of *boy* together with significant repetition of *villain*. The main purpose of this chapter is to consider *boy* and associated expressions in relation to the dramatic situations in which they occur, with the aid of the markedness model.

Certainly, Tybalt's speech threatening a disastrous outcome (1.5.89–92, quoted later) marks the boundary between the *protasis* and the *epitasis*, the crucial point at which the introductory development translates to dramatic action. One might even assert against the common view that it is not the families' feud that kills the young lovers (and three other young men in the play) but rather, the simple monosyllable *boy* spoken in anger, piercing the heart of the young man to whom it was addressed, Tybalt. Except for Benvolio, reserved to sum up at the end of the action, all the young men and women in the play are killed by themselves or each other because of a word.[6]

Shakespeare does not reveal why the Capulets and Montagues are at odds, but it seems that the feud is conducted on the fringes, as it were, of the principal families of Verona, by servants and by such zealots as the fiery Tybalt (1.1.109), not the son but apparently the leading young gentleman of Capulet's clan. Shakespeare assigns each of the principal young men a somewhat limited function in the play, to embody a major attribute of the conventional character of the young man as it developed from classical drama through the sixteenth century.[7] Benvolio ("well-wisher") appears as the good friend; Mercutio as the sociable, volatile humorist; Romeo the young man as romantic lover; and Tybalt, the young man, as the upholder of honor. In the first scene Shakespeare sketches Tybalt's character economically according to conventional Renaissance delineations of character. Tybalt reveals his essential quality and foreshadows his function in the play in his first speeches at his entrance into the fray between the servants of the Montagues and Capulets:

> *Tyb.* What, art thou drawn among these heartless hinds?
>   Turn thee, Benvolio, look upon thy death.
> *Ben.* I do but keep the peace. Put up thy sword,
>   Or manage it to part these men with me.
> *Tyb.* What, drawn and talk of peace? I hate the word
>   As I hate hell, all Montagues, and thee.
>   Have at thee, coward. (1.1.66–72)

Besides his bellicosity, Tybalt's use of epithets to characterize his opponents

---

6. This is not to neglect the influence of the circumstances in which the word is spoken, as I mention later.

7. See Herrick ([1950]1964: 150–154) *Young man*. Among other qualities, the young man is amorous, does everything to excess, is ambitious for honor, and is sociable and fond of laughter.

8. Besides *villain*, mentioned below and in note 14, see Tybalt's *heartless hinds* which can be rendered as *cowardly servants*; for *hind* OED records a transferred meaning of "rustic, a boor." Folk etymology might have associated *coward* and *cow-herd* in Shakespeare's time when (unusually) they shared similar spellings. Later in the play, "slave" (1.5.55) meaning "a servant completely divested of freedom and personal rights" is also "used as a term of contempt" (*OED* I.1.b.).

as social inferiors is obvious.[8] In the three scenes of the play in which he appears (I discuss the other scenes later), Tybalt is depicted as being aggressively conscious of his social standing.

More remarkably, within a few verses, Shakespeare begins a series of uses of the term *villain* that can be shown to be literally marked. At line 79, the head of the opposing house enters. The first words Montague (Romeo's father) utters, in the inflamed Tybalt's presence to the head of his house, are "Thou villain Capulet!" *Villein* (*OED sb.*1. "One of the class of serfs in the feudal system") clearly contributes to *villain* (*OED sb.*1 "Originally, a low-born base-minded rustic; a man of ignoble ideas or instincts. . . . a. Used as a term of opprobrious address."). The next four occurrences of the word (1.5.62, 64, 75, 3.1.61) come significantly from Tybalt's mouth to characterize Romeo, the heir of the house of Montague.

Later, at Capulet's "old accustomed feast" (1.2.20), Tybalt is present as, apparently, the youngest adult male of his family.[9] Although uninvited, Romeo accompanies Mercutio in order to see Rosaline but immediately falls in love with Juliet. Tybalt overhears his infatuated couplets:

> *Tyb.* This, by his voice, should be a Montague.
>   Fetch me my rapier, boy. What dares the slave
>   Come hither . . .
>   Now, by the stock and honor of my kin
>   To strike him dead I hold it not a sin. (1.5.54–59)

Tybalt appoints himself as protector of his family's honor and appealing to the head of his house, old Capulet, expects to be answered with similar devotion to the family's interests. Capulet, however, knows nothing bad about Romeo, "a virtuous and well-governed youth" (68). ("Youth" here is obviously not derogatory).

> It is my will, the which if thou respect,
> Show a fair presence and put off these frowns,
> An ill-beseeming semblance for a feast. (72–75).

To his chagrin, Tybalt finds that his well-intentioned notice of Montague's presence is rejected and, further, that *his* demeanor is criticized. He has assumed that his uncle shared his concern for the family's honor and that he himself had a special responsibility to redress the injury of Romeo's presence. Injured self-esteem is a potent cause of anger and motive for revenge,

---

9. Tybalt is the son of Lady Capulet's brother (3.1.146) and Capulet is his uncle by marriage; he has a younger brother, Valentine, who has no part in the play. The Capulets themselves have no other child than Juliet (3.5.164–165). The point needs to be established because (1) with the death of Tybalt and later of Juliet, Capulet loses his heirs as the Montagues lose theirs on Romeo's death, ensuring the extinction of both households; and (2) Shakespeare may have intended Tybalt to regard himself as having a special responsibility to protect the family's honor. (Shakespeare establishes the general agedness of the guests—except for Juliet and the mute Rosaline—by Capulet's conversation at the beginning of 1.5.)

as Campbell ([1930] 1970) pointed out for *King Lear*.[10] With rising anger, Tybalt sets his judgment against his uncle's and reacts forcefully:

> *Tyb.* It fits when such a villain is a guest.
>   I'll not endure him. (75–76)

Capulet's response is immediate and predictable: Old men, as the conventional theories of character have it and experience confirms, are quickly moved to anger when the young go against their will.

> *Cap.*   He shall be endured.
>   What, goodman boy? I say he shall, go to!
>   Am I the master here, or you? go to!
>   You'll not endure him! God shall mend my soul,
>   You'll make a mutiny among my guests!
>   You will set cock-a-hoop! you'll be the man!
> *Tyb.* Why, uncle, 'tis a shame.
> *Cap.*   Go to, go to,
>   You are saucy boy. (76–83)

Capulet's speeches here are marked rhetorically by the short periods and the profusion of exclamation and interrogation marks (mostly supplied by the modern editor). The ten verses of Capulet's previous speech (1.5.65–74) advising Tybalt to tolerate Romeo's presence contain five periods (here defined as sequences of words terminated by a semicolon, a period, an exclamation mark, or a question mark) of an average length of sixteen words. The first ten verses of Capulet's following speech (1.5.76–85) contain fourteen periods, averaging 5.42 words in length. An actor does not have to supply passionate intensity to these lines: Shakespeare's language virtually directs him to deliver the speeches in the appropriate manner.

Rendered economically by Shakespeare's mastery, the psychological mechanism that drives Tybalt's speeches here is readily recognized. Tybalt assumes that he and Capulet share a distaste for Romeo's presence at the feast and expects that Capulet would respond to the notice of Montague's attendance with pejorative speeches about Romeo, language like his own. But Capulet responds in a different register. The breakdown in the negotiation of a common style of speaking occurs when Tybalt refuses to take Capulet's lead, and it is represented dramatically by Capulet's resort to abusive speech, particularly the marked use of the usually denotative *boy*.

Capulet calls Tybalt *goodman boy* and *saucy boy* and mocks his pretensions

---

10. Describing an Elizabethan philosophy of anger descended from Aristotle (*Rhetorica*, 1378a, 31–34), Campbell uses words that apply well to Tybalt:

> We see [him] demonstrating what we know to have been an accepted principle, that a man is angered by an injury to his self-esteem, that he is soonest angered when that respect in which he has thought himself most worthy seems to be disregarded, that he is soonest angry . . . with those who have previously treated him becomingly and now change, and with those who do not appreciate his kindness. (Campbell [1930]1970: 185–186)

to manhood: *You'll be the man!* (81), thus explicitly marking out the domain of his insults.[11] In Capulet's eyes, and in his speeches, Tybalt has fallen from the prized state of manhood to unprivileged boyhood. Shakespeare elsewhere remarks of Cupid, *his disgrace is to be called boy, but his glory is to subdue men* (*Love's Labor's Lost*, 1.2.179–182). Humiliated publicly, in the midst of his kinsmen, but unable to challenge the patriarch of his family, Tybalt cannot subdue men. He can, however, challenge his coeval, Romeo, who supplied the occasion of his disgrace.

> *Tyb.* Patience perforce with willful choler meeting
> Makes my flesh tremble in their different greeting.
> I will withdraw, but this intrusion shall,
> Now seeming sweet, convert to bitt'rest gall. (89–92)

The quatrain form and the alliteration and assonance that contribute to the intensity of this speech mark its significance for the prosecution of the action. Within a short time, Benvolio and Mercutio know of Tybalt's letter to Romeo challenging him to a duel (2.4.6–7). Interspersed with scenes of romantic lyricism, the tragedy now surges toward its catastrophe.

On his third and final appearance in the play (in 3.1), Tybalt addresses Benvolio and Mercutio correctly (and neutrally) as *gentlemen* (38). Although the play is set in Verona, Shakespeare observed his usual practice of establishing the ranks and familial relationship of the characters with the terms familiar to his London audiences: He did not attempt to supply an Italian veneer with such terms as *signior*. Consequently, the speeches are sprinkled with the common terms of address: *sir, sirrah, my lord, lady, madam, nurse* (for the Nurse) and *father* (for Friar Lawrence), as well as *nephew, niece, uncle, cousin, mother,* and *daughter* often used vocatively between relatives. Such expressions, like Tybalt's *gentlemen* are the tokens of common civility and relationship and therefore are usually not marked. However, on Romeo's entrance Tybalt applies to him in person the derogatory epithet by which he earlier described Romeo three times, the characterization that Capulet rejected: *Romeo . . . thou art a villain* (60–61). Moreover, Mercutio passes on to Romeo the even more strongly marked term by which Capulet so humiliatingly addressed him, challenging him to fight with *boy* (66). The markedness of this word derives first from the dramatic circumstances of its application to Tybalt in 1.5 as well as the contrast with the socially correct term of address used to the other young men in this scene. From the beginning of their exchange here Romeo and Tybalt were talking at cross purposes: Tybalt wanted Romeo to fight him and Romeo wanted Tybalt to regard him as a member of his family (on account of his marriage to Juliet in the previous scene). The use of *boy* here then probably marks the boundary of Tybalt's willingness to negotiate with Romeo, but we cannot be sure. Romeo's conse-

11. G. B. Evans remarks that "*goodman boy* is a double-barreled insult to Tybalt, *goodman* being a title inferior to that of gentleman." (Riverside 1974: 77 note)

quent soft reply infuriates Mercutio who draws on Tybalt, bringing about his own death. At last Romeo, a reluctant revenger, fights Tybalt:

> [*Rom.*] Now, Tybalt, take the "villain" back again
> That late thou gavest me. . . . (3.1.125–126).

The modern editor makes the markedness of the expression transparent in his text.[12] Initially linked with *boy* in scene 1.5, its force continues through the play:

> *Tyb.* Thou wretched boy, that didst consort him here,
> Shalt with him hence.
> *Rom.*   This shall determine that.
> *They fight; Tybalt falls.* (130–131)

There remains only one more significant use of *boy* to notice, a coda to the plot line of Tybalt's revenge. The *boy* Romeo received from Tybalt at 3.1.129 before the duel, he passes on to Paris as he seeks entrance to the Capulet family tomb.

> [*Par.*] Stop thy unhallowed toil, vile Montague!
> Can vengeance be pursued further than death?
> Condemned villain, I do apprehend thee.
> Obey and go with me, for thou must die.
> *Rom.* I must indeed, and therefore came I thither.
> Good gentle youth, tempt not a desp'rate man. (5.3.54–59)

Once more addressed as *villain* (56), Romeo returns *good gentle youth* (59, *youth* 61) to the challenger, whom he does not recognize.[13] But when Romeo is brought to the point of fighting, in his speech the gentle youth is demoted to a mere boy: *Then have at thee, boy!* (70).

THE USE OF "BOY" AND "VILLAIN"

The distribution of *boy* and *villain* in the play, particularly their collocation in crucial episodes, demonstrates that their usage is marked by design rather than by statistical accident. *Villain* in particular occurs seventeen times in the play. It is first used of Capulet by Montague in Tybalt's presence, applied four times to Romeo by Tybalt, and it is twice rejected or returned to Tybalt by Romeo (in 3.1, where also Mercutio uses it twice, once neutrally and once of Tybalt). On learning of Tybalt's death at Romeo's hands, Juliet debates with herself the respective shares of Tybalt's and Romeo's villany in 3.2, using the term three times, and again with Lady Capulet in 3.5, where the term occurs four times in three verses:

12. The same editor notes of *villain* that it is "A very serious insult demanding reprisal, carrying not only the sense of 'depraved scoundrel' but undertones of 'low-born fellow.'" (Evans 1984: 123)

13. Romeo's reference to himself as "man" (59) is generic and neutral in the context.

[*La. Cap.*] . . . the villain lives which slaughter'd him.
    Jul. What villain, madam?
  La. Cap. That same villain Romeo.
    Jul. [*Aside.*] Villain and he be many miles asunder. — (3.5.79–81)

Like others of her clan, Juliet knows how important names are: It was she who first raised the question of nominal value.[14] Finally, as I just mentioned, *villain* is coupled with *boy* in the last scene of the play.[15] In this play, then, *villain* is not a general term of abuse but, rather, a marked one.

CONSIDERATION OF "CONTEXT" IN DRAMA

Whether or not the foregoing discussion correctly illustrates the application of the markedness model to a literary work, it does raise larger issues that deserve consideration. The social context in which the early modern playwright conducts his "conversation" with the reader or spectator is rhetorical. (By "social" I mean the whole complex of factors that govern the relationship of an author and his public in a particular time.) More narrowly, his linguistic choices are constrained by the initial choice of genre, as was foreshadowed earlier by the initial mention of the negotiation principle. By undertaking to write *The Most Excellent Lamentable Tragedie, of Romeo and Juliet* (to give the title of the first, 1599, edition), that is, by selecting the genre of tragedy, Shakespeare undertook to make certain linguistic choices. He knew also that those among his audience who cared would have certain stylistic expectations. As well as the decorum of character that I already mentioned, there is decorum of language: speech or style—register in a sense. The style of speech is expected to be appropriate both to the social status of the character and also to the specific context, emotional, dramatic, and so on. A play by one of Shakespeare's early contemporaries affords a striking illustration of stylistic variation. In Thomas Kyd's *The Spanish Tragedy* (1587?) the elderly Lord Marshall (chief judge) Hieronimo laments the murder of his son in highly wrought formal verses:

> O eyes, no eyes, but fountains fraught with tears;
> O life, no life, but lively form of death;
> O world, no world, but mass of public wrongs,
> Confus'd and fill'd with murder and misdeeds;
> [*17 verses omitted*]

---

14. In fact, an important question in the play for the Capulets is precisely what name Romeo should bear: hence Juliet says, *O, be some other name! / What's in a name? That which we call a rose / By any other word would smell as sweet; / So Romeo would, were he not Romeo call'd, / Retain that dear perfection which he owes / Without that title. Romeo, doff thy name, / And for thy name, which is no part of thee, / Take all myself.* (1.2.42–49).

15. To summarize, *villain* occurs at 1.1.79, 1.5.63, 1.5.65, 1.5.75, 3.1.61, 3.1.64, 3.1.94, 3.1.102, 3.1.125, 3.2.79, 3.2.100, 3.2.101, 3.5.79, 3.5.80, 3.5.81, and 5.3.56.

> Eyes, life, world, heavens, hell, night, and day,
> See, search, shew, send, some man, some mean, that
>   may— *A letter falleth.*(Edwards [1959] 1969:3.2.1–4, 22–23).

But when a letter falls in his path, surprised and suspicious, his style of speech alters remarkably:

> What's here? A letter? tush! it is not so:
> A letter written to Hieronimo. (24–25).

Similarly (returning to *Romeo and Juliet*), though the abrupt change in Capulet's speech in 1.5 with its short, angry phrases is stylistically significant, that does not mark it for auditors or readers: It is the appropriate style of speech for an angry man and therefore should be considered the unmarked choice.[16] Stylistic variation, therefore, may not invariably produce markedness although, as in this instance, it may be remarkable. That is, variation is only marked when it brings in a style that is unexpected or inappropriate for the relationship depicted.

DO DRAMATIC CHARACTERS MAKE CHOICES?

Not all the speeches in plays are conversations, but the conversations are the obvious site for application of the markedness model. Nevertheless, anyone who analyzes conversations in plays must be uncomfortably aware of the influence of the author. The exchanges between speakers that make ordinary conversations worth overhearing become, in light of the negotiation principle, curiously uninteresting. The exchanges are not dynamic for the speakers except within the scope predetermined by their creator. In fact, they are not conversations at all but, rather, the representations of conversations, in plays selectively scripted with greater or lesser skill by the playwright. Generally, they lack the mumblings, false starts, hesitations, irrelevancies, repetitions, syntactical errors, or confusions of conversations in ordinary life, and rarely do characters on a stage speak at the same time as other speakers or interrupt the speeches of other characters. The dramatic speakers are not "rational actors" in the usual sense, possessing the possibility to make linguistic choices as conversations continue, but, rather, they are puppets whose linguistic constructions are governed by such matters as the initial choice of genre, the principle of decorum of language within the general theory of genre, and the specific purposes of the playwright.

Consideration of the relevance of such matters may also bring to question, in their relation to early modern literature, principles as fundamental as Grice's (1975) maxim of quantity. They also identify fruitful areas of investigation

---

16. What would mark Capulet's speech, difficult though it might be to conceive it, would be an orotund, expansive manner of speech employing long periods and ornamental figures.

beneficial to students of linguistics and literature alike.[17] For instance, rhetorical embellishment and ornamented speech were thought desirable for a large part of European history. The plain style *is* a style in early modern practice. Consequently, there may be a paradoxical reversal of modern readers' expectations, so speeches where Grice's maxim pertains may be strongly marked for a modern reader. For instance, when Hamlet declares that he had never loved Ophelia (*Hamlet*, 3.1.118), Ophelia sheds her previously artificial style of speaking: *I was the more deceiv'd* (119), one of Shakespeare's telling "quiet" speeches. More pertinently, in *Romeo and Juliet*, on learning the false news of Juliet's death, her usually prolix lover speaks only the plain but memorable *Is it e'en so? Then I defy you, stars!* (5.1.24). On the other hand, even though readers or spectators might form some expectation—from their understanding of the characters in the plays—of the ways in which Ophelia or Romeo would react to those speeches whose function is largely informational, it is difficult to conceive that spectators or readers could have expectations of the style of expression of their speeches. Readers may form expectations of the actions of speakers in a play and judge them more or less appropriate accordingly, but they cannot form expectations about the *specific* form (language) of the speeches unless the play was written in language so thoroughly conventional or trite as to lack any tinge of originality, individuality, or unexpectedness. Humiliation or grief can be expressed in different ways even within the convention of decorum of speech. In fact, the idea of reader's expectations, though acceptable on a broad level from a shared knowledge of generic or rhetorical conventions, may not readily be invoked in less-expansive dramatic situations which are, as established, controlled by the playwright without mediation (save in his own mind during the process of composition) with spectators or readers. Whether expectation functions on the microlevel of individual speeches and variations of style in early modern plays is questionable, particularly if expectations are formed from readers' understanding of intentions, whether the playwright's or the individual speaker's, as revealed by the prevailing register and such of the dramatic speeches alone.

Moreover, the embeddedness of speeches within the play complicates the analysis of markedness because, more often than not, considerations broader than the local contexts of speeches determine the shapes they take and therefore the identification of markedness. In ordinary conversations, as linguists recognize, facial expression, physical posture and gesture, and verbal delivery contribute to communication and, therefore, to a degree, to verbal negotiations and markedness. In drama, markedness is supplied by such performance means (i.e., nonverbal means) as physical action (movement, stage position, gesture), as well as by lighting, sound effects and accompanying

---

17. To mention existing studies of these matters would divert the thrust of this chapter, which is essentially literary rather than linguistic.

music, and the use of properties and costume, and a theatrically experienced reader cannot escape their influence. The extent to which such considerations affect the analysis of a printed text of speeches written for performance on a stage is uncertain: The relationship of markedness and the semiotics of performance might deserve some examination. I make these remarks with the tentativeness that befits one who has limited knowledge of recent linguistic studies but, nevertheless, great interest in their outcome.

REFERENCES

Campbell, Lily. 1930. *Shakespeare's tragic heroes: slaves of passion.* Cambridge: Cambridge University Press. Reprint, London: Methuen, 1970.

Edwards, Philip (ed.). 1959. In Revels plays. *The Spanish tragedy: Thomas Kyd.* London: Methuen.

Evans, G. B. (ed.) 1984. *Romeo and Juliet.* New Cambridge ed. Cambridge: Cambridge University Press.

Grice, H. P. 1975. Logic and conversation. In *Syntax and semantics, vol. 3,* ed. Peter Cole and Jerry L. Morgan, 41–58. New York: Academic Press.

Herrick, Marvin T. 1950. *Comic theory in the sixteenth century.* Urbana: University of Illinois Press. Reprint, 1964.

Howard-Hill, T. H. 1996. U and non-U: class and discourse level in *Othello.* In *Shakespeare's universe: Renaissance ideas and conventions: essays in honor of W. R. Elton,* ed. John M. Mucciolo [and others], 175–186. Aldershot, Hertsfordshire: Scolar Press.

Myers-Scotton, Carol. 1993. *Social motivations for codeswitching: evidence from Africa.* Oxford: Clarendon Press.

Riverside Shakespeare. 1974. Textual ed. G. Blakemore Evans. Boston: Houghton Mifflin.

Spevack, Marvin. 1969. *A complete and systematic concordance to the works of Shakespeare.* Vol. 4: *A concordance to the complete works: "A"-Hilding.* Hildesheim, Germany: G. Olms.

— III —

Stylistic Choices in Spoken English

— 8 —

Markedness and Styleswitching in Performances by African American Drag Queens

RUSTY BARRETT

THIS CHAPTER CONSIDERS the ways in which African American drag queens (AADQs) use language style in their performances, particularly the ways in which they use choices that would be considered "marked" under the markedness model (Myers-Scotton [Scotton] 1988; 1993; chapter 2, this volume). After discussing *drag queen* as a social category, I consider the concept of *style*, and some of the confusion surrounding the terminology used for linguistic varieties. I argue that the Markedness Model provides a useful tool for examining differences related to the notions of *dialect, register*, and *genre*. Finally, I use examples from AADQ speech to demonstrate how AADQs use both unmarked and marked choices as rhetorical devices in their performances to highlight the instability of social categories related to gender, ethnicity, class, and sexuality.

DISTINGUISHING DRAG QUEENS

First, it is important to clarify the meaning of *drag queen*. Basically, the social category of drag queens is gay men who dress as women, especially those who perform in gay bars. As a social group, drag queens are often confused with other groups: transsexuals, transvestites, cross-dressers, and female impersonators.[1] *Transsexuals* are individuals who feel that the sex they were assigned at birth does not correspond with their true gender identity. The term *transvestite* is used to refer to those who wear the clothing of the opposite sex (i.e., opposite from the sex they were assigned at birth). Unlike transsexuals,

---

1. The terms *transgender person* or *transgenderist* are often used as umbrella terms for various social groups. (For discussion see Bullough and Bullough 1993; Devor 1989; MacKenzie 1994; and Feinberg 1996.)

transvestites (or cross-dressers) categorize themselves as members of the gender corresponding to their assigned sex. *Cross-dressing* refers to anyone who wears the clothing associated with the opposite sex/gender, regardless of their sexual orientation. Neither transsexualism nor transvestitism/cross-dressing is a specifically gay/lesbian phenomenon. In contrast, *drag* is specifically part of lesbian and gay culture. Although it is possible to say that heterosexuals such as Milton Berle or Dustin Hoffman (in *Tootsie*) are "in drag," these men would not be considered drag queens.

The term *female impersonator* is closer to drag queen than any of the other terms considered here. Many professional drag queens refer to themselves as female impersonators or illusionists as a means of distancing themselves from nonprofessional drag queens. For example, one participant in Esther Newton's ethnography of gay female impersonators said that the term *drag queen* sounded "sort of like a street fairy puttin' a dress on" (1972: 17). However, female impersonators generally attempt to produce the illusion of being a "real" woman, usually performing as a specific celebrity (e.g., Marilyn Monroe, Liza Minnelli, or Cher).

Professional drag queens typically have their own unique persona (as opposed to only reproducing the persona of a single celebrity). In addition, most drag queens generally make no pretense about not being male but, rather, use their performances as a means of playing on the irony of crossing genders. Finally, although there are self-described female impersonators who claim to be heterosexual, drag queens are openly (and proudly) gay.

AADQ performances generally include lip synching to records and emceeing a variety of shows, including lip synching by other drag queens, male strippers, or talent shows. The emcee usually presents comedic monologues that involve interaction with the audience. Performances often encode direct information about the relationship between language (and performance as a whole) and social and cultural issues. As Turner noted, the relationship between performance genres and society is "reciprocal and reflexive—in the sense that the performance is often a critique, direct or veiled, of the social life it grows out of" (1986: 22). This is true of AADQ performances, which often present critiques of social structure and are often highly political. As Briggs argues, "performers are not passive, unreflecting creatures who simply respond to the dictates of tradition or the physical and social environment. They interpret both traditions and social settings, actively transforming both in the course of their performances" (1988: 7). Building on the work of Bauman (1975) and Hymes (1981), Briggs (1988: 8–9) notes that one of the primary components of performance is the responsibility of the performer to his or her audience. The audience evaluates a performer not only on the content of the speech but also on the performer's communicative competence in accordance with the criteria for a specific performance genre. A primary goal of drag performance is to highlight mismatches between the performer's "perceived" identity (as a woman) and her "biographical" identity (as a man). A successful drag performance is dependent on the ability to use language in a way that demonstrates that categories based on gender, ethnicity, class, and sexuality are indeed performances (cf. Butler 1993) and cannot be taken as obvious or constant reflections of some "authentic" identity.

DRAG QUEENS IN THIS STUDY

The drag queens in this study all belong to the class of *glam(our) queens*, that is, drag queens who attempt a highly stylish image of glamour, dressing up like movie stars at the Academy Awards or contestants in the evening gown competition at a beauty pageant. "Glam" queens typically wear evening gowns with lots of beads or fringe, exaggerated jewelry (such as big earrings or wide flashy bracelets), and big-haired black wigs.[2] Their clothing is often fairly revealing, with very short skirts or high slit dresses and bare arms. Although they dress in a way to accentuate their ability to look "feminine," they often undermine that image of femininity in their performances. Thus, instead of producing humor through their appearance, they play off the irony that a man could create the believable image of a woman.

Most of the language examined in this chapter is taken from public performances by AADQs in gay bars in Texas. From January to May 1993, I observed between six and ten AADQ performances per month. In addition to dealing with drag queens in Texas, some of the data in this study come from television appearances by RuPaul, a drag queen originally from Atlanta whose dance song "Supermodel (You'd better work!)" became very popular in early 1993. RuPaul recorded two albums, appeared in several films, and was on numerous television shows and even wrote her[3] autobiography (RuPaul 1995). She currently hosts her own talk show on the VH-1 cable channel. In this chapter, data involving RuPaul are taken from two talk show appearances and a speech given at the 1993 March on Washington.

LANGUAGE STYLE AND THE MARKEDNESS MODEL

I take *style* to be an overarching term for all linguistic varieties below the level of *language*, namely the types of variation that Ferguson (1994) categorizes as *dialect, register,* and *genre.*[4] Ferguson states that "identifying markers of language structure and language use" (1994: 18–21) set apart one dialect from another, one register from another, and one genre from another. Among

2. Unlike all of the other drag queens in this study, RuPaul almost always wears a blond wig.

3. I generally use feminine pronouns to refer to drag queens, especially in drag. The use of *he* to refer to a drag queen may be insulting as it insinuates that her performance is somehow flawed. (For a study of uses of *she* among gay men in general, see Rudes and Healy 1979.)

4. Here I depart from Ferguson's use of the term *conversational variation* in his definitions of variation. For me, conversation is a particular mode of discourse (or genre) included under the cover term style.

themselves, the three varieties differ in this way: (1) dialects distinguish one *social group* from another; (2) registers distinguish one *communication situation* from another; and (3) genres distinguish one *message type* from another. I follow Ferguson in distinguishing the three types of varieties in this way.

Whether a given set of linguistic variables (on any of the levels of phonology, morphosyntax, or lexicon) is classified as dialect, register, or genre is determined by the discourse (i.e., through usage). For example, for speakers with multiple group identities (i.e., with more than one dialect), a given dialect may be reserved for speech in a particular communication situation (e.g., with particular interlocutors). However, because that dialect is also a feature of the situation, that dialect functions as a register for those speakers. This means that in different interactions the terms *dialect, register,* and *genre* may apply to the *same* set of linguistic variables. For this reason, I use the term *style* to represent all the sets of linguistic variables included in any of the three categories. Thus, I employ the following definition of *style:*

> Style: The set of linguistic variables that are characteristic of a given dialect, register, or genre.

This definition is similar to Ferguson's use of the term *variety;* however, for many researchers, *variety* includes language as well as dialect, register, and genre. For this reason, I prefer *style* for my purposes. Recognizing style as a cover term for dialect, register, and genre enables us to make distinctions in speaker variation more explicit. Such an interpretation contrasts with Labov's (1972) use of the term *style.* He used it to refer to a continuum between "formal" and "informal" speech and operationalized the continuum in terms of specific tasks (or genres), such as talking in an interview situation, or reading word lists or narrative materials. He also brought in the notion of social setting (or communication setting in Ferguson's definition of register). Thus, for Labov, register and genre were collapsed into a single dimension of "formality," which was then used to compare speech across social groups (dialects). The lack of explicit distinctions between the categories of dialect, register, and genre and the vagueness of distinctions such as formal/informal reduces the usefulness of *style* in this sense as an analytical concept. Similar problems arise in research that examines register in terms of "oral" versus "literature" genres (e.g. Finnegan and Biber 1994).

STRUCTURAL CHARACTERISTICS OF DIALECTS, REGISTERS, GENRES

As Ferguson notes, dialects, registers, and genres differ "in the degree of cohesiveness they show as systems and the sharpness of the boundaries between them" (1994: 23). Thus, these three systems, which I consider together under the rubric *style,* consist of linguistic variables that form "fuzzy" sets, and the degree to which variables belong to a given set must be considered before meaningful discussions of style can proceed. However, as already noted, overlap is inevitable such that one linguistic variable is found across more than one type of style. For example, Sherzer (1989) points out that some verb suffixes in Kuna occur exclusively in specific genres, whereas others occur in everyday speech in general but with greater frequency in a given genre.

Certainly, the more a variable is restricted to a particular style, the higher its degree of membership in that style will be. For example, compare two variables from African American Vernacular English (AAVE) in the Southern United States: the copula verb *be* with continuative or durative aspect (e.g., *I be working there for five years*) and double modals (e.g., *might could* as in *She might could do that*). Both forms have been attributed to AAVE. Yet, compared to double modals, this use of *be* would be the more salient (and less "fuzzy") marker of the AAVE style set, at least in the Southern United States, as it has less overlap with the speech of whites.

Because they are more salient, variables with the more exclusive membership in the set of variables defining a particular style are typically more useful in studying the ways in which speakers use styles, although combinations of low membership variables might also produce a salient index of identity. Dialects that are more distinct from one another have fewer salient, high membership variables in common. There is a continuum from very similar dialects (e.g., "men's language" versus "women's language" in English), which will have many variables in common, to distinct, unrelated languages, which may have no variables at all in common.

MOTIVATIONS FOR SWITCHING BETWEEN STYLES

Myers-Scotton's markedness model (Scotton 1988; 1993; chapter 2 of this volume) analyzes switches between different codes (languages or styles) of a given language based on the relationship between the code and the rights and obligations sets (RO sets) indexed by the code. Sets of linguistic variables may be seen as indexing the particular RO set associated with a given group identity, situational context, or speech event. Thus, individual dialects, registers, and genres index particular RO sets. Within the markedness model, each type of interaction has an unmarked RO set. According to the model, "the unmarked RO set is derived from whatever situational features are salient for the community for that interaction type" (Myers-Scotton 1993: 84). Paramount among those features are the identities of participants. Speakers use codes to index the RO sets that are unmarked for a given interaction or to attempt to change or explore the nature of the RO set present in an interaction. Thus, the RO set is dynamic: At the outset of an interaction an unmarked RO set is in place, but it is open to change as well.

In regard to motivations for codeswitching, Myers-Scotton (1993) claims that there are four major types of switches: sequential unmarked code switching, codeswitching itself as the unmarked choice, codeswitching as the marked choice, and codeswitching as an exploratory choice. These are described in the discussion that follows. By analyzing all switching as one of these four types, the markedness model enables us to explain the choices of stylistic variables speakers make from their linguistic repertoires to achieve specific goals in the course of particular interactions.

In addition, however, the markedness model could provide a means for exploring the relationships and distinctions among the fuzzy sets comprising style: dialect, register, and genre. For example, consider sequential unmarked codeswitching, which refers to switches from one code to another as unmarked when the unmarked RO set changes within an interaction. That is, with a change in situational factors, the unmarked RO set changes, and with this change comes a change in unmarked code to index the new RO set. This type of switching would be predicted for both dialects and registers. For dialect switching, sequential switches from one dialect to another as unmarked would be predicted when there are changes in the group identities that are salient; for register switching, sequential unmarked switching would be predicted when there are changes in the situational context.

The second type of switching, codeswitching as the unmarked choice, would be predicted to occur with dialects. This type of switching consists of a pattern of switching back and forth between two styles in the same conversation, with the overall pattern carrying the message of multiple identities for the speakers. However, such switching is not predicted when styles function as registers. By definition, a register occurs in a particular situational context and therefore we cannot speak of a change of register without a change in situation. Switching as the unmarked choice takes place *without a change of situation* and therefore cannot involve registers. However, we would predict that the third and fourth types of switching, marked switching and exploratory switching, would occur with register rather than dialect in the majority of cases. Codeswitching as a marked choice is a switch to a code that is not the unmarked choice for the current RO set and therefore is a call for another RO set in its place. Codeswitching as an exploratory choice occurs when an unmarked RO set (and therefore an unmarked choice) is not clear. In such cases, speakers use switching to propose alternate choices as candidates for an unmarked choice and thereby as an index for the RO set which they favor.

I suspect that all types of switching can occur between genres. For example, the inclusion of a personal narrative style in the academic writing of some feminist theorists would have originally been a marked change from one genre to another (within a given work); such an inclusion might be seen as an attempt to alter the exclusion of women from the RO set indexed by academic writing. Over time, however, this type of switching has become conventionalized, making switches between personal narrative and more academic styles an unmarked norm in the writing of some scholars. Unmarked sequences of genre switching should be quite common, such as moving from jokes to stories within the course of a conversation. When the appropriateness of a given genre is unclear, or the responsiveness of an audience is uncertain, speakers might use exploratory genre switching as well.

The asymmetry of dialect and register switching, within the terms of the markedness model, reflects the fact that expressions of a particular identity are often reserved for specific situational contexts. The fact that the markedness model has (unintentionally) encoded the division between dialects and registers provides external support for the model, suggesting that the model might provide a principled basis for studying the ways in which dialects, registers, and genres relate to one another in actual use.

STYLISTIC CHOICES OF AFRICAN AMERICAN DRAG QUEENS

Although AADQs usually employ a wide variety of styles, three basic styles recur in their speech, reflecting membership in three different social groups. These are an AAVE style, a gay male style, and a style based on stereotypes of white women's speech. The AAVE and gay male styles index the identities of AADQs as African Americans and as gay men, respectively. The *white woman style* indexes their identity as drag queens while also indexing the RO set associated with actual white women and implying a variety of social attributes associated with white women, including stereotypical notions of femininity and glamour (cf. Barrett 1994).

When used by AADQs, each of these styles reflects a stereotype of the linguistic behavior for the prototypical member of the social groups indexed by the style. As Le Page and Tabouret-Keller note, when speakers construct their identities through language "what they recognize and imitate are stereotypes they have created for themselves" (1985: 142). As linguists, we often pride ourselves on the fact that we study language as it is actually used, often attempting to demonstrate the falseness of stereotyped attitudes. When discussing choices of linguistic style, however, it is important to remember that speakers often base their linguistic behavior on stereotypes (as they do not have our privileged access to detailed sociolinguistic studies). Thus, each of the styles I am presenting does not reflect the *natural* speech of any actual white woman, gay man, or African American. Rather, the styles reflect prevailing stereotypes concerning the speech of members of these three social groups and are used by AADQs to index the RO sets of those social groups.

Because each of these styles indexes a social group, each constitutes dialects in Ferguson's (1994) framework.[5] Nevertheless, because each can serve to index a particular situation, each also can be considered as a register as

5. Traditionally, style and dialects are differentiated as follows. *Dialect* is used for specific social groups (differentiated along ethnic, regional, and sometimes class divisions). *Dialect* also often connotes an opposition to the *standard dialect*. Typically two styles differ from each other by fewer linguistic variables than two dialects do.

well as a dialect (depending on usage). This is why I use the broader term *style* as a cover term. As is often the case with styles, there is a certain amount of overlap in the sets of linguistic variables making up these three styles. Although I will not arrange the variables in a given style in a hierarchy of "salience," it is important to keep in mind the fact that the degree of indexicality is not constant across variables. In addition, it should be noted that not all variables will be present in any given style at any given moment (and the presence/absence of variables will not be constant across speakers). Speakers may even choose a subset of linguistic variables from a style to index specific attributes associated with speakers of that style. For example, Sunaoshi (1995) demonstrated that Japanese women in managerial positions choose particular features (but not the complete set of variables) from the "Motherese" style in Japanese to index the authoritative status of mothers. By not using the full set of variables associated with Motherese, these women are able to assert their authority without fully indexing the powerful differential between mothers and children (which might be seen as condescending to their employees).

In the data that follow, I generally classify a particular utterance as belonging to a given style according to the following (rather arbitrary) criteria: (1) a linguistic variable represents a particular style if the variable's distribution does not overlap with it in some other style and (2) a particular style is present if two linguistic variables from that style are present that do not both overlap with another style (although they may each individually overlap with two different styles). The basic features of each of these styles are outlined in the following sections. Those features characterizing the white woman style come from Lakoff (1975), because Lakoff's description reflects a stereotyped image of how white women should speak (cf. Barrett 1994; Bucholtz and Hall 1995). The features associated with stereotypes of gay men's speech are those I have discussed elsewhere (Barrett, 1997); they are compiled from a variety of sources (Lakoff 1975; Rodgers [1972]1979; Hayes 1981; Walters 1981; Goodwin 1989; Moran 1991; Gaudio 1994). The features of AAVE have been widely studied by linguists; the list presented here is primarily that of Walters (1992). Wyatt provides a similar list (1994).

In the remainder of this chapter, I present examples that demonstrate the ways in which AADQs choose particular stylistic variables from this repertoire to enhance their performances.

White Woman Style (Lakoff 1975: 53–56)

Specific lexical items related to their specific interests, generally relegated to them as "woman's work": *dart* (in sewing) and specific color terms (*ecru, magenta*)

"Empty" adjectives like *divine, charming, cute . . .*

Question features for declaratives: tag questions (*It's so hot, isn't it?*), rising intonation in statement contexts (*What's your name, dear? Mary Smith?*)

The use of hedges of various kinds (e.g., *well, y'know, kinda*)

The intensive use of *so*

Hypercorrect grammar, superpolite forms, and euphemisms: women are not supposed to talk rough.

Women don't tell jokes.

Gay Male Speech Style (Barrett 1997)

The use of lexical items and structures included as part of Lakoff's women's language, e.g., specific color terms and the "empty" adjectives (*marvelous, adorable,* etc.), as well as hedges and boosters.

The use of a wider pitch range for intonational contours than in speech of straight men.

Hypercorrect pronunciation; the presence of phonologically nonreduced forms and the use of hyperextended vowels (the probable source of the "lisping" stereotype).

The use of lexical items specific to gay language (Rodgers [1972]1979 gives a somewhat dated lexicon of many such expressions).

The use of a H*L intonational contour, often co-occurring with extended vowels (as in *FAAABulous*).

African American Vernacular English (AAVE) Style (Walters 1992)

AAVE Realizations of Standard English Phonological Features :

Interdental fricatives as labiodental fricatives: "teeth" [tʰijf], "other" [ʌvə]

Final consonant reduction: /r/ deletion, "sister" [sIstʰə]; /l/ palatalization or deletion, "all" [ɑ]; /l/ cluster vocalization or reduction, "film" [fIm] or [fI.lm]; unreleased stops as glottal stops, "cat" [kʰæʔ]; cluster simplification, "best" [bɛs]

Intervocalic weakening: /r/ deletion, [v] → [ß] "every" [ɛßij]

Strident cluster metathesis or modification: "ask" [æks], "stray" [ʃtrej]

Prenasal raising of [ɛ] to [I], "pen" [pʰIn]; or lowering to [æ]: "thing" [θæŋ]

Monophthongization of [ai]: "my" [ma]

Stress fronting: "police" [pʰów:lijs]

AAVE Morphological and Lexical Innovations and Realizations of SE Features:

Absence of nonsyllabic inflectional endings: third person singular {-s}, noun plural {-s}, possessive {-s}

Reduction of unstressed syllabic inflections {ing}: [In], or [.n], and {to}: [ə] "going to" [gʌnə]

Lexical verbs as aspect markers: perfective "done," *I done finish my work;*

inceptive "come" *don't come coming in here . . .;* future perfect *be done;* intensive continued progressive *be steady;* habitual copula: *she be nervous* vs. *she nervous* (non-habitual) (Green 1994)

Negation: multiple negation, *didn't do nothing; ain't* as negative of forms of *to* be and *to have*

"You" plural distinctions: *y'all* and *y'all's*

Special intonation patterns, e.g., H*HL in rhetorical speech

CONTEXT AND UNMARKED CHOICES

For in-group communication outside performances, AADQs typically exhibit styleswitching as the unmarked norm. This switching consists of all three of the styles discussed here, mirroring the fact that AADQs are all African American, gay men, and drag queens. Thus, by unmarked switching between styles, they index these three aspects of their group identities.

This continuous switching between the three styles is typical of AADQ speech, so much so that the styles may even co-occur, with phonological variables from one style overlapping with syntactic variables from another style. In the utterance in [1] (from RuPaul on the *Arsenio Hall Show*), the phonology is that of the white woman style (i.e., it is typical of Standard English, but not the hypercorrect pronunciation sometimes associated with the speech of African American women or gay men). The syntax, however, is typical of the AAVE style.

[1] You know, in my mind's eye I always been a superstar, you know. And nobody couldn't tell me no differen[t].

The white woman phonology occurs up until the final word *different*, which is pronounced [dIfrIn] (i.e., without the final [t]). After the word *different*, the speech continues in AAVE style, so that the switch actually occurs before the end of the sentence. This meshing of styles is possible because of the fuzzy boundaries between styles and points to a problem that was not addressed by purely quantitative studies of language style. A quantitative analysis would most likely misanalyze the utterance in [1] as belonging to only one style, depending on whether the coding was for syntactic or phonological characteristics. This suggests that possible cases of styleswitching as the unmarked norm may have gone unnoticed because the styles were studied as closed sets that can be easily isolated from one another.

Consider the following example, a speech given by RuPaul at the 1993 March on Washington for Lesbian, Gay and Bisexual Rights:

[2] Speech given by RuPaul

1 Hello America

2 My name's RuPaul

3 Supermodel of the worl[d]

4 [begins chant, audience joins in] Hey . . . Ho . . . Hey . . . Ho . . .
Hey . . . Ho

5 You know people ask me all the time

6 Where I see myself in ten years

7 And I say I see myself in the White House, baby!

8 Miss Thing goes to Washington

9 Can you see it? Wha- we gonna paint the mother pink, OK?

10 We put one president in the White House, I figure you can do it again.

11 Everybody say love! [audience responds, "love!"]

12 Everybody say love! [audience responds again, "love!"]

13 Now drive that down Pennsylvania Avenue!

14 Peace, love and hairgrease!

15 I love you!

In this example, RuPaul moves back and forth between each of the three styles, often allowing the styles to overlap. For this reason, and the fact that the situational context does not change, this type of switching would be referred to as dialect, as a subset of style, switching as the unmarked choice.

RuPaul begins her speech with typical standard, albeit feminized, English pronunciation reflecting the white woman style. The phrase *supermodel of the world*, however, is produced without a final [d] on the word *world*, a form typical of the AAVE style. The chant in line 4 reflects the call–response tradition, a genre often associated with African American preachers (and frequently used by drag queens). After the chant, RuPaul returns to a white woman style up until line 7 and the phrase *in the White House, baby*. This phrase is spoken with an increasingly widening pitch range, typical of the gay male speech style ending with the word *baby* spoken with an extended vowel and long falling (H*L) intonation (typical of the gay male style). In line 8, RuPaul refers to herself as *Miss Thang*, a term that indexes gay male identity and/or African American identity. She pronounces the word *thing* with standard English [I], however, rather than with the [ei] or [æ] vowels typical of both the gay and AAVE pronunciations. Thus, a term related to both gay and African American identity occurs with a "white woman" phonology, letting the various styles overlap. In line 9 the question *Can you see it?* is spoken with a white woman phonology. The phonology then switches to AAVE with the word *mother,* which is pronounced without the final [r] and ends with the exaggerated H*L gay male style intonation on the word *OK*. RuPaul's phonology returns to a white woman style in lines 10 and 11. Although line 11 has white woman phonology, it begins a call–response routine, thus again indexing African American identity. In lines 12 and 13, the intonation becomes more like that found in African American preaching (cf. Queen 1992). Through the use of codeswitching as the unmarked norm, RuPaul uses the speech to simultaneously index her membership in several different social groups.

Even though codeswitching as the unmarked norm is typically used for in-group communication and some performance contexts, a change in the situational context may mean a change in style. In this case, we can say that the performer is switching registers from one context to the next. For example, the table below compares the speech of RuPaul during her first appearances on the *Joan Rivers Show* and on the *Arsenio Hall Show*. These two televised interviews occur about one year apart from each other. The *Arsenio Hall* episode aired in March 1993; the *Joan Rivers* episode aired in May 1994. The *Arsenio Hall* interview was RuPaul's first appearance on national television. Although both were recorded before live audiences, the two programs constitute quite different contexts. The *Arsenio Hall Show* was hosted by an African American male, aired late at night, and was generally targeted to young adults. The *Joan Rivers Show* was hosted by a white woman, aired during the morning, and was generally targeted to women (especially women who do not work outside the home). The differences in context on the two programs can be seen in the stylistic choices made by RuPaul on the two programs. Table 8-1 compares RuPaul's use of the three styles discussed above on each of the two programs. Because the styles overlap a great deal and may co-occur (as already noted above), the table compares utterances (rather than particular phonological or syntactic linguistic variables). The utterances are sorted according to those that occur exclusively in a given style, those in which a switch between two styles occurs or in which two styles overlap, and those in which all three styles occur. The tokens were collected from the first six minutes of the interviews.[6]

On the *Joan Rivers Show*, which has a predominantly white studio audience, RuPaul does not use the AAVE style at all. More than 80% of the time, she uses the white woman style exclusively. This can be seen as a form of accommodation (cf. Giles, Coupland, and Coupland 1991) to the speech of Joan Rivers, an actual white woman. Nevertheless, RuPaul does continue to reference gay identity, demonstrating that drag queen identity must, at the very least, combine some elements of gay male speech with stereotyped women's speech.[7] In contrast, on the *Arsenio Hall Show*, RuPaul used the white woman style exclusively only half of the time and used the AAVE style exclusively 13.3% of the time. Thus, although the white woman style continues to

6. This is the time up until the first commercial break on the *Joan Rivers Show* (in which the entire interview lasts an hour minus commercials). On the *Arsenio Hall Show* the interview was only about ten minutes long in its entirety.

7. For example, as noted by Queen (1997), the actors in the film *To Wong Foo . . . Thanks for Everything, Julie Newmar* do not sound like actual drag queens, largely because they use white women's speech (and in the case of Wesley Snipes, AAVE), but they do not employ gay male speech as would an actual drag queen.

Table 8-1
Stylistic Variation in the Speech of RuPaul
on Two Television Talk Shows

style	Joan Rivers		Arsenio Hall	
	N	%	N	%
WW	70	81.4	38	50.6
GM	8	9.3	7	9.3
AAVE	0	—	10	13.3
WW/GM	8	9.3	6	8
GM/AAVE	0	—	4	5.3
WW/AAVE	0	—	2	2.6
AA/AAVE/GM	0	—	2	2.6
Totals	86	100	75	99.8

WW = white woman style, GM = gay male style, AAVE = African American Vernacular English style, N = number of utterances in a give style or combination of styles.

predominate, it co-occurs with the AAVE style, reflecting the context and shared African American identity between RuPaul and Arsenio Hall. Although some of the stylistic choices on the *Arsenio Hall Show* reflect marked choices, it is clear that the context of the program allows for a much wider range of stylistic choices. Thus, context in a broad sense may influence what is the unmarked choice as well as the general range of stylistic choices possible. Moreover, although switching as the unmarked norm is quite common among AADQs, the styles may also occur in isolation, acting as registers indexing the RO set of a given situation. This is the case with the absence of the AAVE style on the *Joan Rivers Show*, in which RuPaul does not index her African American identity, reflecting the RO set of the interaction with a white woman.

Because each style may work individually, switches between any of the three styles may be a marked switch or a sequence of unmarked styles. Recall that unmarked sequences are predicted with changes in audience, topic, or context. A number of unmarked sequences occur in a specific genre of comedic monologues, that which offers critiques of the political and economic situations of African Americans. In this genre, certain comments may be directed to certain members of society, whether or not they are present in the audience. The white woman style is used to index the power held by whites, whereas the AAVE style is used to index the social situation of African Americans. The following example is from a drag queen performing in a gay bar. The style shifts correspond to a change in topic; as such they are changes in register. The AADQ is posing as a salesperson trying to sell rat traps to the audience. She offers three different types of rat traps for use in three different neighborhoods.

[3] Segment of performance by African American drag queen in Texas

1 OK! What we're gonna talk about is, um, rat traps, um . . .

2 [holds up a mouse trap] This is a rat trap from <name of upper-class white neighborhood>

3 It's made by BMW. It's real compact.

4 It's, thank you . . . <obscured> . . .

5 It's really good, it's very convenient, and there's insurance on it.

6 And this is from <name of same white neighborhood>

7 OK, now for the <name of housing project> . . . [holds up a large rat trap]

8 This rat trap is made by Cadillac, it's a big mother fucker.

9 [holds up a gun] Now for the <name of inner city area>

10 You just don't need no rat trap.

11 Cause those mother fuckers look like dogs out there.

12 Shit!

13 I put in a piece of cheese, the mother fucker told me,

14 "'Next time put in some dog food."

This example begins in the white woman style, switching to the AAVE style beginning in line 7. The sentences in 1–7 all end with a final rising tone, typical of the white woman style (Lakoff's "question intonation"). The phonology and intonation switch to AAVE in line 7, although the first syntactic features of AAVE do not occur until line 10, when the speaker begins to talk about the third location (which has the strongest reputation as a primarily African American low-income area). Thus, the number of linguistic variables used to index African American identity increases when discussing the neighborhood that is the strongest representative of the social conditions stereotypically associated with African Americans. This increase supports the claim of the markedness model that linguistic choices are indices of particular RO sets. In addition, it demonstrates that the density of variables from a particular style may increase with an increased desire to index the RO set corresponding to that style.

In situations of performances or public appearances, the unmarked choice should generally be clear, as the expected audience (and corresponding RO set) is probably known to a speaker before the performance begins. Thus, cases of exploratory switching are quite rare in public performances by AADQs. One example of exploratory switching, however, occurred during the opening moments of RuPaul's appearance on the *Arsenio Hall Show*. This appearance was RuPaul's first on national television and, according to her autobiography (RuPaul 1995: 176–7), she was extremely nervous. At the very beginning of the interview, RuPaul greeted the audience by saying how much she loved their enthusiastic response to her introduction:

[4]

```
      H*L
1 I love it.
        H*    HL
2 I feel aaaall the love . . .
      H*L
3 I love that.
      L            H
4 I feel all the love you're sending me.
```

Here, the first utterance of *I love it* carries a H*L intonational contour that reflects stereotypically gay speech (as in *FAABulous*). In line 2, the word *all* is extended with a H*HL intonation that is particular to certain types of rhetorical speaking in AAVE. This intonational pattern, which Michaels (1986) described in African American children's show-and-tell narratives, contains a high pitch on an extended vowel followed by a shortfall. In addition to indexing African American identity, H*HL indexes the genre public speaking, typically in formal settings, such as sermons (cf. Queen 1992). In line 3, RuPaul returns to the "gay" style of line 1. Finally, in line 4, the final H of the white woman style is used. In this example, the same referential information is conveyed four times, with alternations between each of the three styles. These alternations can be seen as exploratory switching that indexes a variety of possible identities as a means of addressing the variety of potential audience members in the studio and watching on television. Thus, exploratory switching may occur when the unmarked choice is not clear. This is not surprising, considering that these data represent RuPaul's first utterances during her first appearance on national television, a context in which she may not have been certain as to which stylistic choice would be most appropriate.

MARKED CHOICES IN AADQ PERFORMANCES

Although off stage AADQs generally use styleswitching as the unmarked norm for ingroup communication, in their performances they make more use of marked stylistic choices to draw attention to their speech. The performers use language style to play on the audience's assumptions surrounding issues of gender, ethnicity, and sexuality. A major part of the communicative skill displayed in AADQ performances relies on the speaker's ability to anticipate audience members' interpretations of the situation and then to use marked stylistic choices to disrupt the audience's assumptions.

Often, these marked choices reflect instances of *signifyin(g)*, an African American speech event in which the full meaning of an utterance cannot be understood from referential meaning alone (cf. Gates 1988; Mitchell-Kernan 1972).[8] In signifyin(g), an utterance takes on special value through indexing a particular rhetorical figure or a speaker's skill at verbal art. In particular, the examples of signifyin(g) in these marked stylistic choices are cases of what Morgan (1994) discusses as "reading dialect," in which the linguistic style itself may be crucial in conveying the full meaning of a given utterance.

AADQs often directly address particular audience members, using marked stylistic choices to put the addressee "on the spot." This technique is quite common in drag performances. For example, this device is used by The Lady Chablis, a Savannah, Georgia, drag queen discussed in the best-selling *Midnight in the Garden of Good and Evil* (Berendt 1994). In her autobiography, The Lady Chablis describes how she approaches audience members during performances:

> Whenever I performed my monologue, I made sure to comb the audience for a "victim." I'm always gonna pick on someone—that's part of my act. Still is. I'll usually find somebody in the front row who's got a certain *afraid* look on their face, like "Oh my God, please don't say nothing to me." *That's when I move in for the kill.* If I see a woman, and she's draped in diamonds, I might ask, "Girl, what didja do to get those jewels? Didja suck dick that good? Share y'secrets with The Doll!" (The Lady Chablis 1996: 103)

Here, The Lady Chablis uses a highly marked stylistic choice for comic effect. The highly informal style and coarse language directed at a woman "draped in diamonds" is unexpected, indexing a (false) closeness and familiarity between the drag queen and the audience member. As such, it represents both a dialect switch (imaginary change in participant identity) and a register switch (imaginary change in type of interaction). For example, discussing sexual exploits and using the term *girl* would normally be reserved for conversations with a close friend (most likely another gay man or another drag queen). The drag queen suggests that the audience member is not a wealthy upper-class woman but someone who simply received her jewels as a reward for her sexual abilities. As Myers-Scotton argues, such a marked choice is often a powerful feature of language "because it deviates from the expected and because its motivations may not be clear, therefore leaving the addressee off balance and unable either to predict the RO set in effect for the rest of the exchange or to explain the speaker's precise motivations" ([Myers-Scotton]Scotton 1985: 112). By using a marked choice, AADQs disrupt the expected RO set between audience and performer. Such marked choices are most often used to address white audience members, especially if they are clearly heterosexual or upper middle class. In these cases the marked choice produces comic effect because the AADQ used stylistic language choices to assert power over individuals belonging to more dominant social groups.

8. For a fuller discussion of *signifyin(g)* in AADQ performances, see Barrett (1994).

In a similar example from a performance in Texas, the drag queen approaches a white heterosexual couple sitting near the stage. The setting is a gay bar with a predominantly African American clientele. When speaking to the white couple, the drag queen switches to the white woman style and then asserts that she herself is also white. Note that the switch does not occur within example [5] but rather the example itself represents a marked dialect, given that a dialect associated with African Americans would be unmarked in this setting.

[5] African American drag queen approaching a white couple during a performance in a gay bar:

1 Oh, hi, how are you doing?
2 White people. Love it.
3 I . . . I'm not being racial cause I'm white.
4 I just have a <obscured> . . . I can afford more sun tan.

In line 1, *how are you doing* is spoken with an exaggerated L*H intonation pattern typically associated with wealthy suburban young white women such as sorority members (cf. McLemore 1991). This marked choice implies that, as whites, the audience members must be spoken to in white English. The stylistic change indexes the issues of power created by the presence of a white heterosexual couple in a bar for gay African Americans, a dialect switch. The heterosexual couple assumes a certain privilege in invading what is otherwise a "safe space" for gays and lesbians. By producing humor at the expense of the white audience members, the AADQ makes it clear that their decision to come and "observe" (and appropriate) gay African American culture is, at the very least, problematic.

In the next example a Texas drag queen uses a marked choice to undermine the image of femininity indexed by the white woman style. The switch here is from one dialect to another, as if the drag queen belongs first to one social group and then to another.

[6] Drag queen in Texas introducing a male stripper in a gay bar

1 Are you ready to see some muscles?
2 (audience yells) Some dick?
3 Excuse me I'm not supposed to say that, words like that in the microphone,
4 Like shit, fuck, and all that, you know?
5 I am a Christian woman.
6 I go to church.
7 I'm always on my knees.

In this example, the AADQ uses the white woman style in line 1. After using the word *dick* in line 2, she apologizes for using words that aren't "ladylike" (cf. Lakoff's "women don't talk rough"). Here the apology emphasizes the fact that the use of obscenities is a marked stylistic choice (given that it occurs within the white woman style). The performer further undermines the white woman style by explaining the apology in line 4 by using even more obscenities. These marked choices disrupt the RO set indexed by the white woman style, emphasizing the fact that the drag queen does not actually hold claim to the image of genteel femininity that the style indexes. The remainder of this example further exploits this irony with a joke about the drag queen being a *Christian woman* who is *always on her knees*. Here, the reference to being on her knees carries the dual meaning of "always praying" and "always performing fellatio," thus playing off of the stereotypes of white women and drag queens, respectively. The stylistic choice highlights the fact that the audience cannot assume that the "performed" identity of an upper-class, sophisticated woman is "authentic" because the chosen style produces inferences (about the character of the drag queen) that violate the expected behavior associated with the white woman style.

In example [7], RuPaul uses a marked switch into the AAVE style to emphasize her identity as a biologically male African American. Hall is using the standard dialect of American English, but RuPaul switches to AAVE.

[7] RuPaul during her first appearance on the Arsenio Hall Show

> *Arsenio Hall:* I'm sure there're some people who would like the question answered do you . . . would you have rather been born a woman?
>
> *RuPaul:* No. No no. I'm very happy with being (.) a big o' black man.

Up to this point, RuPaul uses primarily the white woman style, indexing an RO set associated with a high level of sophistication and femininity. Following the pause after *being*, however, she switches into the AAVE style to say *a big o' black man*. This marked switch enhances the referential content of the utterance by using a linguistic style associated with being black. In addition, the choice undermines the audience's assumptions concerning RuPaul's performance of a sophisticated feminine identity by reminding them (both referentially and stylistically) that she is indeed both African American and male.

In the next example, an AADQ in Texas also uses AAVE as a marked choice to point out that she is biologically male. This example comes from a bar with a predominantly white clientele. As the drag queen is introducing a male stripper, a young African American man enters the bar and walks past the front of the stage. In line 7, the performer makes a marked switch to another dialect to address the newcomer.

[8] Another introduction of male stripper in a bar in Texas

> 1 Please welcome to the stage, our next dancer,
>
> 2 He is a butt-fucking tea,[9] honey.

9. *Butt-fucking tea* refers to anything that is exceptionally good.

3 He is hot.

4 Masculine, muscled, and ready to put it to ya, baby.

5 Anybody in here (.) hot (.) as (.) fish (.) grease?

6 That's pretty hot, idn't it?

7 (Switches to exaggerated low pitch) Hey what's up, home boy?

8 (Switches back) I'm sorry that fucking creole always come around when I don't need it.

9 Please, welcome,

10 hot, gorgeous, sexy, very romantic,

11 and he'd like to bend you over and turn you every which way but loose.

Given that lines 1–6 are primarily in the white woman style, the switch to AAVE (accentuated by an accompanying drop in pitch) makes the switch highly emphasized. The switch creates momentary solidarity with the African American who entered the bar, thus disrupting the prevailing RO set in a bar filled primarily with whites. In line 8, the AADQ apologizes for *that fucking creole*. In this line, however, the word *creole* is pronounced with a vocalized [l], and the verb *come* occurs without the Standard English /+s/ inflection. Although the drag queen apologizes for using AAVE, the apology itself occurs in the AAVE style. This stylistic choice continues to index solidarity with the African American patrons in the bar, undermining the sincerity of the apology to the predominantly white audience. In lines 9–11, the performer returns to the white woman style, returning to the RO set that was in place before the marked switch in line 7. This return to the white woman style serves to further emphasize the markedness of the switch to AAVE and the change in RO sets relating to the show of solidarity with the African American patron.

As these examples demonstrate, the use of marked choices disrupts the status quo during a given performance. By using such marked stylistic choices to call the prevailing RO sets into question the performers can draw attention to themselves and their communicative skills. In addition, these marked choices highlight the various questions of social difference brought out in the performances by indexing disunities between perceived/performed and "actual" (biographical) identity.

CONCLUSION

One of the goals of glam drag is to present an image that is as "real" as possible. Through the use of clothing, jewelry, hair, and cosmetics glam queens create an external image of exaggerated femininity, often taking great pride in how much they appear to be "real women." The Lady Chablis, for example, often announces that she is not only a real woman, but "a pregnant uptown white woman" (Berendt 1996). Thus, glam queens often make a specific effort to create the illusion of a femininity associated with upper-class white heterosexual women. Language style plays a crucial role in the construction of this image of femininity. AADQs demonstrate their ability to draw on the power and prestige of white society through the creation of an external image of a wealthy woman (i.e., clothes, jewelry, and makeup) and the use of the white woman style of speaking. The white woman style is thus crucial in creating a real, believable presentation of uptown white womanhood.

While the use of the white woman style adds to the external image of femininity in drag performances, styleswitching into AAVE or stereotyped gay male speech undermines the rich white feminine persona indexed by the white woman style. By switching into these other language styles, AADQs demonstrate that although they are capable of creating the visual and linguistic symbols of white upper-class society, they are not actually attempting to create a personal identity associated with white society. In AADQ performances, demonstrating pride in one's African American identity is usually as important as the ability to produce white women's language. AADQs who wear blond wigs or who prefer to lip-synch to songs by white artists are often criticized as "trying to be white." Styleswitching thus demonstrates that although an AADQ is capable of producing language that fits into white society (and thus, take on the prestige associated with white society), she consciously chooses to maintain her identity as an African American gay man (see Barrett 1994, 1995b). The white woman style of speaking is thus used both to index the power and prestige of white upper-class society and to produce a critique of the social inequalities associated with white society.

AADQs use styleswitching to undermine audience assumptions concerning the personal identity of the performer. Marked switches are often used to renegotiate assumptions concerning AADQ identity, demonstrating that the performer refuses to be categorized according to a single, given set of social attributes. Styleswitching thus plays a crucial role in AADQ performances, keeping the audience aware that the performer cannot be tied down to a single identity. In turn, interest in the performance is heightened by the awareness that the current persona of the performer could change at any moment through a change in language style.

The examples presented here demonstrate the ways in which AADQs choose from sets of linguistic variables to attune their language to particular social settings. Using their knowledge of what the unmarked or marked code choice will be in a given interaction, they choose linguistic forms to produce specific effects. The markedness model provides a means of understanding the ways in which these stylistic choices convey the performers' attitudes about the issues brought up in the course of a performance. In some cases, they may choose the unmarked choice, whether that be a particular style or codeswitching as the unmarked norm. It is the marked choices, however, that are used to add emphasis and rhetorical force to AADQ performances. By using marked choices, AADQs tune their performances to undermine audience assumptions concerning issues of social difference such as ethnicity, sexuality, class, or gender.

ACKNOWLEDGMENT: Thanks to Grainger Saunders, Gregory Clay, and Kathryn Semolic for help and support in conducting this research and to Carol Myers-Scotton for comments on earlier drafts. Finally, special thanks to Keith Walters for helpful suggestions and advice. (Barrett 1995a is an earlier version of this chapter. See also Barrett 1994, 1995b.)

REFERENCES

Barrett, Rusty. 1994. "She is *not* white woman!": the appropriation of white women's language by African American drag queens. In *Cultural performances: proceedings of the third Berkeley women and language conference*, ed. Mary Bucholtz, A. C. Liang, Laurel Sutton, and Caitlin Hines, 1–14. Berkeley, Calif.: Berkeley Women and Language Group.

———. 1995a. The Markedness Model and style switching: evidence from African American drag queens. In *SALSA II: Proceedings of the second annual symposium on language and society–Austin (Texas Linguistics Forum 34)*, ed. Pamela Silberman and Jonathan Loftin, 40–52. Austin: University of Texas Department of Linguistics.

———. 1995b. Supermodels of the world, unite!: political economy and the language of performance among African American drag queens. In *Beyond the lavender lexicon: authenticity, imagination and appropriation in lesbian and gay languages*, ed. William L. Leap, 203–223. Newark, N. J.: Gordon and Breach.

———. 1997. The "homo-genius" speech community. In *Queerly phrased: language, gender, and sexuality*, ed. Anna Livia and Kira Hall. New York: Oxford University Press.

Bauman, Richard. 1975. Verbal art as performance. *American Anthropologist 77*. 290–311. Revised and expanded as *Verbal art as performance*. Prospect Heights, Ill.: Waveland Press, 1977.

Berendt, John. 1994. *Midnight in the garden of good and evil*. New York: Random House.

———. 1996. Chablis and me. In *Hiding my candy: the autobiography of the grand empress of Savannah,* by The Lady Chablis with Theodore Bouloukos, 12–18. New York: Pocket Books.

Briggs, Charles. 1988. *Competence in performance: the creativity of tradition in Mexicano verbal art*. Philadelphia: University of Pennsylvania Press.

Bucholtz, Mary, and Kira Hall. 1995. Introduction: twenty years after *Language and woman's place*. In *Gender articulated: language and the socially constructed self*, ed. Kira Hall and Mary Bucholtz, 1–22. New York: Routledge.

Bullough, Vern L., and Bonnie Bullough. 1993. *Cross dressing, sex, and gender*. Philadelphia: University of Pennslyvania Press.

Butler, Judith. 1993. *Bodies that matter: on the discursive limits of "sex."* New York: Routledge.

Devor, Holly. 1989. *Gender blending: confronting the limits of duality*. Bloomington: Indiana University Press.

Feinberg, Leslie. 1996. *Transgender warriors: making history from Joan of Arc to RuPaul*. Boston, Mass.: Beacon Press.

Ferguson, Charles A. 1994. Dialect, register, and genre: working assumptions about conventionalization. *Sociolinguistic perspectives on register*, ed. Edward Finegan and Douglas Biber, 15–30. New York: Oxford University Press.

Finegan, Edward, and Douglas Biber. 1994. Register and social dialect variation: an integrated approach. In *Sociolinguistic perspectives on register*, ed. Edward Finegan and Douglas Biber, 315–347. New York: Oxford University Press.

Gates, Henry Louis, Jr. 1988. *The signifying monkey: a theory of African-American literary criticism*. New York: Oxford University Press.

Gaudio, Rudolf P. 1994. Sounding gay: pitch properties in the speech of gay and straight men. *American Speech* 69: 30–37.

Giles, Howard, Nikolas Coupland, and Justine Coupland. 1991. Accommodation theory: communication, context, and consequence. In *Contexts of accomodation: developments in applied sociolinguistics*, ed. Howard Giles, Justine Coupland, and Nikolas Coupland, 1–69. Cambridge, England: Cambridge University Press.

Green, Lisa. 1994. Study of verb classes in African American English. *Linguistics and Education* 7: 65–81.

Goodwin, Joseph P. 1989. *More man than you'll ever be: gay folklore and acculturation in middle America*. Bloomington: Indiana University Press.

Hayes, Joseph J. 1981. Gayspeak. In *Gayspeak: gay male and lesbian communication*, ed. James W. Chesebro, 45–57. New York: Pilgrim's Press.

Hymes, Dell. 1981. *"In vain I tried to tell you": essays in Native American ethnopoetics*. Philadelphia: University of Pennsylvania Press.

Labov, William. 1972. *Sociolinguistic patterns*. Philadelphia: University of Pennsylvania Press.

[The] Lady Chablis, with Theodore Bouloukos. 1996. *Hiding my candy: the autobiography of the grand empress of Savannah*. New York: Pocket Books.

Lakoff, Robin. 1975. *Language and woman's place*. New York: Harper and Row.

Le Page, R. B., and Andrée Tabouret-Keller. 1985. *Acts of identity: Creole-based approaches to language and ethnicity*. Cambridge, England: Cambridge University Press.

MacKenzie, Gordene Olga. 1994. *Transgender nation*. Bowling Green, Oh.: Bowling Green State University Popular Press.

McLemore, Cynthia Ann. 1991. The pragmatic interpretation of English intonation: sorority speech. Unpublished PhD dissertation. Austin: University of Texas Department of Linguistics.

Michaels, Sarah. 1986. Narrative presentations: an oral preparation for literacy with first graders. In *The social construction of literacy*, ed. Jenny Cook-Gumperz. Cambridge, England: Cambridge University Press.

Mitchell-Kernan, Claudia. 1972. Signifying and marking: two Afro-American speech acts. In *Directions in sociolinguistics*, ed. John J. Gumperz and Dell Hymes, 161–179. New York: Holt, Rinehart & Winston.

Moran, John. 1991. Language use and social function in the gay community. Paper presented at NWAVE 20 (New Ways of Analyzing Variation). Philadelphia.

Morgan, Marcyliena. 1994. No woman no cry: the linguistic representation of African American women. In *Cultural performances: proceedings of the third Berkeley women and language conference*, ed. Mary Bucholtz, A. C. Liang, Laurel Sutton, and Caitlin Hines, 525–541. Berkeley, Calif.: Berkeley Women and Language Group.

[Myers-Scotton, Carol]Scotton, Carol Myers. 1985. "What the heck, sir": style shifting and lexical colouring as features of powerful language. In *Sequence and pattern in communicative behaviour*, ed. R.L. Street, Jr., and J. N. Cappella, 103–19. London: Arnold.

———. 1988. Codeswitching and types of multilingual communities. In *Language spread and language policy*, ed. P. Lowenberg, 61–82. Washington, D.C.: Georgetown University Press.

———. 1993. *Social motivations for codeswitching: evidence from Africa*. Oxford: Oxford University Press.

Newton, Esther. 1972. *Mother camp: female impersonation in America*. Chicago: University of Chicago Press.

Queen, Robin M. 1992. Prosodic organization in the speeches of Martin Luther King. *Proceedings of the IRCS workshop on prosody in natural speech*, 151–60. Philadelphia: Institute for Research in Cognitive Science, University of Pennsylvania.

———. 1997. "I don't speak spritch": locating lesbian language. In *Queerly phrased: language, gender, and sexuality*, ed. Anna Livia and Kira Hall. New York: Oxford University Press.

Rodgers, Bruce. 1972. *The queen's vernacular*. Reprint as *Gay talk: a (sometimes outrageous) dictionary of gay slang*, New York: Paragon Books, 1979.

Rudes, Blair A., and Bernard Healy. 1979. Is she for real?: the concepts of femaleness and maleness in the gay world. In *Ethnolinguistics: Boas, Sapir and Whorf revisited*, ed. Madaleine Mathiot, 49–61. The Hague: Mouton.

RuPaul. 1995. *Lettin' it all hang out: an autobiography*. New York: Hyperion.

Sherzer, Joel. 1989. The Kuna verb: a study in the interplay of grammar, discourse, and style. In *General and Amerindian ethnolinguistics*, ed. Mary Ritchie Key and Henry M. Hoenigswald, 261–72. Berlin: Mouton de Gruyter.

Sunaoshi, Yukako. 1995. Your boss is your "mother": Japanese women's construction of an authoritative position in the workplace. In *SALSA II: Proceedings of the second annual symposium about language and society–Austin (Texas Linguistics Forum 34)*, ed. Pamela Silberman, and Jonathan Loftin, 175–88. Austin: University of Texas Department of Linguistics.

Turner, Victor. 1986. *The anthropology of performance*. New York: PAJ Publications.

Walters, Keith. 1981. A proposal for studying the language of homosexual males. Master's thesis, University of Texas at Austin.

———. 1992. Supplementary materials for AFR 320/LIN 325: Black English. Master's thesis, University of Texas at Austin.

Wyatt, Toya A. 1994. Language development in African American English child speech. *Linguistics and Education* 7: 7–22.

—9—

Styleswitching in Southern English

MARGARET MISHOE

W HAT MOTIVATES the same speaker to sometimes remark on heavy rain by saying *I ain't never seen nothing to beat all this rain* and, at other times, to say something more like *I've never seen a rain like this*? In this chapter, I argue that speakers switch between the styles in their linguistic repertoire to project different dimensions of themselves. The subjects studied here are a close-knit group of rural southern whites who have relatively little education and little exposure to how others negotiate the fast track of modern life. Yet, their language use patterns demonstrate that their tacit knowledge of the intentional messages in contrasting style choices serves them as well as it does any urban high-flyer. The subject here is strategic switching between the two varieties in the community's linguistic repertoire to index how they wish to present themselves in relation to new topics or other participants' contributions in an ongoing conversation.

When speakers have access to two different styles in the dialect of their language, factors in a large-scale social pattern help to account for individual choices in styleswitching. These social patterns can be discussed in terms of marked versus unmarked style choices ([Myers-Scotton]Scotton 1983). Most speakers have at least two forms of their language, switching from one to the other in predictable settings. For example, they may use one form in the home and another in the market. Blom and Gumperz (1972) refer to this as situational switching. Distinct varieties of the language are employed for distinct situations (church, school, home) or activities (public speaking, ceremonial speech).

However, switches also occur among family members and close friends in the same conversation, often with no change in setting or even participants. This occurrence indicates that the phenomena of styleswitching is not confined to interactions in selected places but, rather, is a natural part of conversation that can occur for a variety of reasons. Myers-Scotton (1993) discusses non-situationally motivated switching under three rubrics: switching itself as the unmarked choice, switching as the marked

162

choice, and switching as an exploratory choice. Most of the switching discussed in this chapter can be characterized as switching as the marked choice.

Data for this study were collected from lower socioeconomic white speakers who live in a small community located in the foothills of North Carolina. I call the community Cedar Falls. Over a two-year period, the subjects were videotaped taking part in various social activities, including two Christmas Eve parties, a small church service, casual interactions among friends and family members, and a Thanksgiving dinner. All the participants in this study are family members or close friends living in the same speech community.

GOALS AND METHODS

Using examples from the data gathered for this study, I offer support for the existence of strategic switching between the two linguistic varieties spoken in Cedar Falls. Whether these varieties are best characterized as different dialects or styles of the same dialect is open to discussion. Sociolinguists form no consensus on this issue, and, in fact, most largely sidestep it altogether. This sidestepping is what the term *variety* accomplishes, after all. Generally speaking, if two varieties are labeled styles of the same dialect (rather than dialects of the same language), their similarities outweigh their differences. Clearly, the two varieties in question here have many structural features in common. Yet, identifiable differences separate them at all three levels of linguistic structure (i.e., phonology, morphosyntax, and lexicon); the examples given here make that separation apparent. However, assessing these differences via quantification is beyond the scope of this chapter and not relevant to its purpose. Therefore, I simply refer to one dialect, the Cedar Falls dialect, but recognize two styles. The style that is the common medium for in-group conversations in this community is called *home style*, and the style more reserved for outgroup interactions there is called *local standard*. Because the speakers studied used home style for 95% of their conversational exchanges, home style is considered the unmarked choice for conducting conversation between family and close friends. Local standard represents the participants' approximation of Standard American English. However, local standard only approaches the standard dialect, as exemplified on national network television news programs. Speakers in this study may styleswitch into a different variety that they *believe* is Standard American English but still use words or patterns that are part of the rural southern vernacular—what I call home style here.

Sentence [1] exemplifies some of the most distinctive features of home style:

[1] What I need me is some time and some money, but I ain't got neither one right now.

The use of the personal dative *me*, the negative form of *ain't*, and the double negatives, *ain't* and *neither* mark this sentence as home style. When speakers use other forms that approach Standard American English, as in sentence [2], I claim that they are using local standard, the local version of Standard American English.

[2] I don't go to saloons to eat—even if they have good food, I don't want that kind of environment.

To point out distinguishing features of home style is not to suggest, however, that every sentence spoken in home style contains these features. In fact, if a speaker were to use such features in every sentence, it would be very unusual indeed. A strong indicator of a switch to local standard is that speakers speak more slowly than usual. Thus, sentences that may appear to be in local standard in the following examples may be considered as part of a home style discourse because they lack the feature of slower speech rate that is a defining feature of the local standard. The question for this study is: If home style is the unmarked choice for these speakers, and if they are surrounded by family and close friends, why would these speakers styleswitch at all? If the situation is unchanged and the participants remain constant, what is the motivation for styleswitching? The following examples involve styleswitches from local standard, from home style into local standard, or are examples wherein we might anticipate a switch that is not forthcoming. Examining these examples gives us clues as to why speakers choose the marked choice of styleswitching during certain speech events.

The participants in this study are my family members and friends and acquaintances of those family members. The participants were chosen on the basis of the following sociocultural factors: their geographic identity (they were all born and presently live in rural North Carolina), their educational background (one female member of the group went to nursing school at the local technical college; none of the other participants graduated from high school), and their occupations and income (if employed, they have low-paying blue-collar jobs). Their community was once a thriving cotton mill town, but the mills closed in the early 1960s, and the people who were not closely tied to the community left for the cities. The people who remained behind usually owned a piece of land and a small home. They now work in the nearest small town, about 12 miles from the community. These jobs are generally in fast-food restaurants and retail stores (Wal-Mart or K-Mart). There is also seasonal work in the furniture industry. The members of this community are generally very close and depend on each other emotionally and spiritually. The older members attend church together regularly; the younger members attend sporadically.

Instead of attempting to present all the features that constitute home style, I give fairly long segments of the conversation showing styleswitching, and for each conversation, I refer to the features of the switch to make it clear to the reader that a switch took place. The switch into a different variety (most commonly from home style to local standard) is in caps. The data were gathered by me, or by a person in the community who was a member of my family. A videorecorder was used.

ANALYSIS OF DATA

The first example centers on Pearl, the matriarch of the family, greeting two of her guests for a small Christmas Eve party at her door. She greets them in local standard, and then immediately switches to home style. Note that (.) = pause, // // indicates overlap. Switches are in caps.

[3]   Pearl: 1 it's so nice to see y'all
              2 I'm so glad you could make it
              3 please come in and find a seat
              [The guests seat themselves and Pearl continues]

[4]   Pearl: 4 AIN'T THIS RAIN AWFUL?
              5 I'M AWISHIN I COULD GO SOMEWHERE AND SEE ME SOME SUN
              6 I AIN'T NEVER SEEN NOTHING TO BEAT ALL THIS RAIN

The only nonstandard variant that we see in sequence [3] is the use of the plural form *Y'all*, but this is not a stigmatized form in southern English, because it is used across class boundaries in the South and thus is considered a component of local standard. In sequence [4], Pearl sits down with the same guests that she just greeted at the door. Now we see five separate examples of the more distinctively local variety, home style. First, Pearl uses the negative *ain't* to begin her conversation about the weather: AIN'T THIS RAIN AWFUL. Then *a* is prefixed before the verb *wishing*: I'm AWISHIN I could go somewhere. In this same sentence Pearl uses the personal dative *me*, as in AND SEE ME SOME SUN. Also, standard auxiliary verb selection is not followed in I AIN'T NEVER SEEN. Finally, there is another occurrence of the negative form *ain't* in a negative sentence to end the exchange: I AIN'T NEVER SEEN NOTHING.

In sequence [3], Pearl greets her guests in local standard. When she goes to the door, even though she is greeting close friends, she is aware that the situation requires a relatively formal greeting. She wants to be seen as someone who is a "hostess," someone who knows and understands her duties as hostess. Therefore, she uses local standard to establish this identity. However, in the same exchange, as her guests are seating themselves, it is also important for Pearl to reaffirm her identity as close friend and community member.

Her code choice in sequence [3] is a choice that permits her to present herself with the status of hostess. Notice that Pearl uses three formulaic utterances which are all echoic of what even an upper-class hostess at a formal party might say to guests whom she does not know well. Pearl's choice in [4] is a move toward declaring solidarity with her guests; she accomplishes this by switching to home style, the style the guests recognize as their unmarked medium of in-group social exchanges.

In sequence [5], we see Pearl facing a similar set of options. The participants in this sequence are Pearl and Dan; Tessa; Tessa's husband, Ed; and Pearl's daughter Sheila. Pearl brings Tessa a chicken breast covered in sour cream and bacon. Everyone is speaking in home style. The phone rings and Pearl answers it, switching to local standard.

[5] Pearl: 1 [to Tessa] How ya like that?
     Tessa: 2 It's good. [looking at her husband] You wouldn't like it (.) so don't bother.
        Ed: 3 I noticed you hadn't offered me none.
    Sheila: 4 Mitch [her brother] don't eat em good neither.
             5 His girlfriend keeps bringing em to him.
       Dan: 6 What's that?
    Sheila: 7 Them chicken breast with sour cream.
       Dan: 8 [to Ed] You wouldn't like em so don't insult your taste buds.
                 //[laughter]//
        Ed: 9 I don't plan on it (.) I can't eat no sour cream.
    Sheila: 10 Speakin' of food (.) has anybody tried sushi?
     Tessa: 11 Idn't that raw fish?
    Sheila: 12 Oooh yes.
     Tessa: 13 D'you like em?
    Sheila: 14 Oooh no:o.
                 //[laughter]//
    Sheila: 15 I kept thinkin' iffen they'd abattered em up an dropped em in a deep fryer we'd all be eatin' good.
            16 I mean might jus as well swallow up a goldfish.
            17 I don't want me no raw fish.
                 [phone rings]
     Pearl:18 LOFTIN RESIDENCE (.) HAPPY THANKSGIVING.
            19 HOW IS SHE?
            20 UH HUH
            21 DO THEY THINK THAT'S BASED ON HER MEDICATION?
            22 I SEE (.) YOU KNOW I'M PRAYING FOR YOU BOTH
            23 MY HEART IS WITH YOU
            24 WHATEVER HAPPENS HERE WE'LL ALL MEET IN THE RAPTURE, WON'T WE?
            25 TELL HER TO REST . . .
        Ed: 26 //[to Sheila]// I member when you threw eggs on us at Easter.
    Sheila: 27 I never did!

Pearl: 28 [still on the phone] GOODBYE DEAR.

Sheila: 29 I ain't never chunked the first egg at nobody (.) never.

//[laughter]//

[Pearl hangs up the phone as Sheila says line 29. She turns back to the people in the room]

Pearl: 30 Well good Lord (.) what in tha(.)

31 I'm athinkin' y'all are all crazy.

In this sequence, Pearl is again faced with a limited number of options when she answers the phone. The subset of ways to answer a telephone is relatively small. Pearl, who is conversing with her family in home style, can choose to answer the phone in home style or she can switch to local standard. Because Pearl works part time at a shelter for battered women, there is the possibility that she is being called about a problem at work. Pearl's work puts her in contact with people of varying social status, including workers from the local hospital and law enforcement agents. Features of home style, such as multiple negation and nonstandard subject–verb agreement, are stigmatized by the educated people in the town in which Pearl works, and Pearl is aware of this; therefore, the cost of staying in home style when she answers the phone could be a loss of status among her colleagues.

That explains why Pearl switches into local standard when she answers the phone. The question is, Why does she choose to stay in local standard when she finds out that the person calling is a close friend who was invited for dinner? Faced with a set of choices similar to that in sequence [3], Pearl this time chooses to continue to use local standard in the exchange. The answer to this question lies in the topic of the conversation. Pearl is a retired practical nurse and the topic that immediately comes up concerns a medical problem. Local standard would be used by most of the community members if they went to the hospital or a doctor's office; it is the variety used for more formal occasions. Here, Pearl can claim expert status (particularly among people in her speech community, most of whom did not graduate from high school). So in line 21, when Pearl asks about her friend's medical condition, she does so in local standard.

21 DO THEY THINK THAT'S BASED ON HER MEDICATION?

In lines 22 through 24 the topic shifts away from medicine, yet it still concerns the physical well being of the caller's wife. Pearl shows her concern by saying in line 22 that she *is praying for you both* and in line 23 that her *heart is with you*. Line 24 is a serious religious reference that comes directly from the Bible and therefore Pearl treats it with formality.

24 WHATEVER HAPPENS HERE WE'LL MEET IN THE RAPTURE WON'T WE?

We don't know what the caller's response to this utterance is, but we do know that even though the conversation going on behind Pearl is taking place in home style and is very lighthearted, Pearl is not influenced by it. We can see this is line 28 when Pearl closes the phone conversation with *goodbye dear*. In this community, this is a marked way to end a conversation with a friend. Phone calls in home style usually end with phrases like *bye bye, love ya*, or *I'll call ya soon*. Pearl's choice of a marked closure indicates the seriousness of the topics that were discussed in the phone call. When she turns back to her family and rejoins their conversation, she immediately switches back into home style.

As we can see, even though the situation limits the subset of responses, the speaker still has choices. Before each switch in sequences [3], and [4], Pearl is presented with these choices, and she makes them based on her knowledge of her community and the social message she wants to convey. The situation limits, but does not control, her choices.

In sequence [6], we see another example of styleswitching to establish identity. This time the speaker wants to move from his identity as a close friend of the family into the identity of someone who is an expert or who has exceptional knowledge in a particular situation. Again, the situation propels the styleswitch. The participants in this situation are family members: Dan (father), Pearl (mother), Sheila (daughter), Mitch (son), and friends of the family, Frank and Myra (husband and wife). Frank uses his styleswitch to commandeer the new camcorder that Dan and Pearl received for Christmas. The conversation begins in home style.

[6] Frank: 1 What in the world have y'all got now?

Pearl: 2 We got us a prize (.) the young'uns tol us ta open it up early.

Frank: 3 Well lookit that (.) ain't that sompin?

Dan: 4 January one (.) This says January one.

Pearl: 5 Well (.) that ain't us.

Dan: 6 This here things a year behind.

Pearl: 7 Hell (.) maybe it is us.

//[laughter]//

Sheila: 8 It says ta press initial button.

Mitch: 9 //no (.) that ain't it//

Myra: 10 Honey, [speaking to her husband Frank] don't you know sompin' bout these things (.) ain't there sompin on tha side?

11 There's spose ta be sompin on tha side.

Frank: 12 WE NEED SOME EXTRA LIGHT (.) DO YOU HAVE AN OVER-HEAD LIGHT?

Pearl: 13 We usta (.) but Ralph knocked it out with his numchucks.

Dan: 14 Is the thing on?

Pearl: 15 I think it's been steady on.

Frank: 16 JUST LET ME SEE WHAT I CAN DO.

Pearl: 17 Honey do your thing.

//[laughter]//

Frank: 18 I DON'T BELIEVE IT WILL GIVE YOU A PICTURE WITHOUT MORE LIGHT.

Sheila: 19 Idn't it spose ta work in any light (.) don't it say something bout candle light?

Frank: 20 No (.) that's another model (.) this'un NEEDS MORE LIGHT.

21 PUT A LAMP ON EITHER SIDE OF THE ROOM AN IT'LL WORK FINE.

22 (.) I THINK IT'LL WORK FINE.

In line 1, Frank enters the conversation by inquiring about the present that Dan is opening:

1 what in the world have y'all got now?

Pearl responds in home style, and in line 3, Frank assesses the gift using home style:

3 Well lookit that (.) ain't that sompin?

Lines 4 through 10 demonstrate that Dan has no knowledge about the camcorder, in line 12 Frank styleswitches into local standard and takes control of the situation.

12 WE NEED SOME EXTRA LIGHT (.) DO YOU HAVE AN OVER HEAD LIGHT?

The other participants remain in home style throughout the rest of the exchange while Frank continues using local standard through line 22:

22 I THINK IT'LL WORK FINE.

Speakers have multiple identities; one way to change identities in an exchange is to change the linguistic variety that is indexing one identity to a linguistic variety that will index another. Frank wants to move from someone who is a guest and close friend to someone who knows more than the other speakers about the camcorder. None of the other speakers challenge his right as expert; they continue to use the unmarked home style. The host, Dan, turns over the operation of the camcorder to Frank, and the other speakers start to move lamps and set the room up as Frank requests. In other words, Frank's styleswitch successfully establishes his identity as the expert in charge. This example illustrates the point that different speakers in the same exchange may have different marked and unmarked choices. When Frank uses local standard to negotiate a new identity, that variety becomes his unmarked choice. His bid for a new rights and obligations set (RO set) is successful, even if it seems that he is using marked choices for the situation without response. His status as expert is accepted by the other speakers, as evidenced by their behavior. To negotiate a new RO set for an exchange does not necessarily mean to negotiate a new variety for all participants in the exchange. In fact, in these particular circumstances, if other speakers were to switch as well it would be interpreted as a challenge to Frank's authority, as though the speakers who switched were also establishing themselves as experts, and an argument would almost certainly ensue.

In sequence [7], someone is making the marked choice to enter a conversation using local standard in response to a face-threatening act. This sequence starts with a conversation between Pearl and her niece Tessa. Dan (Pearl's husband) is listening to this conversation but does not enter until the last exchange. He joins the conversation using local standard.

[7]   Pearl: 1 We usta would go ridin in tha mountains.
             2 But I hate the ole interstate (.)
             3 There ain't a blamed thing ta see on an ole interstate.
             4 But Dan (.) he won't never drive off the interstate.
             5 He's always afraid he's agonna get lost.
             6 I tol him (.) honey there ain't no way—
             7 I mean you jus can't get lost in America.
                //[laughter]//
             8 but we jus ride ride that ole interstate jus ride that ole interstate
   Tessa: 9 Is he worried bout gettin lost do ya think?
          10 Maybe he's worried bout havin ta ask some mountain man for directions.
                //[laughter]//
   Pearl: 11 That's more likely.
          12 He says you get back up in there where nobody don't know ya and y'll get shot.
                //[laughter]//
   Tessa: 13 Are ya jus a little paranoid Dan?
                //[laughter]//
    Dan: 14 NO (2) I'M A REALIST.
          15 I KNOW PEOPLE UP IN THERE DO THINGS THEY DON'T WANT FOLKS TA KNOW ABOUT AN YOU RIDE UP ON A STILL UP THERE Y'LL BE MISTOOKEN FOR SOMEBODY ELSE.
          16 YOU CAN GET YOURSELF SHOT

In this sequence, Pearl and Tessa laugh about Pearl's husband. They have insinuated that he might be unnecessarily afraid of both driving in the mountains and asking for directions. Although Dan cannot dispute the facts of the story because he did indeed tell his wife he would not drive off the interstate for fear of being attacked, he can still establish himself as a reasonable person with reasonable fears. He does this in a number of ways. First, he starts the exchange with a simple denial in 14, *no*. He then pauses for a full two seconds before he continues. When he says, *I'M A REALIST*, he is using a lexical item, *realist*, which is not normally in his code; this is the first indication he has switched to local standard from home style. (Note that Dan has only two switches in eight hours of data.) The fact that he switches here indicates that he feels a strong need to take control and assert power; therefore, he assumes the prerogative of initiating a change in the code that is being used. He tells us in lines 15 and 16 that he knows something about the hills of North Carolina, and that there is a real danger in venturing off the main roads and stumbling on a moonshiner's still. When Dan says, *I'M A REALIST,* he implies that Pearl and Tessa are not being realistic when they talk about driving through the mountains. Pearl and Tessa have to choose whether they will continue the exchange, possibly counterattacking Dan, or whether they will yield to Dan's bid for power. They choose to yield, possibly because Dan's use of local standard alerts them to the fact that they have insulted him. After he speaks, Pearl and Tessa nod seriously at each other and at Dan. They then take up another topic.

The styleswitches seen in sequences [3] through [7] are all switches wherein the speakers are negotiating power in the interaction. With this power comes a change in the speaker's position in the RO set in effect for the conversational exchange, an acknowledgment of authority and expertise. Therefore, to negotiate such a change they make a marked choice, in this case the use of local standard, so that they might gain in some way. They "rock the social boat" (Myers-Scotton 1988: 202). In the first sequences, Pearl's styleswitches gain her a strengthened social role. When Frank switches to local standard in sequence [6], he gains status as an expert. And when Dan uses local standard in sequence [7], he establishes himself as a thinking person who knows how to act responsibly. By virtue of initiating a change in the relationship, the speakers indicate a desire to communicate superiority or authority. The success of the choices they make can be seen in the responses of the other participants.

However, other reasons to initiate a codeswitch in a conversation exist. In sequences [8] and [9], the speakers styleswitch from home style into local standard when they become contemplative, remembering a poignant past event. In sequence [8], the participants are Pearl, her daughter Sheila, her niece Tessa, and her friend Myra. It is Thanksgiving Day, and they are remembering a Christmas Eve party they attended the year before. While this conversation goes on with all the speakers using home style, another family friend, Louise is seen turning into the driveway of Pearl's residence. At first the arrival of this friend triggers sarcastic remarks because Louise's husband (Richard) makes a point of not joining these gatherings. He always has an excuse; usually he begs off by claiming illness. Pearl suddenly urges her other guests not to expect too much of Louise during the holidays because this is her first Thanksgiving and Christmas since the death of her father. Pearl reminds everyone how hard the holidays are for someone who is grieving for a loved one and this reminder triggers a memory about her youngest daughter who was killed twelve years earlier. Pearl styleswitches into local standard as she remembers her daughter, the funeral, and the first Christmas she spent without her. In this example, the conversation goes from being very lighthearted to sarcastic to very serious, and we can see that the topic change triggers the styleswitch. The discussion of death and the memory of the funeral of Pearl's daughter motivates the switch.

[8]   Pearl: 1   Frank was crazy over there with Sheila.

2   Tryin ta open her presents.

3   And she opened one and it was panties and he says what size are they? an she says my size!
//[laughter]//

Sheila: 4   He din't need ta know.

5   They was my size.

Pearl: 6   An he was opening up uh uh

7   Eve'rything she'd open he was into it.

8   An he says "coulda been mine."

Sheila: 9   //I think it's Louise//

Pearl: 10   "If it hadn't been for the name tag."

Pearl: 11   An he wadn't gettin his present fast enough.

12   Mitch was passin um out an he was makin all manner of fun at it ya know.

13   Mitch said (.) "finally it's yours" an held it over to look at it.

14   An he said "I don't believe it (.) I wanna see tha tag"

15   Louise is all by herself

Tessa: 16   She are? [sarcastic]

Pearl: 17   [very sarcastic] Ri:chard jus coul:dn't fa:ce it.

Sheila: 18   [High pitch] Wimpy wimpy wimpy.

Tessa: 19   Do we do we do we hear a hint of?
//[laughter]//

Pearl: 20   She is real (.) she's kinda down in the dumps.

21   IT'S HER FIRST HOLIDAY WITHOUT HER DADDY

22   IF SHE DON'T ACT PLUMB NORMAL IT'S CAUSE SHE CAN'T HARDLY (.) IT'S AWFUL. IF YOU'VE NEVER BEEN THROUGH IT

23   THERE'S HOLIDAYS STILL AIN'T THE SAME.

24   I BROKE DOWN THE OTHER DAY AN ASKED SHEILA (.) WHEN DOES THE GRIEF EVER END?

25   IT'LL SOON BE 12 YEARS SINCE DEBRA(.)

26   I AIN'T (2) GOT OVER IT YET(.) I REALLY MISS HER HOLIDAYS.

Myra: 27   DIDN'T DADDY DIE THA SAME YEAR? 81?

Pearl: 28   YEA(.) YOUR DADDY DIED WHEN?

Myra: 29 June.

Pearl: 30 SHE DIED JULY 8TH.

Tessa: 31 Lord it don't seem like its been that long.

Pearl: 32 81 IN JULY AND IT'LL BE 12 YEARS COMING UP (.) TO ME
IT SEEMS LIKE A MILLION YEARS (.) AN OTHER TIMES IT
SEEMS LIKE YESTERDAY.

    33 I can still smell them horrible flowers at the funeral home. (2)

    34 NOT THAT I WADN'T GRATEFUL FOR THEM I WAS (1) BUT
THAT'S A HARD SMELL TO FORGET.

    35 THAT'S A HARD CHRISTMAS THAT COMES NEXT

The recollection of a formal and sad occurrence triggers a shift to formal and serious language (local standard). This type of switch is brought on by the internal factors of contemplation and memory. Pearl makes the marked choice to switch to a formal code to signal that she is talking about a formal and solemn occasion.

It is important to recognize that there is a difference between conversation about a formal and solemn topic and conversation that is serious. Participants do not switch to local standard every time the topic shifts to a very serious subject. For example, sequence [9] is a conversation about two friends of Pearl whose son was arrested for murder. The friends, Lynn and Pam, cannot attend the Thanksgiving day dinner because Pam is too upset about her son (Cody) being in jail (for murdering his friend, Sid) to socialize. In this sequence, Sheila explains to Tessa why Lynn and Pam will not be at the gathering and what happened to Cody. Even though she is talking about a very serious chain of events, she does not shift to local standard.

[9]   Sheila: 1 They're saying he [Cody] killed that guy [Sid].

          2 But Sid weren't no account.

          3 He was meaner than a snake.

          4 If Cody did kill him it weren't no more than he deserved (.) got
what he deserved.

          5 Did you know sompin?

          6 He [Sid] rode him around with a head in tha trunk of his car for a
week once.

          7 Everybody knowed he was bad (.) awful.

          8 But folks was scared of him.

          9 Now tha law is actin all crazy cuz they found him shot dead in
his car.

        10 I don't know if Cody did it or what.

        11 But his poor momma is going wild.

        12 An for what (.) for some trash that's dead an nobody cares.

        13 He [Sid] was a sorry son of a bitch.

        14 Whoever shot him oughta get a medal.

Sheila recounts this narrative to Tessa without any styleswitches to local standard, even though the topic itself could not be more serious. A topic shift to a serious subject is not enough in itself to trigger a shift. Sheila becomes more vehement as she talks, but she does not styleshift.

However, in sequence [10] we have another narrative with a serious topic that does cause the speaker to shift from home style to local standard. Sequence [10] is taken from data gathered at a small rural church. The church has a very small membership and shares a pastor with two other small churches. When the minister is unavailable, the members gather in the sanctuary and share personal testimony about the power of God in their lives. This sharing is referred to as testifying. The following transcript comes from a male in his early sixties who rises and tells the congregation about the time that he knew he was saved by the Lord. Testifying in church calls for a certain discourse structure. If the testimony is about the moment in time when the speaker was saved by God, the speaker starts by recounting his life before he was saved. He then discusses the moment or time of salvation and recounts how his life changed from that moment to the present. In the following sequence, the speaker starts his testimony using home style. When he remembers the time that he found God, he styleswitches to local standard. The switch seems to be triggered by the recollection of this solemn event in his life.

[10] 1 Hello friends (.) I come ta talk to you today bout tha power of the Lord

2 I member tha time as a youngun (.)

3 My momma and daddy'd pray for me ever night.

4 I wuz wilder than a hare.

5 I wuz headed for that no good place (2) an they knowed it (.) an they prayed.

6 Didn't nothing they said make no differance ta me.

7 I made ma poor momma and daddy cry many's tha night.

8 I got married (.) but it didn't change me none.

9 I kept on with ma ways (.) kept on.

10 THEN THERE CAME A DAY

11 IT WAS SEPTEMBER 9TH 1963

12 I WAS RIDING IN MY CAR COMING BACK FROM RALEIGH

13 AND I SUDDENLY FELT THE POWER OF THE LORD IN THA CAR WITH ME

14 AND GOD SPOKE AS PLAIN (2).

15 AND HE SAID IT'S TIME TO COME HOME.

16 AN I FELT THE POWER OF SALVATION RIGHT THEN AND THERE IN MA HEART AND I KNEW NOTHING WOULD EVER BE THE SAME.

17 FOLKS (.) YOU HAVE TO FEEL THA POWER OF THE LORD FOR YOURSELF.

18 AS MUCH AS THEY WANTED TO (.) MY DEAR MOTHER AND

FATHER COULDN'T PRAY ME INTO HEAVEN.
19 I HAD TA FIND THAT ROAD.
20 I HAD TA HEAR THA VOICE.
21 AN I THANK GOD EVER DAY.
22 AN I PRAISE THA LORD EVER DAY.

The speaker in this sequence starts his narrative using home style. This use allows him to signal his solidarity with the rest of the congregation. By keeping the details of his past vague and by using the more casual form of the dialect (home style), he allows them to share in the first nine lines of his story. In this small rural Baptist church all the listeners believe that you must first fall and then accept Christ in your life. By starting his story with his failure to lead a good life and the worry that caused his parents, he is telling the hearers something that they can understand and with which they can identify. In lines 3 and 7, the speaker refers to his parents as *momma and daddy*. He seems to be using home style to identify that time when he was a child, not young in years, but too young in his mind to accept God, so that his parents had to try to pray for his salvation because he would not do it himself. In line 11, the speaker recounts the exact day and year that he found God. The memory of this powerful event marks the styleswitch into local standard, and the speaker stays in local standard throughout the rest of his narrative. This switch is powerful and shows the speaker is manipulating his language to make a point. On the day he found God, he became an adult; his life changed completely. To further demonstrate this change, in line 18 the speaker refers to his parents as my dear *MOTHER AND FATHER*, terminology used by an adult.

In sequences [8] and [10], styleswitching is triggered by contemplation and memory. It is used by the speakers to signal that they are discussing a time or an event that is both important and serious. The topics in these shifts (death and salvation) are solemn subjects, and the speakers styleswitch to local standard when they remember and want to convey how serious the events were.

In sequence [9], Sheila recounts a serious narrative to Tessa, but even though she is discussing the problems faced by friends of the family, the message is neither personal nor formal for her: Therefore, Sheila makes the unmarked choice and stays in home style. We might predict that if Cody's mother was telling the story related by Sheila, she might styleswitch into local standard. For her, these events are personal, solemn, and tragic, and her code choice would probably indicate this for the listener.

The final two examples come from the patriarch of the family, Dan. In sequence [11], Dan is telling about a retirement dinner given for an executive in the company for which he worked. The dinner was being held at the local country club, a place to which Dan had never been invited before. The menu was pre-selected, with prime rib as the main course. Dan tells the family about the evening.

[11] Dan: 1   So we's all at this party at the Country Club an they's serving prime rib.

2   An I hadn't never had none of that though I'd heard of it

3   So they come abringin' it out an the boy sets mine down in front of me

4   An let me tell you the thing was aswimin' in pure ole red blood an there weren't no way I was gonna eat it

5   So I looked at the boy an I says to him

6   SAYS I (.) YOUNG MAN (.) I BELIEVE I'LL HAVE MINE COOKED.

//[laughter]//

Dan is attempting to achieve at least two goals with his shift. First, he is making fun of the posh surroundings. At this event, it probably feels to him that everybody is putting on airs, and he shows that he can put them on, too. But also, he shows his family and friends that even though he thought the behavior of those around him was funny, he is a man who knows how to use what would be considered proper speech in this type of situation. He knows how to send unsatisfactory food back and how to behave properly at the country club.

Sequence [12] is an example of someone refusing to styleshift when to styleswitch suddenly becomes the unmarked choice. The reason we can say that styleshifting into local standard here is the unmarked choice is that the speakers are all talking about travel overseas. Some of the members of the community have traveled overseas, but only if they were in the military and stationed at an overseas base. Usually this means Germany, which is one of the few destinations to which servicemen and -women can take their families. The people in the group start discussing their travels to Germany, and they switch into local standard. This may be because a variety approximating Standard American English is the unmarked choice when they are overseas, and thus local standard is the unmarked choice when they are reminiscing.

The participants who were abroad begin to talk about daytrips to France, and they discuss how beautiful Switzerland is. The listeners respond in short sentences in local standard, such as *it sounds wonderful* and *I would love to go someday.* At one point in the conversation, Pearl turns to her husband and says, "Oh Dan wouldn't you just love to go there." Dan responds in sequence [12].

[12] Dan: 1   I done been ta the ocean on the one side and the mountains on t'other

2   An that's all the fartherest I intend ta go

Dan's refusal to switch to the style that is prevailing in the group marks a powerful manipulation of his language. In home style, the term *done been* marks finality, that is, something that was done and probably will not be repeated in the near future. The adjective *all* in line 2 indicates the full amount, or rather the total limit of what Dan intends to do. And finally the invention of a new superlative, *fartherest*, indicates that Dan will absolutely not travel any farther from home than the mountains or the beach. He could have said he has gone "as far as he wants to go," or that he wants "to go no farther." But Dan combines the terms *done been, all,* and *fartherest* to let his listeners know that he is not interested in travel to Europe or anywhere else too far from home.

When we examine Dan's word choice, along with his refusal to accommodate his style (once we know that styleswitching is a possible choice in his repertoire), we see a powerful manipulation of language. Dan's refusal to styleswitch puts not only himself but also his world in a positive position. He has the mountains on one side and the ocean on the other. This puts him and his home in the center of the universe, and his staunch refusal to move far, either in language or in location, lets the hearer know that this is exactly where he wants to be.

CONCLUSION

The data from this study show us that people alternate between styles to make very subtle changes in day-to-day relationships. The ability to shift styles, to change both mood and tone, to switch identities to what appears to be the most favorable incarnation for an interaction, is at the heart of styleshifting. The ultimate reason for styleshifting is to promote ones self in the most positive light, and here we see ordinary people negotiating language in their home, showing themselves to be linguistic virtuosos.

REFERENCES

Blom, J. P., and J. J. Gumperz. 1972. Social meaning in linguistic structures: codeswitching in Norway. In *Directions in sociolinguistics*, ed. John J. Gumperz and Dell Hymes, 407–435. New York: Holt, Rinehart and Winston.

[Myers-Scotton, Carol] Scotton, Carol Myers. 1983. The negotiation of identities in conversation: a theory of markedness and code choice. *International Journal of the Sociology of Language* 44: 115–136.

———. 1988. Codeswitching as indexical of social negotiation. In *Codeswitching: anthropological and sociolinguistic perspectives*, ed. Monica Heller, 151–186. Berlin: Mouton de Gruyter.

———. 1993. *Social motivations for codeswitching: evidence from Africa*. Oxford: Oxford University Press.

10

Marked versus Unmarked Choices on the Auto Factory Floor

JANICE BERNSTEN

D ISCOURSE RESEARCH on talk at work largely focuses on the analysis of naturally occurring language in settings such as law and medicine (Drew and Heritage 1992). It is easy to see how special conditions apply in a venue such as a courtroom, with all the rules constraining the talk of judges, lawyers and witnesses. What is less evident is that the rules of engagement are just as stringent in such work settings as an automobile plant. There, it is not the law books that provide the rules but the contracts between union and management. Equally important from the point of view of the workers are the unwritten expectations for appropriate talk between management and labor. The purpose of this chapter is to show how talk in the automobile factory is constrained by participants' tacit knowledge of expected or unmarked language choices and how participants interpret marked choices. I demonstrate that communication in the factory was hampered in the last few years by the entrance of supervisors lacking assembly-line experience and, therefore, lacking the mental representations for making appropriate choices under the markedness matrix characteristic of the factory setting.

Drew and Heritage (1992) point out the special nature of institutional talk, which makes it of interest to researchers. Institutional goals lead to constraints and expectations such that participants may be expected to follow a different set of rules than those that apply to conversations in a social setting. As Miller writes:

> Institutional discourses are shared and standardized frameworks for anticipating, acting in, and reflecting on social settings and interactions. They allow and constrain setting members to organize their interactions as instances of standardized types of social relationships and produce conditions for responding to issues in predictable ways. (1994: 282)

In the case of a unionized automobile plant, the standardized social relationships on the factory floor are those between worker, supervisor, and union representative. Each of these players contributes to institutional talk based on scripts developed over years of negotiation between union and management. The data that follow show that a principal goal of the workers is to fight against the power asymmetry that Drew and Heritage note as a customary characteristic of institutional settings. The resulting scripts show unmitigated language to be the code choice for all the players.

I became interested in investigating shop talk because of linguistic examples provided in my sociolinguistics classes in Flint, Michigan, by students who had strong family connections in the local auto industry. Most of these students are the first generation in their family to attend college, and most come from the families of auto workers or are auto workers themselves, coming to college to retool for the changing demands of today's economy. These students reported that linguistic principles were very valuable in explaining some of the communication problems they were experiencing on the job. At the end of a lecture on Myers-Scotton's markedness model (1993), a student came up and said, "It was a marked choice!" He had a new manager who was perceived as totally ineffective on the factory floor. The man would approach two workers talking on the line and wait until one was finished before addressing them. Then he would say something like "I hate to bother you, but could you possibly do X." My student explained that on the factory floor, the unmarked directive form is *Do X*. The marked language choices of the manager were clear evidence to his workers that he lacked the skill to manage. I became very interested in finding out more about what did constitute effective management language in the eyes of local factory workers. How could the markedness model be applied in this setting to account for the workers' evaluation of appropriate and inappropriate linguistic choices by supervisors?

MYERS-SCOTTON'S MARKEDNESS MODEL

Myers-Scotton (1993) argues that speakers have, as part of their linguistic capacity, a markedness metric which allows them to judge linguistic choices as more or less expected for given interaction types. Each setting has norms specifying the expected or unmarked set of rights and obligations for each participant. Both marked and unmarked choices emanate from Myers-Scotton's negotiation principle:

> Choose the *form* of your conversation contribution such that it indexes the set of rights and obligations which you wish to be in force between speaker and addressee for the current exchange. (1993: 11)

Speakers sometimes make the unmarked choice, which has the effect of maintaining the status quo in terms of rights and obligations between speakers. On the other hand, they may make an unexpected or marked choice, which has the effect of changing the set of rights and obligations between speaker and addressee.

Of course, each speech community has its own set of norms and its own set of choices which will be viewed as marked or unmarked within given contexts. Markedness can only be interpreted within specific interactions in specific communities. As noted, talk at work has a discourse structure that differs substantially from ordinary conversation. An outsider in the work setting may err, as did the supervisor in my student's story, by making a code choice that in a general setting could be viewed as unmarked. However, in the auto factory setting, his directive choice was viewed as a marked choice, leading workers to view him as abdicating the power a supervisor should display by using bald imperatives in the work setting. Although it was not his intention to alter the rights and obligations between himself and the workers, his marked choice led to that result.

DATA COLLECTION

Whereas the students provided brief anecdotal examples of encounters in the factory, I needed more evidence to determine the whats, hows and whys of discourse in the automobile factory. To discover the marked and unmarked language in the factory setting, it was essential to collect more examples of naturally occurring talk and also the workers' evaluation of this speech. Although there is a fair amount of literature on talk in the courtroom and medical office (Atkinson and Drew 1979; Fisher and Todd 1983; Mishler 1984; West 1984; Levi and Walker 1990; Conley and O'Barr 1990), relatively little work has been done on shop talk. This lack of data is due in large part to the fact that factory managers consistently prohibit outsiders from doing such studies within their facilities. Auto production companies fear industrial espionage, litigation, and negative publicity which, according to Form (1976: 140), kept investigators out of plants for many years. I ran into similar resistance when I applied for permission to collect data in local auto production facilities.

When it became clear that doing research within the factory setting was not possible, I proceeded to collect data by interviewing factory workers outside the workplace. Fifteen male and fifteen female workers were interviewed, resulting in thirty-five hours of transcripts. The workers initially talked with me individually at a local coffee shop and then started keeping notebooks with linguistic examples, particularly those in which there was a communication breakdown between supervisor and worker which could illuminate marked and unmarked linguistic choices. This sort of data collection was advocated by Cameron et al. (1992) who criticized traditional social science research methodology, particularly as it is applied in studying relatively powerless groups, such as factory workers. They encourage moving away from research on subjects to research on, for, and with subjects. This sort of research implies "the use of interactive or dialogic research methods, as opposed to the distancing or objectifying strategies" (Cameron et al. 1992: 22) traditionally used in social science research. Indeed, the interviewees and data collectors for this study were enthusiastic participants. One man said, "I am so glad someone is interested in our opinions and sees us as skillful workers and worthwhile individuals—not as stupid, lazy factory workers."

Workers were equally enthusiastic when it came to participating in a more traditional data collection procedure—filling out questionnaires designed to follow up on insights gleaned in the original interviews. A mid-Michigan local of the United Auto Workers (UAW) allowed me to take up the first twenty minutes of its monthly meeting administering a brief questionnaire which combined free response and multiple-choice items.

Sixty-four workers completed the questionnaire (forty-one males and twenty-three females). These workers are representative of the current UAW membership in mid-Michigan in being part of a shrinking work force. General Motors has done a great deal of downsizing in the last twenty years and very little hiring. The average age of the workers is forty-four; only one worker below age thirty participated in the survey. The workers have an average of twenty-two years on the job and are thus intensely steeped in factory culture.

According to my informants, institutional talk on the factory floor is highly constrained by the rules in national and local union–management contracts. These codes have the effect of depersonalizing communication and creating "scripts" for many encounters between workers, supervisors, and union representatives. Before taking a look at the actual talk, it is useful to take a step back into the history of the auto industry to find the sources of current factory discourse.

HISTORICAL DEVELOPMENT OF SHOP TALK

In the early days of the auto industry, the production process was not yet standardized. Making cars was a craft in which the work was varied and workers controlled production. Management was paternalistic. Gartman notes that in those early days, Henry Ford "relied on personal intimacy and association to control his workers" (1986: 180). The result was talk between workers and managers which focused on solidarity rather than power. Nevins and Hill write of Henry Ford in 1904:

> Everybody used to call him Hank or Henry . . . and he used to know everybody by name. He seldom gave a direct command. Instead, he would say, "I wonder if we could get this done right away," or, "It would be fine if you could do so-and-so." These hints were effective. The men would just break their necks to see if they could do it. They knew what he wanted. (1954: 270–271)

As the factories grew, the work also became more mechanized and workers had far less control over their labor. Foremen took over supervision and in those days, the power of the foreman was arbitrary and unchallengeable. The speed of the line, one's chances for promotion, indeed, keeping the job itself—all were under the control of the foreman (Gartman 1986: 182). One woman told me about a foreman who would pay a different piece work rate for exactly the same job, depending on how well he liked the worker. When the women complained, he told them, "There are plenty of people waiting outside the plant for this job if you don't want it." Another man told me of a foreman who gave higher wages to men willing to mow his lawn and bring him cases of beer.

Pressure to standardize arbitrary work practices came from both above and below. Management established employment departments to centralize worker discipline and base sanctions on written rules and records instead of the manager's personal opinions. The UAW, established in 1937, worked for job classifications so that wages were associated with work done rather than the individual doing it. The UAW also put in place the seniority system and overtime pay policies. These efforts stripped the foremen of power and distanced their personal involvement in conflict. As Form writes: "Grievances are not resolved by on-the-spot consultation with the foreman because grievances are often categoric and not individual matters. An elaborate grievance machinery involving increasingly high echelons of the union and management handles thousands of complaints annually" (1976: 140).

SHOP TALK SCRIPTS

Three different publications outline the "grievance machinery": the national agreement between UAW and the auto production company, the local agreement between a plant and a specific union local, and the employee handbook for the plant (UAW 1993; North American Truck Platforms/Flint Assembly 1994; Employe Handbook n.d.). When a conflict arises, the first step is for worker and supervisor to attempt to solve the problem themselves. If the conflict is task related, supervisors must make expectations clear; this comes in the form of the statement *I'm giving you a direct order*. If the worker doesn't comply with the order, he or she is in danger of being written up and eventually suspended from the job. In that case, the supervisor must say *I'm writing you up*. Workers can be written up not only for disobedience but also for any of thirty-six other code violations in the Employe [sic] Handbook (n.d.) of the Flint Truck and Bus Group. These range from being late to fighting to throwing refuse on the floor.

I'm giving you a direct order and *I'm writing you up* have the force of performatives as described by Austin (1962) because their utterance results in a change in the world. In the factory setting, when the supervisor utters these statements, the result may be the loss of the worker's job. The seriousness with which workers take these utterances is illustrated in an ex-

ample from Kearns, quoting a worker who cut her hands doing her job on
the assembly line.

> On both my hands, I'm bleeding all over the place, through my gloves and I said,
> "I've got to go to first aid now. Now I have to go."
> He said, "No, you finish your job, then you can go."
> But what am I going to do? I don't want to get fired for not following a direct
> order. Okay? And that is an automatic fire. (1990: 67)

The woman kept working, the parts she was assembling continuing down the
line covered with blood, much to the dismay of the workers after her on the line.

If a worker disagrees with the supervisor's view of a situation, or if the
worker wants to initiate a grievance, the script is *Get me the committee man*.
The committee man, as the union representative is called in the factory, comes
to the floor to negotiate the conflict between worker and supervisor. Conflicts not solved by discussion among worker, supervisor, and committee
man may be appealed through several levels—first, to the shop committee,
then to the corporation and international union, and, finally, to an impartial
umpire at the highest level (UAW 1993).

One source which details several conflicts on the shop floor is *Rivethead*,
Ben Hamper's account of his twenty years on the auto assembly line. The
following example is a conflict script featuring the talk described previously
plus another feature of shop talk described by all the interviewees in the study:
the pervasiveness of profanity on the factory floor.

> *Supervisor:* Hamper, that was the General Foreman on the line. According to
> him, you've run three wrong axles in the past hour. Goddamnit, I'm writin'
> your ass up NOW!
>
> *Worker:* I don't give a shit how many times you try to write me up. The whole
> problem is that I am too fucking short to see what the hell I'm doin' on that
> job. How can I hit the carrier arms when I can't even SEE the bastards?
>
> *Supervisor:* Don't try to peddle me that line of bullshit. I've had short people run
> that job before.
>
> *Worker:* I want my committee man down here—NOW! (Hamper 1986: 107)

This shop talk differs quite dramatically from Henry Ford's hint directives of days gone by. In fact, these linguistic forms are consistent with institutional talk on the factory floor in general: Language is direct and unmitigated. There are several origins of this direct language. First, as noted earlier, clear orders and directives are mandated by union contracts. Second,
the factory environment is often so loud that it is difficult for workers to hear
heavily embedded directives. Third, according to Ervin-Tripp (1976), we
can expect unmitigated directives when persons are asked to do something
generally expected to be their responsibility. Children say to mom *I need a
cookie*, customers say to a McDonald's clerk *Give me a hamburger*, and
supervisors in the factory say to the worker *Go and sweep*. Workers expect

direct language from supervisors and as shown later, mitigated language often receives a negative evaluation.

What may be less expected is the unmitigated language, which workers use to address supervisors. We find that workers address everyone—worker, supervisor, plant manager—up to the top management by first names. One woman showed me a piece she wrote in the plant newsletter called *Why can't we compete, Pete?* criticizing the policies of the general manager of the plant whose first name is Peter. When asked on a questionnaire how they would request time off from a supervisor, more than half of the union workers chose not a question (e.g., *Could I have some time off tomorrow to go to the doctor's? Would it be possible to have some time off tomorrow?*) but the statement *I won't be here tomorrow afternoon. I'm going to a doctor's appointment.* Cavendish, in describing eight months working in a British auto firm in the late 1970s, relates an incident with her supervisor which illustrates the unmitigated nature of talk between workers and supervisors:

> He [the supervisor] acted as if he was doing us a great favour whenever he brought components or took away boxes, and stood waiting for us to say "please" and "thank you." We bawled him out because it was his job to fetch and carry and no one said please and thank you to us every time a tray came down the line. (1982: 104)

It is clear that talk on the factory floor is full of unmitigated directives and vulgarity and lacks politeness markers such as please and thank you. Again, looking at history can put this language into perspective. Literature from the UAW paints the traditional relationship between workers and management as a long-term class struggle dating back to late sixteenth-century Europe (UAW n.d.: 3). According to Nash, "the auto worker, despite high pay and other benefits, remains among the most militant and angry members of the American labor movement" (1976: 61). Nash points out that the major source of job dissatisfaction among auto workers is powerlessness in the work situation. The UAW was formed in the first place to offer resistance to the power asymmetry in the factory. Workers can fight against this asymmetry of power by using the language of equals to their supervisors, knowing the union will back them when conflict arises.

The desire to be treated with respect as individuals and workers was a common theme in Collinson's (1992) work in a British factory and was echoed in mid-Michigan interviews and questionnaire comments. When asked to describe their least effective supervisors, 44% of the UAW members included comments involving respect. A thirty-six-year-old female assembler wrote of her supervisor, "She was disrespectful and treated employees like children that needed to be babysitted." A forty-year-old male wrote, "He acts like *I'm the boss and it doesn't matter what you think.*" Workers respond to perceived inequalities with straight talk. A forty-eight-year-old male assembler wrote:

My supervisor was acting like a "boss" not as a supervisor. I'm not asking him to "kiss my ass" but I'm certainly not going to kiss his. I finally told him, "I can be a cooperative employee or an uncooperative employee. Which do you want?" We at present time get along much better.

The unmitigated nature of shop talk marks the discourse as very different from that expected in ordinary conversational interaction. In their politeness model, Brown and Levinson (1987) describe in detail the efforts speakers usually make to defuse or mitigate face threatening acts through positive and negative politeness strategies. Coulthard notes that bald on-record acts "are not frequent" in conversation (1985: 51). Brown and Levinson observe: "The majority of natural conversations do not proceed in this brusque fashion at all" (1987: 95).

If the conversational rules between supervisor and worker in the auto factory differ from those in other discourse settings, we can assume that there is a potential for misunderstanding when a person who lacks experience in the factory becomes one of the players. Traditionally, supervisors came from the ranks of workers on the line who were looking for advancement. Recently, however, due to increased educational requirements and reluctance of workers to leave the security of the union, supervisors coming to the floor lack experience on the line (Chinoy 1992). Some of the misunderstandings described by the workers can be traced to a lack of knowledge of shop talk. On the other hand, other conflicts arise between supervisors and workers who know the factory discourse "rules" perfectly well but choose not to follow them. The interviews and questionnaires provide examples of both intentional and unintentional marked choices on the part of supervisors.

MARKED CHOICES ON THE FACTORY FLOOR

An Intentional Marked Choice
The following exchange really puts into focus the unmitigated directive as the unmarked and expected code choice of a supervisor in an auto factory.

[1] Conversational sequence between experienced supervisor and experienced worker who is serving as an all-purpose replacement (Bernsten 1995).

Supervisor: "Go do Bill's job." [Worker complies]
Supervisor: "Go do Tom's job."
Worker: "I can't do Tom's job."
Supervisor: "I'm giving you a direct order." [Worker tries to comply—returns to supervisor]
Worker: "I can't do Tom's job."
Supervisor: "Go sweep."   [Worker complies]
Supervisor: "Do you think you can do Helen's job?"

Worker: "Get me the committee man."

[Worker complies; supervisor writes request for union rep]

In this case, we have an experienced manager supervising a woman who came to his department as a replacement for the day. This highly skilled woman knows all the jobs on the line and can do almost all of them. The supervisor in the first encounter with this worker makes the unmarked choice in giving orders in the form of a bald imperative. The manager started the day by telling her to replace Bill so he could go on a break; the request took the form *Go do Bill's job*, which she did. Then the manager asked her to cover one of the few jobs she cannot do on the line because of the heavy lifting involved. According to the worker, the supervisor knew she couldn't do it. In fact, he wanted to keep the man who was doing it on the line. When he gave her the direct order, she had to make the attempt. She returned, and he sent her to sweep, saying *Go sweep*. At this point, she was mildly irritated with him but continued to comply with his orders. His next request took the form of a question directive, the type of mitigated request form which on the surface looks far more polite than his previous directives. He said *Do you think you can do Helen's job?* The worker took this request as a highly marked form and a direct insult to her capabilities as a replacement worker. She told me, "Of course I could do Helen's job. How could he say such a thing to me?" She complied with the request, but on her way out, she said *Get me the committee man.* When the union representative arrived to negotiate, the foreman agreed he had been out of line and gave her a formal apology.

An Unintentional Marked Choice

Example [1] shows a supervisor making a deliberately marked choice, which the worker took as unnecessary sarcasm and throwing his power into the exchange. His remark certainly had the effect of challenging the rights and obligations set between the conversational participants, with a visit from the union representative as the result. In contrast, we find some supervisors making linguistic choices which from their standpoint would be unmarked; in fact, these choices would be unmarked in the general speech community. However, in the context of the factory, the choices are perceived by workers to be marked.

[2]   Conversation between new supervisor and experienced worker.

Supervisor: "Are you going to be here tomorrow?"

Worker: "I hadn't planned on it."

[Supervisor leaves abruptly and returns with committee man]

Supervisor: "You have disobeyed a direct order."

Worker: "What was it?"

Supervisor: "To come back to this department and work here tomorrow."

Example [2] is a conversational sequence between a new supervisor and an experienced worker who was told he would be serving as a replacement in a department for three days. At the end of the third day, the supervisor came up to the worker and asked, *Are you going to be here tomorrow?* When the worker replied *I hadn't planned on it,* the supervisor left angrily to return with the committee man. She said to the worker, *You have disobeyed a direct order.* The worker said, *What was it?* The supervisor believed she had told the worker to be back in the department for a fourth day; her question directive was, of course, ambiguous and the worker took it as an information question rather than a directive. The unmarked choice on the factory floor would have been *Be back here tomorrow.*

When asked to give examples of ineffectual management language, workers talked about supervisors who used polite or ambiguous directives which actually sound a lot like the ones attributed to Henry Ford in the early days of the auto industry. These supervisors were given nicknames like "Mr. Rogers" and/or "The Lamp Post" and were generally regarded with contempt by the workers.

Exploiting Ambiguity

Although the misunderstanding in example [2] was due to a true communication breakdown between supervisor and worker, interviewees gave other examples in which workers exploited the ambiguity of mitigated directives to ignore ones they felt were too indirect. Example [3] features such an exchange.

[3]   Conversational sequence between supervisor and repair person.

    Supervisor: "Aren't you going to fix that?"
       Worker: [Ignores supervisor]
    Supervisor: "I'm telling you to do that."
       Worker: [Makes repair]

In this case, the worker chose to interpret "Aren't you going to fix that?" as an information question rather than a directive. He waited until the supervisor produced the unmarked directive for the factory setting, the direct order *I'm telling you to do that.* Workers told me the indirect requests in the form of questions or hints were sometimes ignored.

In an effort to learn more about workers' perceptions of marked directive choices, I included the following problem on the union workers' questionnaire:

Suppose you had a supervisor who said, "I wonder if you could possibly do this job." How would you evaluate his or her effectiveness? Do you think workers would comply with this type of directive?

Twenty percent of the workers commented on the ambiguity of the request and stated that their effectiveness rating and their compliance would depend on their relationship with the supervisor. A forty-two-year-old male wrote,

"A good supervisor who has a rapport with workers can use this approach. If a supervisor has to rely on positional power, this approach will not work." A male zone committee man wrote, "It depends on if it is a genuine question or if after you answer 'no' you know a direct order will follow."

Forty-two percent of the respondents reacted negatively to the *if you could* request. They labeled a supervisor who used such a directive form as ineffectual and believed workers would not comply with the request. A forty-one-year-old female noted two possible negative interpretations. She wrote, "There is the negative of *if you could possibly* which could be taken as an insult, but the question also sounds like the supervisor is scared to death to ask the question." Indeed, some workers responded as did the worker in example [1], taking such a request as a personal insult. A forty-six-year-old male, wrote "I might be defensive in thinking he was questioning my ability to complete the job." Another group viewed such a request as a sign of weakness. A male electrician wrote, "No leadership, workers would not completely respect them." A final group assumed that such a request would only be for work out of one's job classification—something definitely to be avoided. A thirty-seven-year-old woman wrote, "Being that this would be a rare request, my first response would be 'sorry, I don't do favors for engineers.' This practice could come back to haunt you in added duties."

Interestingly, 37% of the workers reported that they would be very pleased to be addressed in such a way by a supervisor. A female worker with thirty years of experience on the assembly line wrote, "For me, it would be very effective. I would do more for him or her when asked in that manner." A male wrote that the supervisor would be effective because "it's not an order, it's a request to do your best effort." Another said, "I feel more workers would respond to this type of language because it is working with the workers and our jobs are important to us."

DISCUSSION

Workers describing actual encounters with supervisors and those responding to hypothetical situations on the questionnaire showed a great deal of insight in discussing the alternative implications of language choices. Workers described minor differences in syntactic and lexical choices which could result in major differences in interpretation. Also, many workers wrote at length about possible interpretations based on the differences in the supervisor's perceived assumptions and motivations. It is evident that given social identity features (e.g., age and gender) and given linguistic choices do not mechanistically determine listeners' interpretations. Myers-Scotton writes: "While norms largely determine the interpretations of choices, speakers, not norms, make choices" (1993: 102). It is clear from this data that perceived attitudes of the speakers play a large part in the listeners' evaluations of possible meanings.

The markedness model is characterized as a universal cognitive structure in which the "actual assignment of readings of markedness of codes is only developed in reference to a specific community through social experiences in interactions there" (Myers-Scotton 1993: 79). The social competence to communicate effectively in the factory requires workers to activate their knowledge of the way in which factory discourse differs from the other discourse worlds which they inhabit. The workers' intricate responses reveal cognitive calculations based on their underlying knowledge of marked and unmarked behavior in the factory.

Although all the conversational maxims in the markedness model are affected by the discourse structure of the factory, one which is particularly impacted is the deference maxim: "the switch to a code which expresses deference to others when special respect is called for by circumstances" (Myers-Scotton 1993: 147). There appear to be very few settings in the factory in which the deference maxim is activated. The factory discourse patterns revealed in this study are the result of the historical development of talk between managers and workers where management and union have maintained a basically adversarial relationship for many years. I would argue that the lack of politeness markers and the bald imperatives used by both management and workers can be indexed with the attempt of each group to assert and maintain equal power. Unmitigated talk is the unmarked choice for both management and worker in an effort to maintain the status quo in rights and obligations established in rigorous union–management negotiation and codified in the omnipresent union–management contract (UAW 1993). Any deviations from the unmitigated code choices are perceived as marked and are interpreted as an abnegation of the power stance expected from both the supervisor and the workers.

These data offer implications for training employees in the most effective discourse patterns, particularly new managers coming from outside the factory culture. It is clear that managers need to be prepared for unmitigated language from workers as the unmarked choice. They also need to know the expectations of workers regarding the unmarked choices for directives from them. On the other hand, mastering scripts does not automatically make a respected supervisor. Workers described the best managers as those who used good judgment in managing workers by giving clear orders on the one hand and treating workers with respect on the other. The best managers were those who avoided conflict talk altogether. One woman described her favorite supervisor as a man who "let's [*sic*] his line run itself. He sees potential problems and deals with them in advance."

It would be beneficial to see how talk on the shop floor differs in two other types of auto factories. What is shop talk like in factories where workers lack the protection of the union, particularly in these days of uncertainty about job security? Can we expect more politeness and mitigated talk from workers in such factories? Will the unmarked choices for management and worker show a more asymmetrical relationship? An alternative venue is the factory run under Japanese management. How does the cooperative/team approach brought in to Japanese-owned plants in the United States play out on the factory floor? Does it result in both workers and supervisors being less direct and more polite? Do the unmarked choices in these factories reveal mitigation on the part of both management and worker? Contrasting shop talk in these plants with that in unionized Michigan auto production facilities will constitute the next phase of this research.

ACKNOWLEDGEMENT: Thanks to Kevin Beard, Barbara Eastman, Loren Shipprett, Gary Bernath, the members of UAW Local 605, Lansing, Michigan, and all the other workers who provided the insights that made this chapter possible.

REFERENCES

Atkinson, John Maxwell, and Paul Drew. 1979. *Order in the court: the organisation of verbal interaction in judicial settings.* London: Macmillan.

Austin, John L. 1962. *How to do things with words.* New York: Oxford University Press.

Bernsten, Janice. 1995. "You know you're in trouble when she swears": female and male managers on the automobile factory floor. Paper presented at the American Association of Applied Linguists Annual Meeting, Los Angeles.

Brown, Penelope, and Stephen C. Levinson. 1987. *Politeness: some universals in language usage.* Cambridge: Cambridge University Press.

Cameron, Deborah, Elizabeth Frazer, Penelope Harvey, M. B. H. Rampton, and Kay Richardson. 1992. *Researching language: issues of power and method.* London: Routledge.

Cavendish, Ruth. 1982. *Women on the line.* London: Routledge and Kegan Paul.

Chinoy, Eli. 1992. *Automobile workers and the American dream.* 2nd ed. Urbana: University of Illinois Press.

Collinson, David L. 1992. *Managing the shopfloor: subjectivity, masculinity and workplace culture.* Berlin: Walter de Gruyter.

Conley, John M., and William O'Barr. 1990. *Rules versus relations: the ethnography of legal discourse.* Chicago: University of Chicago Press.

Coulthard, Malcolm. 1985. *An introduction to discourse analysis.* London: Longman.

Drew, Paul, and John Heritage. 1992. Analyzing talk at work: an introduction. In *Talk at work: interaction in institutional settings,* ed. P. Drew and J. Heritage, 3–65. Cambridge: Cambridge University Press.

Employe [sic] *Handbook.* n.d. Truck and Bus Group, Flint Assembly Plant, G-3100 Van Slyke Road, Flint, Mich.

Ervin-Tripp, Susan. 1976. "Is Sybil there?" The structure of some American English directives. *Language in Society* 5: 25–66.

Fisher, Sue, and Alexandra Dundas Todd (eds.). 1983. *The social organization of doctor–patient communication.* Washington, D.C.: Center for Applied Linguistics.

Form, William H. 1976. *Blue-collar stratification: autoworkers in four countries.* Princeton, N.J.: Princeton University Press.

Gartman, David. 1986. *Auto slavery: the labor process in the American automobile industry, 1897–1950.* New Brunswick, N.J.: Rutgers University Press.

Hamper, Ben. 1986. *Rivethead: tales from the assembly line.* New York: Warner Books.

Kearns, Josie. 1990. *Life after the line.* Detroit: Wayne State University Press.

Levi, Judith N., and Anne Graffam Walker (eds.). 1990. *Language in the judicial process.* New York: Plenum.

Miller, Gale. 1994. Toward ethnographies of institutional discourse. *Journal of Contemporary Ethnography* 23: 280–306.

Mishler, Elliot G. 1984. *The discourse of medicine: dialectics of medical interviews.* Norwood, N.J.: Ablex.

Myers-Scotton, Carol. 1993. *Social motivations for codeswitching: evidence from Africa.* Oxford: Oxford University Press.

———. 1995. What do speakers want? Codeswitching as evidence of intentionality in linguistic choices. *SALSA II: Proceedings of the second annual symposium on language and society*–Austin, ed. Pamela Silberman and Jonothan Loftin, 1–17. Austin: University of Texas Linguistics Department.

Nash, Al. 1976. Job satisfaction: a critique. In *Auto work and its discontents*, ed. B. J. Widick, 61–88. Baltimore: Johns Hopkins University Press.

Nevins, Allan, and Frank Ernest Hill. 1954. *Ford: the times, the man, the company.* New York: Scribner's Sons.

North American Truck Platforms/Flint Assembly. 1994. Local Agreement between NATP Flint Assembly and Local 598 United Autoworkers.

United Auto Workers. 1993. Agreement between UAW and the General Motors Corporation.

———. n.d. *Heritage of struggle: the historical setting for the Flint sitdown strikes.* Detroit: UAW Education Department.

West, Candace. 1984. *Routine complications: troubles in talk between doctors and patients.* Bloomington: Indiana University Press.

— IV —

Stylistic Choices and
Second-Language Acquisition

11

"Not quite right": Second-Language Acquisition and Markedness

MARY SUE SRODA

N̲O ONE CONTESTS the assertion that acquiring a second language as an adult is an arduous and extremely complex process. This chapter considers one part of that complex process—the acquisition of native-like use of a second language, also known as *pragmatic ability* or *pragmatic competence*.[1] I propose that reanalysis through the markedness model (Myers-Scotton 1993b) yields an explanatory account of the complexity of second language use through a simple cognitive mechanism underlying complex sociopragmatic effects.

The nature of language use is so flexible and unpredictable that it is almost impossible to exhaustively describe what is "appropriate" language use in any situation. That is, the fundamental issue of language use for teachers of second-language (L2) learners is, "why do we say what when?" Teachers of a second language often get questions from students in the following form: "What should I say in situation *X*?" At first, the answer for highly formulaic situations seems easy. In the case of purchasing stamps at the post office, for example, a teacher might give an answer such as *I would like a book of 20 stamps please*. However, there are many other lexical and morphosyntactic variations that are just as acceptable as in examples [1]–[4]:

[1]   Do you have books of 20 stamps?
[2]   Could I have a book of 20 stamps?
[3]   A book of 20 stamps, please.
[4]   20 stamps, please.

The set of allowable, appropriate responses is even larger in situations that are less formulaic. In fact, in everyday communication, situations in which

1. This ability contrasts with other linguistic abilities, the ability to produce well-formed utterances, for example.

there is only one appropriate lexical or morphosyntactic code choice are the exception rather than the rule.

That is, instead of there constantly being one "correct" answer, there is often a range of "right" answers, some answers that are "not quite right," and other answers that would not be considered acceptable at all. Following the post-office situation, examples [5] and [6] could be considered less "right" than [1]–[4].

[5]   Give me 20 stamps.

[6]   Pardon me, would you be so kind as to allow me to purchase a book of 20 stamps?

Example [7], on the other hand, would not be considered acceptable at all for this type of service transaction:

[7]   20 stamps, now!

One point from which to start examining this phenomenon is to examine what is meant by right in light of the post-office example; a code choice that is right would mean that it is appropriate for the status of the speakers and appropriate for what is communicated. Even though it violates no structural rules of English, example [7] is not right in two ways: First, bald imperatives are not normative (unmarked) for this type of service transaction; second, inclusion of the lexeme *now* stands in contrast to the typically unvoiced assumption that the transaction would normally take place immediately after the request is made.

Identifying code choices that are absolutely not right or appropriate for a given situation such as the post-office transaction, is quite easy. The type of language that is harder to discuss involves examples that fall into the "not quite so right" category as seen in examples [5] and [6]. Unfortunately, language use that is not quite so right is exactly the type of language use that teachers of nonnative speakers of English often encounter. Students say or write things in their L2 which strike their teachers, as one colleague put it, as "odd English." That is, many times, especially in the case of intermediate or advanced nonnative speakers, what the students say or write is not grammatically wrong in the sense of violating the rules of well-formed English but, rather, odd in the sense of not being the way a native speaker would say it. In such cases, the effect of the odd language choices L2 learners make can vary in degree from simply emphasizing the fact that the learner is not a native speaker of English to completely obscuring the learner's intended meaning.

The issue of differences in the sociopragmatic effects of various morphosyntactic or lexical choices in L2 acquisition and the difference in the interpretation and/or perception of these structures by native and nonnative speakers of English is well studied in the field of L2 acquisition (see Blum-Kulka et.al. 1989; Kasper and Blum-Kulka 1993, among others). But Turner (1995,

1996) points out that these studies have limited implications for pedagogy as applied to natural language use.

The goal of this chapter is to look at the acquisition of pragmatic competence by L2 learners within a theoretical framework that provides an explanation of the variations in the morphosyntactic/lexical choices in natural language use such that teachers of English as a Second Language may have a new way to talk to L2 learners about how the choices they make are (and are not) like the choices native speakers make. That is, this chapter shows how Myers-Scotton's markedness model provides an explanatory framework for the range of linguistic choices that L2 learners can make which are "not quite right."

THE MARKEDNESS MODEL

In the last ten years much research was done concerning the development of theories and models of communication that involve the intentionality of speakers when communicating and their cognitive awareness of linguistic choices. Such a model is Myers-Scotton's markedness model (MM; 1993b) proposing sociolinguistic motivations for codeswitching among multilingual speakers. To limit the MM to simply motivating choices made in codeswitching would be a mistake, however, as it is applicable to all linguistic choices that speakers make.

A detailed description of the MM is included in chapter 2 (Myers-Scotton in this volume). The discussion here is intended to emphasize the parts of the model that specifically concern this analysis. The idea behind the MM is that speakers make linguistic choices to negotiate social distances in linguistic interactions. For each interaction, an expected, normative, unmarked rights and obligations set (RO set) exists for each speaker. However, RO sets are community specific.

During an interaction, speakers either endorse or reject the expected RO set for the interaction by making linguistic choices that are or are not compatible with that RO set. A choice that is compatible with an RO set is unmarked for that particular set, and a choice not compatible with the RO set is marked for that RO set. If a speaker makes a marked choice, he or she is making a bid for another RO set. For example, in an employer–employee discussion, an employer may use a more casual style of speech and lexical choice to indicate a willingness to switch from a very formal employer–employee RO set to a more informal RO set that colleagues would use, thus making a bid for a decrease in social distance.

THE MARKEDNESS EVALUATOR

The markedness evaluator (ME) is the mental faculty involved with assigning assessments of markedness to linguistic choices. On this faculty, Myers-Scotton writes:

This metric [evaluator] is part of the innate cognitive faculty of all humans. It enables speakers to assess all code choices as more or less *unmarked* or *marked* for the exchange type in which they occur. A critical distinction is that, while the metric [evaluator] is a cognitive structure and therefore a universal, it underlies an ability which is particular. The ability, consisting of the actual assignment of readings of markedness to codes, is only developed in reference to a specific community through social experience in interactions there. Thus, while it is a universal feature of language use that all choices are interpreted in terms of their markedness, one can speak of the markedness of a particular code *only* in reference to a specific speech event in a specific community. (1993b: 80)

Speaking of choices as marked or not assumes that they take place in a normative framework . . . while speakers are innately equipped with a markedness metric [evaluator], they only make actual readings through experience with language use in that community. They then view the codes in their community's repertoire as more unmarked or marked, according to community norms, as the index of the unmarked RO set between certain participants in a given talk exchange. This argument implies that conversations are more or less conventionalized, that speakers have some sense of the unmarked "script" or "schema" for them. (1993b: 109)

The analysis of L2 morphosyntactic lexical choices is concerned with two key ideas from the previous passages: "the actual assignment of readings of markedness to codes" and the "normative framework" within which the readings of markedness make sense. I propose that both concepts are part of the markedness evaluator and provide explanations for why nonnative speakers (NNSs) have difficulty using an L2 the way that native speakers (NSs) use the same language. The innate non-language-specific cognitive mechanisms of the MM, which are in place before a speaker acquires even one language, underlie sociopragmatic competence in any language. As a basic cognitive faculty of speakers of any language, the markedness evaluator (ME) does not change when a speaker begins to acquire and use an L2. Instead, during L2 acquisition, all the things that serve as input to these abilities and mechanisms that allow NNSs to make choices reflecting their communicative goals are what change. In this sense, then, part of what an L2 learner acquires in becoming a native-like L2 communicator is not only information about the RO sets specific to that L2 community but also community-specific "readings," as it were, about which lexical and morphosyntactic structures index those sets.

In short, I propose that the examples of "odd," awkward, or ineffective language can be redefined as choices marked for a given RO set and, therefore, interfere with or confound communication. Yet they represent a speaker's "best attempt" at a code choice that reflects his or her communicative intention. As markedness is delineated in the MM, the ways in which an utterance can be marked are complex but not infinite, and this markedness is always defined relative to some sort of unmarked starting point.

My hypothesis is that many of the seemingly infinitely complex problems of awkwardness and ineffectiveness that occur in student writing of Standard

American Academic English can be accounted for within the structure of the MM. I predict that both NS and NNS writing may show these errors but that there will be differences in the type of errors that NSs and NNSs make. I further contend that the way the MM accounts for these differences provides clues for teachers of NNSs to help their students become more native-like in their language use.

METHODOLOGY

The data from composition writing for this chapter were gathered from NSs and NSSs of English from a one semester, first-year composition class (English 101) at the University of South Carolina. Normally, there are special sections of English 101, called English 101B, which are solely for international students enrolled at the university. Yet, through a computer error at the registrar's office, four native speakers of English were allowed to enroll in a section of 101B in the fall of 1994. The corpus consists of drafts and in-class writing collected throughout the semester from thirteen NNSs and four NSs.

The example from the corpus that brought the possible applications of the MM for the L2 acquisition of pragmatic competence to my attention was an essay from a female student, Miko, a native Japanese speaker. Miko was beginning her freshman year at the university after having spent one year as a student in the university's intensive English program for international students. From her writing on the first day of class, she expressed a love of writing but also recognized the differences between communicating in Japanese and English. She expressed frustration common to many students who have an intermediate-level command of English in writing: "I tried to get used to American writing style, but it was very hard for me."[2] However, one particular paper of Miko's, an assignment asking students to write a narrative essay, brought into relief the way the MM may help explain the developing sociopragmatic ability of L2 learners.

In the first draft of her narrative essay, Miko told the story of losing her wallet one afternoon while at the university. After a frenzied search of places she had been shortly before she noticed the wallet was missing, she remarked, "I wanted to call my boyfriend, but I didn't have even 25 cents."

The possible applications of the MM can be seen in her use of internal dialogue to decide what to do then while standing in front of the campus student activity center:

> "If I ask somebody, will he or she give me money?" There was a lot of people there.
> "Who can I ask?" I've never asked somebody for money like a homeless person in my life. I was scared. I was thinking of a polite English sentence in my Brain.
> "Could I have your 25¢?" "Is that correct?" I had no idea. I was totally lost.

---

2. All examples from student writing are presented exactly as they occurred, including all nonstandard punctuation, spelling, and grammar. Except when indicated otherwise, examples come from writing that students did not edit or revise.

Another English sentences came to my mind. "Excuse me, today I lost my wallet. I'd like to call my boyfriend, but I don't have money. Can I borrow money?" This time, kind of long sentences came to my mind. It sounded ok for me. However, if the person say No, what should I do?

Because she could not decide about the best way to ask a stranger for money for the pay phone, Miko never asked anyone. In her essay, Miko came up with two possibilities for asking for a quarter: *Could I have your 25¢?* and *Excuse me, today I lost my wallet. I'd like to call my boyfriend, but I don't have money. Can I borrow money?* Either choice may have resulted in Miko achieving her communicative goal, getting a quarter from a stranger, but Miko didn't just want to get a quarter, she wanted to ask *the right way.* Stated in the terminology of the MM, Miko could not make a code choice that she thought was unmarked for the RO set she considered to be in place when asking a stranger in English for money to make a phone call.

Ironically, the second option Miko proposed, *Excuse me, today I lost my wallet. I'd like to call my boyfriend, but I don't have money. Can I borrow money?*, was relatively unmarked and probably would have resulted in someone understanding what she needed and giving her a quarter to call.

MEASURING UNMARKEDNESS

I felt that augmenting my intuitions about what constituted an unmarked choice in Miko's situation should be possible by designing a task to elicit the intuitions of other speakers of English. My prediction was that comparing the responses should yield quantifiable characteristics of unmarked choices consistent with the MM. Once the characteristics of the unmarked choice were described, the unmarked choice was compared to NNS responses to the same task.

The eventual goal of this chapter is to apply the operationalized description of unmarked choices from the elicitation task to the problems in markedness that L2 learners have in their writing to help them understand precisely how their linguistic choices are not native-like.

ELICITATION TASK AND RESPONSES

Every speaker has intuitions about markedness, but often explicitly discussing those intuitions can be very difficult. To help average speakers avoid this difficulty, I developed the task that described a situation similar to the one Miko described in her narrative essay. Subjects for this task were NSs of English enrolled in two sections of English 101 ($n = 30$). For purposes of comparison, the same task was given to students enrolled in one section of 101B containing only NNSs of English ($n = 21$).

All students were given a blank index card, told to put their native language at the top, and asked to write their responses to the following situation:

One day you drive your car to school and lock your keys inside. You can call home to have someone bring your spare set of keys, but there is only a pay phone and you have no money. You have to ask a stranger for the money to call . . . what would you say?

Two NS responses and one NNS response were excluded from this analysis because the subjects wrote down summaries of their communication strategies as opposed to writing the actual words they would use; that is, *I would try to politely ask to borrow a quarter* versus *Excuse me, I locked my keys in my car.* Examples [8]–[10] and [11]–[13] illustrate responses which were included in the analysis from the NS and NNS groups, respectively.

NS Responses

[8] Excuse me sir, but I locked my keys in my car and I don't have any change. Would you happen to have some change I could have.

[9] Excuse me do you have a quarter so I can call home? I have locked my keys in my car. I have some change in my car and will give it back to you when my car is opened.

[10] Excuse me. I've locked my keys in my car and need to call someone. May I please borrow a quarter for a phone call?

NNS Responses

[11] Would you please give me a quarter to make a phone-call, 'cause I've forgotten my car's key and I want my family to pick me up.

[12] Sorry to bother you, but I really need to borrow a quarter. See I locked my keys in my car and I just need to phone a friend to come pick me up.

[13] Excuse me sir. I have a slight problem. I wonder if you could help me. I seem to have locked my keys in my car and I don't have any money. May I please borrow a quarter so I can call home.

RESULTS OF "LOCKED CAR" TASK

As seen in Table 11-1, the responses made by the NSs and NNSs of English do not on the surface seem very different. Responses in both groups varied from the brief to the verbose with responses from the NNS group spreading

Table 11-1
Analysis of Responses

	Native Speakers (N = 30)	Nonnative Speakers (N = 21)
Briefest response	16 words	11 words
Longest response	41 words	63 words
Mean length of response	25.9 words	27.8 words
Median length of response	29 words	37 words

out toward the two extremes more than the NS group. The striking difference between the two groups in this type of analysis is a difference in the median of each group, but this difference is mostly due to one extremely long response from one of the NNS subjects. If that one very long response is not counted, the next longest response is forty-two words and the median for the NNS group drops to twenty-seven words. Even though NNSs tended to use slightly more words in their responses, the variation of length of response in both the groups indicates that the number of words is not particularly revealing in terms of distinguishing features of unmarked responses.

CODING THE "LOCKED CAR" DATA

The problem still remains of how to describe these responses such that an unmarked NS response for this situation can be characterized and compared to the NNS responses. To do this, the responses were analyzed in terms of the information they contained. Following the model of communication proposed in Sperber and Wilson (1995), one can define the information content of the responses in terms of the effect that a piece of information has on the assumptions of a hearer. Sperber and Wilson describe assumptions of a hearer as thoughts treated by the individual as representations of the world. When linguistic input is processed, it has the effect of causing the hearer to construct a new assumption, strengthen or weaken existing assumptions, or abandon existing assumptions. I propose that linguistic input can be divided into "information features." For example, all responses contained an information feature that I call ASK FOR MONEY. When the hearers process the information feature of ASK FOR MONEY, they construct a new assumption: *This person is asking me for money.* Describing the information in an utterance by the effect that it has on the assumptions of the hearer provides a way to compare utterances that are, in terms of meaning, roughly equivalent. In fact, I propose that this method is the only way to compare such utterances because different combinations of lexical items can have the same social effect. For example, no two NSs chose the same way to ask for money, as the following nine randomly selected NS examples help illustrate.

[14] May I please have a quarter

[15] . . . and need some change to call home, do you have some I could have?

[16   Could you please spare me a quarter.

[17] I was wondering if you had a quarter I could use for the pay phone.

[18] . . . but I have no money to use the pay phone. Could you please help me out?

[19] Would you happen to have some change I could have.

[20] do [you] happen to have a quarter

[21] do you think you can spare a quarter

[22] could you lend me a quarter

All the information features in the request introduce or modify assumptions. For instance, if the overall request contains a feature that mentions specific use for the money in addition to the ASK FOR MONEY feature, the assumption introduced by the ASK FOR MONEY feature is modified to something like *this person is asking me for money to make a phone call*. The assumptions introduced or modified by information features serve as input to the ME that produces readings about the relative markedness of the information features.

The information features that appeared in the "locked car" data are described next, illustrated with examples from the NS data:

POLITE OPENING. This category includes instances of opening the request with a polite attention-getter such as *excuse me* or *excuse me ma'am or sir*, although other alternatives such as bare honorifics like *Sir?* occurred. Other examples of Polite Opening in the data were *could you help me?*, *I'm sorry to bother you,* and *could I have a second of your time?*

ASK FOR MONEY. This represented the actual request for the money to make the call. Responses varied widely, as examples [14]–[22] discussed earlier show.

NO KEYS. This category included any mention that the subject has locked the keys in the car such as *I've just locked my keys in the car, I seem to have locked my keys in my car,* or *I acidently* [sic] *locked my keys in my car.*

USE FOR MONEY. This category represents all mention of what the subject will do with the money such as *so that I can call home, for a phone call,* and *I need to call home for an extra set of keys.*

NO MONEY. Items in this category included all mention of why the subject has no money and thus provides the stranger with a reason for asking for money for the phone. Examples include *I locked my keys and my money in my car, I don't have any money for the pay phone,* and *I don't have any change.*

PROMISE TO GIVE MONEY BACK. This category includes assurances that the subject will get the money back to the stranger—*I'll pay you back* and *I'll give it back to you once my car is opened.*

THANK FOR TIME. One NNS subject thanked the stranger for taking the time to listen to the request even if the request were to be to be refused.

Table 11-2 shows the breakdown of information categories by speaker group. As seen previously, not all requests included all information features.[3] The only information feature that all subjects in both groups included

---

3. For the purposes of this analysis, I leave further theoretical explication as to how information features may be cognitively represented and stored for future study. However, I do see strong similarities between what I consider to be the content of an information feature and the semantic-pragmatic feature bundles of the matrix language frame model described in Myers-Scotton ([1993a]1997) and Myers-Scotton and Jake (1995).

Table 11-2
Analysis of Responses by Mention of Information

Type of Response	Native Speakers N = 30		Nonnative Speakers N = 21	
	Number	% of N	Number	% of N
Polite opening	24	80.0	14	67.0
Ask for money	30	100.0	21	100.0
Mention keys	25	83.3	16	76.1
Use for money	25	83.3	21	100.0
No money	7	23.3	2	9.0
Promise . . . money back	2	6.7	0	0
Thank for time	0	0	1	4.8

in their responses was ASK FOR MONEY, which the final sentence of the instructions explicitly told them they were to do—*You have to ask a stranger for the money to call . . . what would you say?*

ANALYSIS OF "LOCKED CAR" DATA—NS GROUP

I propose that the frequency of occurrence of certain types of information categories delineates an unmarked choice for the RO set in the locked car scenario. Thus, the unmarked choice for this scenario can be described as ASK FOR MONEY, USE FOR MONEY, and MENTION KEYS. I did not include the category of POLITE OPENING in the unmarked description here because it seemed more a general characteristic of attention getting when starting an interaction, and several of the NS responses seemed (to me) perfectly fine without it as seen in examples [23] and [24].

[23]   Could I please borrow a quarter to use the phone? I've locked my keys in my car.

[24]   I locked my keys in the car. Do you happen to have a quarter so that I can call home and have my roommate bring the spare set?

A somewhat unexpected outcome of this analysis was that the features of the unmarked choice for the car key scenario did not come in any special order. Thirteen NSs started their response with an explanation about locking the keys in the car, but seventeen began with a request for the money to call.

Five NS subjects gave responses that omitted one of the above characteristics describing the unmarked choice for the locked car scenario. Two speakers did not include USE FOR MONEY, as seen in example [25].

[25]   Do you have a quarter I can borrow please, because I locked my keys and my money in my car.

Even though example [25] explicitly omits one information feature judged to be required for the entire utterance to be unmarked, I claim that it is still an unmarked response because the feature USE FOR MONEY is pragmatically recoverable by the hearer. That is, the hearer will use assumptions of shared cultural knowledge, namely that quarters are used in pay phones, to understand that the speaker wishes to make a phone call.

Three NS subjects omitted the feature MENTION KEYS, as seen in examples [26] and [27].

[26] do you think you can spare a quarter so I can make a phone call? I haven't got any money.

[27] Could you help me? I need a quarter to call home, can I get it from you?

Responses that omitted MENTION KEYS are marked because the hearers of examples [26] and [27] cannot pragmatically recover the situation that caused the speakers to ask for the quarter. Thus, the reason for the request was not communicated by the speaker contrary to the element of the RO set that requires unmarked requests to be justified to maintain social distance. The social distance between strangers can be maintained in spite of the imposition of the request if the speaker provides a "good" reason, as defined by the community. In this case, the emergency of locking one's keys in the car is sufficient, but the omission of this information prevents the hearer from knowing this.

In contrast to responses that were marked because of information that was omitted, two NS subjects gave marked responses by providing extra information by promising to pay the money back, as seen in example [28].

[28] Could you please lend me a quarter? I've locked my keys in the car and I need to call home so that my mother can bring me my spare keys. I'll pay you back.

Even though half of both subject groups (fifteen NSs and twelve NNSs) actually phrased the request as *borrowing a quarter*, this request is not usually seen as solicitation of a loan.[4] Therefore, the specific offer to pay back the quarter is marked.

ANALYSIS OF "LOCKED CAR" DATA—NNS GROUP

So far, this analysis focuses on the responses provided by the NS subjects to determine what characterizes the unmarked choice in the locked car situation. How do NNS responses compare with respect to the unmarked choice? Examples [11]–[13] and Table 11-2 show some differences between the two groups, but few of the differences seem consequential. A great deal of similarity between responses of the two groups is not surprising, given the simplicity of the task and the intermediate level of the L2 learners. The NNS also showed the same varied order of information features as the NS group—ten NNSs mentioned the keys first, eleven NNSs mentioned the need of a quarter first. However, out of the group of twenty-one NNSs, five gave marked responses and the analysis of the NNS marked responses is revealing.

4. I am indebted to Amy Albert for her observations and comments about this.

In addition to NNS responses as a group being relatively similar to the unmarked choice, four NNS subjects gave marked responses like those made by the NSs when omitting one of the information features (see earlier discussion). Example [29]–[31] illustrate the NNS responses omitting the information feature MENTION KEYS:

[29] Excuse me, but could you give me some quarters? I need to call my home.

[30] Can you give me some quarters to make a phone call?

[31] Excuse me, would you mind giving a quarter to make a call? Because I don't have any coin.

An interesting aspect of example [29] is that it is the only example in the corpus from a Japanese speaker. Example [29] is also the only response in which the subject wrote out a response in her native language and then translated it into English. This example is somewhat similar to Miko's first formulation of a request, *Could I have your 25¢?* It is possible that part of the difference between Miko's two formulated responses, *Could I have your 25¢?* and *Excuse me, today I lost my wallet. I'd like to call my boyfriend, but I don't have money. Can I borrow money?* may have been that for the first response Miko may have been relying on features of unmarked choices from her native language and culture.

When comparing NS and NNS responses that are marked due to the omission of an information feature, a question of why any of the native speakers omitted an information feature remains. One possible explanation is that a few native speakers in the group did not have a complete understanding of the unmarked features indexed by the locked car RO set.

The goal of soliciting so many responses in this task is to demonstrate that, in the face of so much lexical and structural variation, features can be extracted which describe a normative response and identify its associated RO set. This claim is not to imply, however, that all individuals will make that normative response.

Example [32] is the only marked response from the NNS group that is marked because of additional information features.

[32] *Excuse me sir*! *May* I take of *your precious time* a minute. *I'm affraid* [sic] I locked my keys inside my car if you *could possibly* give me a quarter so that I can make a call to my wife who would come and bring me the other keys from home, *if you cannot I understand* and *I thank you for listening to me.*

It was not only the longest response but the most excessive response in terms of including eight politeness markers (indicated in italics). What makes example [32] marked is that whereas politeness markers are usually unmarked in indexing social distance or an imposition, the politeness should be proportional. That is, in a culture that looks favorably on citizens helping one another with problems and perceives a quarter as a very small amount of money, there is not a great degree of social distance or imposition in the locked car situation. Therefore, not only may incorporating a great degree of politeness be interpreted as marked, it may be interpreted as a sign of sarcasm.

The claim of the MM is not that NSs always try to make code choices that they consider to be unmarked, but that they have the ability to make marked and unmarked choices in interactions and through these choices do "social" work. Recall that some NS choices were marked in various ways. For example, speakers who offered to pay the quarter back may have been making a bid for a slightly different RO set in which they would be on a more equal footing with the stranger because they were explicitly not asking for the stranger to give them the money outright. Or, perhaps these subjects supposed that their offer to pay back the money would not be taken seriously but would emphasize the paucity of the sum they had asked for and thus increase their chances of being successful. In either case, it is possible to intuit a purpose behind these marked choices regardless of whether the marked choice helps the subjects achieve their communicative goals.

Second-language learners want to do the same: make marked and unmarked choices when they wish to. However, the instances of odd English, which I now define as marked choices that confound communication or seem to communicate information that does not seem intentional, indicate that L2 learners do not have the same sort of ability that native speakers do over their linguistic choices.

In this section I tried to show that it is possible to come up with intuitive and empirical descriptions of unmarked choices while still allowing for the lexical and structural variations that occur in natural speech. The ability of the MM to describe normative choices while allowing for surface variation can be of use in explaining to L2 learners how their choices are marked. That is, the problems L2 learners have making unmarked choices is of primary importance. Their goal is not only to make unmarked choices when they communicate but to have native-like marked choices as part of their linguistic repertoires. Without the ability to have the option of marked choices in their linguistic repertoires, L2 learners will never acquire a native-like pragmatic ability. The next question to consider, then, is the following: Can the MM be applied to natural language use and help nonnative learners be more native-like?

MARKEDNESS FOR NATIVE AND NONNATIVE SPEAKERS OF ENGLISH

Because, as discussed earlier, the cognitive faculties underlying the MM are the same in a person's L1 as in her L2, the elements that affect an L2 learner's ability to produce marked and unmarked utterances have to do with the inputs to the process that produce readings about marked and unmarked forms. Furthermore, because of the allowable variation in unmarked forms, these inputs can rarely be a closed set of specific lexical items or morphosyntactic structures. I propose these readings about relative markedness should be described in terms of information features. Specific lexical items or combinations of lexical items will be associated with information features in an L2 learner's encyclopedic memory or mental lexicon.

In applying the conclusions of the locked car task to spontaneous language use, an examination of an L2 learner's ability, or lack thereof, in making unmarked choices in natural language use starts with the odd English examples that are marked. The rest of this chapter examines instances in written discourse when marked choices made by L2 writers did not work. In such examples two explanations are possible: Writers make what they think is an unmarked choice but is not, or, writers are intentionally making a marked choice that is not serving the purpose they intended. In either case, both choices are dependent on the L2 writers' having the same understanding as their intended NS audience of what constitutes an unmarked choice in that particular situation.

On this view, the elements of the MM as discussed previously (L1 community-defined RO sets, information features, and specific lexical/morphosyntactic choices) become descriptors around which a principled discussion of non-native-like markedness is centered. The next section uses examples from the corpus of writing from NNSs described earlier to illustrate each of the levels at which marked choices can be unsuccessful—that is, at the level of the L1 community-defined RO set that indexes certain information features as unmarked, at the level of the unmarked information features associated with that particular RO set, or at the level of the lexical/morphosyntactic choices chosen to reflect those information features.

RO SETS

Essays from L2 students enrolled in an American university provide insight into the writers' perceptions of the RO sets they believe to be in effect. RO sets are not linguistic choices—they index information features and provide input to the ME for markedness readings on all possible linguistic choices, marked or not. As opposed to other types of RO sets, the RO set of writing in American academic discourse has the advantage of being well established and very normative, and bids for other RO sets are generally not acceptable in academic discourse. Therefore, student academic writing reflects an effort to generally stay within the linguistic choices indexed by the RO set. For example, one of the elements that characterizes the academic RO is the establishment of authority. That is, one of the expectations of the academic community is to present information in a way in which it is credible. If the writers are not authoritative sources themselves, the RO set indicates that they should present evidence or cite authoritative sources to give credibility to the information they are presenting. In addition, this expectation of authority indexes formality in information features and the linguistic choices they underlie. Example [33] shows the NNS student trying to work within what she perceives to be the required formality of the RO set in place.

[33] Just when I feel about something deeply, the good words seem to come to my mind one after another, and I pretend to be a very good poet, but actually what I am writing is nothing but a piece of feces.

The student's use of the clinical term *feces*, instead of a more colloquial word, reflects her attempt to stay within the formality required by the RO set in place. However, her use of a more formal term was not compatible with the RO set, in spite of its formality, because references to bodily waste in nonliteral ways are almost *never* appropriate in formal academic writing. Note that other formal terms, such as *excrement*, would have been just as unacceptable. The student seems to realize that different tasks require different code choices, but is not able to make a code choice that works.

Linguistic choices can be marked with respect to the academic RO set in different ways, as in examples [34] and [35].

[34] For example, I paid $1000 to take psychology 101 and I hate that class. It doesn't help me with my major; HRTA. Even though I study hard, it is difficult to get a good grade for me and if I don't pass it, I have wasted the money. I can buy a car with that money. I feel like I neglect my important classes just to study for a meaningless Psychology class.

Example [34] does not work because of the hierarchical nature of the RO set for academic discourse. That is, in addition to the requirement for presenting information in an authoritative way, there is some social distance between the writer and the addressee, and the addressee has more status. I claim this is true even when students are told that the audience for their essays is composed of other college students (as opposed to the professor or a general academic audience). In the RO set of academic writing, writers behave as if their readers have higher stature even if this is not true in the real world. Unmarked linguistic choices must show deference and reflect the degree of social distance in the author/reader relationship as understood by the academic community.

Therefore, linguistic choices that index solidarity, as in example [32], are marked. In that example, the student was trying to express her frustration at certain university regulations. Yet, instead of presenting a compelling argument for her position, she simply seems to be venting her frustrations to her audience and appealing to the audience's sympathy—choices that are consistent with an equal degree of social status between author and reader. Therefore, appeals to sympathy are marked in the academic RO set because audience has more social status than the author.

Example [35] is marked with respect to the social relationships indexed by RO sets in a different way.

[35] We would like to involve ourselves in the Travel and Tourism segment of this

booming industry and the title of our research paper gives an indirect hint to what we want to pursue as a career choice. [The title of the paper was *The Friendly Skies*]

In example [35], the oblique reference to the intended title comes across as coy, raising the question, "Why didn't the authors come right out and say they wanted to work in the airline industry?" The authors' use of indirectness makes a bid for a decrease in social distance by requiring readers to work harder to understand what they mean. The RO set of academic discourse has requirements of directness consistent with the higher status of the addressee. For their code choices to be unmarked, authors should be as direct as possible and, thus, not waste the time and effort of their readers.

This section is not intended to describe exhaustively all the characteristics of the academic discourse RO set. I am not sure that doing so is useful pedagogically *or even possible* because I have only been able to describe characteristics of RO sets *in the context of mistakes* in natural language use. Because they only index linguistic choices, RO sets work more as boundaries than as predicators of language use—linguistic choices "within" the boundary are unmarked, and those outside the boundary are marked. The way to get L2 learners to understand where an L1 community sets its boundaries depends on showing them when their L2 language use crosses those boundaries while they are trying make their linguistic choices stay inside.

INFORMATION FEATURES

Information features that make up unmarked choices indexed by RO sets represent another type of markedness problem that L2 learners encounter. For example, L2 learners could have a native-like understanding of the elements of the RO set in place but have a non-native-like knowledge of *how* certain information features reflect the unmarked choices they are trying to make, as examples [36] and [37] illustrate.

[36]   Some people do this gradually while some do it overnight by getting involved in an unfamiliar field or by getting involved into *something negative*.

[37]   This question poses a problem to many students and therefore requires *adequate thinking*.

The issues that [36] and [37] raise have to do with leaving out information features that are required for the choices to be unmarked. *Something negative* in [36] and *adequate thinking* in [37] do not follow the requirement to be specific. An information feature of the unmarked choice should be a specific referent. Note that no requirement for exactly what that referent should be exists; specific lexical choices depend on what the writers actually meant by *something negative* and *adequate thinking*.

[38]   If it [the Writing Studio] is for our benefit, why do most people avoid this free help?

Example [38] reflects an error in the information feature requirement I call claim-proof. That is, for a linguistic choice to be unmarked, claim-proof requires the authority of the writer's claims to be supported by some sort of information about how he or she knows this to be so.

Some information features affecting markedness can appear in writing on a more global level—across clauses and paragraphs and sometime throughout the essay, as example [39] shows.

[39]   Finally, it's true because it changed not only his life but also affirmed his writing style.

Out of context, the sentence in example [39] looks perfectly fine except that it was part of an autobiographical essay about the writer's writing experiences. Referring to oneself in the third person throughout the entire essay when it is clear that the author and the subject are the same person was certainly marked.

LEXICAL/MORPHOSYNTACTIC CHOICES

The third type of markedness problem that L2 learners encounter is seen in the way that information features are reflected in specific lexical and morphosyntactic choices as examples [40] and [41] demonstrate:

[40]   Like many other college students I find higher education expensive and like many others who *don't live in SC*—twice as expensive

[41]   The other day I heard a mad professor saying that we are not in high school.

In example [40], I remarked to the student that she did live in South Carolina—she just wasn't *from here*. She responded that she had picked *live* as a synonym for *reside* because the school policy allows state residents to pay lower tuition. In this case the student chose a lexeme that did not communicate the information feature she intended. The same is true in example [41]; the student knew of the semantic relationship between *mad* and *angry*, but the word order he chose unintentionally communicated something else.

NATIVE SPEAKER CHOICES

Although the focus of this chapter is the developing pragmatic abilities of NNSs, the data collected from the NSs of English were not free from problems in markedness. Although the NSs seemed to have fewer problems overall, I found a least one example of each type in the part of the corpus made up of writing from the four NSs in the mixed 101B class. The most salient feature of the markedness problems in the NS writing was that all the choices appeared to be made with clear intentions of the choice being marked; however, the markedness simply did not work from an academic point of view as seen in examples [42] and [43]:

[42]   [From a persuasive essay that argues against hunting] He is an older buck, this may be the last season that his hormones will turn him into *the aggressive love machine of his younger days*.

[43]   I interviewed Mr. Owen in his office in the main building of the high school which was *permeated* with trophies, plaques, and certificates exhibiting a lifetime of success.

The tone of the language in example [42] stood out in such sharp contrast to the overall tone of a persuasive essay against hunting that it came across as flippant. The student explained that he was trying to be expressive and got carried away. In example [43] the student explained that she chose the word *permeated* because she wanted a really impressive word.

So although it seems that NSs and NNSs overall do make the same types of mistakes concerning markedness, they make them for different reasons. Native speakers do not make marked choices *because they think those choices are unmarked*. Rather, in errors concerning markedness, the NSs *intentionally make marked choices* to achieve their communicative goals, but these marked choices are sometimes unsuccessful. Handbooks of academic writing, which students often use in introductory writing classes, such as the class from which these data were collected, encourage students to use expressive, effective language while avoiding "tired expressions and meaningless language" (Carter and Skates 1996: 217). The mistakes NSs make often reflect their unsuccessful attempts to do this without straying too far outside the norms of academic writing.

IMPLICATIONS FOR PEDAGOGY

The markedness model provides a principled explanation as to why employing student-generated language is successful as a basis for illustrating and teaching native-like language use. This intersection of theory and application is crucial to teachers who need simple explanations for the commonalties that seem to run through seemingly endless variations in possible linguistic choices. For example, there are countless discussions in the literature of composition and rhetoric about the influence that cultural knowledge has on language use, but the MM operationalizes the interaction between language and culture in the concept of L1-defined RO sets, the effect that RO sets have on the selection of information features, and the way that information features underlie specific lexical items.

The MM is not a predictive framework in the following way: It does not claim to say when, how often, or under what conditions L2 learners will have problems with markedness in their language use. However, the MM *is* predictive in the sense that it does state that if RO sets index unmarked choices and an unmarked choice is selected, that unmarked choice will not produce marked effects. Because they have tacit knowledge regarding how markedness "works" in their native language, native speakers know they have a range of marked and unmarked options for any communicative task. Nonnative speakers, even ones who know "a lot of words," are not always aware of what their options are. From the MM perspective, developing a native-speaker-like pragmatic competence means having the same range of choice as a native speaker.

The corpus of writing from L2 learners and native speakers used in this analysis contained many examples of marked and unmarked choices that were successful. Using language that students generate themselves, teachers can talk about the features of lexical choices, which of these features are considered unmarked, and how marked choices might be interpreted by the hearer/reader.

It is impossible to list all the possible "correct" lexical choices that students can make in a given situation, be it asking a stranger for a quarter to make a phone call or writing the opening of a paper for a sociology class. By the same token, it is impossible to list all the choices that students should not make in a certain situation. As example [28] shows, a teacher would have to be psychic to tell students before the fact not to mention bodily wastes in their academic essays.

One way to discuss the intuitions that NSs have about RO sets, information features, and lexical choices may be to do a detailed analysis of a particular communicative situation and the possible unmarked choices associated with it, as discussed earlier. However, the very detailed analysis of situations, such as the locked car scenario, is not necessary (and would be impossible) for *every* foreseeable type of communicative situation. Instead, teachers can use their own intuitions about markedness to help students understand the sociopragmatic effects of the linguistic choices they make. Students use this information as input to their own productive, innate cognitive mechanisms that underlie the complex choices about markedness available to them.

Note that the projected outcome of this type of pedagogical approach is not to have learners make only unmarked choices; the marked/unmarked distinction is vital to give students the linguistic flexibility to reach *all* their communicative goals. As competent speakers, L2 learners intentionally make marked choices when it reflects the best way to reach their communicative goals. Instead, this approach should help students build and use their linguistic repertoires as native speakers do.

REFERENCES

Blum-Kulka, Shoshana, Juliane House, and Gabrielle Kasper (eds.). 1989. *Cross-cultural pragmatics: requests and apologies.* Norwood, N.J.: Alex.

Carter, Bonnie, and Craig Skates. 1996. *The Rinehart guide to grammar and style.* Orlando, Fla.: Harcourt Brace College Publishers.

Kasper, Gabrielle, and Shoshana Blum-Kulka (eds.). 1993. *Interlanguage pragmatics.* Oxford: Oxford University Press.

Myers-Scotton, Carol. 1993b. *Social motivations for codeswitching: evidence from Africa*. Oxford: Oxford University Press. Reprint, 1995.

————. 1993a. *Duelling languages: grammatical structure in codeswitching*. Oxford: Oxford University Press.

Myers-Scotton, Carol, and Janice Jake. 1995. Matching lemmas in a bilingual language competence and production model: evidence from intrasentential codeswitching. *Linguistics* 33: 981–1024.

Sperber, Dan, and Deirdre Wilson. 1995. *Relevance, communication and cognition*. 2nd ed. Oxford: Blackwell.

Turner, Ken. 1995. The principal principles of pragmatic inferencing: co-operation. *Language Teaching* 28: 67–76.

————. 1996. The principal principles of pragmatic inferencing: politeness. *Language Teaching* 29: 1–13.

INDEX

DATE DUE

JUL 2 2 2015	
MAY 2 5 2015	